Character Studies

Books by Mark Singer

CHARACTER STUDIES

ENCOUNTERS

with the CURIOUSLY OBSESSED

Mark Singer

Houghton Mifflin Company

Boston • New York   2005

For information about permission to reproduce selections from this book, write to Permissions, Houghton Mifflin Company, 215 Park Avenue South, New York, New York 10003.

Visit our Web site: www.houghtonmifflinbooks.com.

Library of Congress Cataloging-in-Publication Data
Singer, Mark.
Character studies : encounters with the curiously obsessed / Mark Singer.
p.   cm.
ISBN 0-618-19725-7
1. Characters and characteristics—United States. 2. Eccentrics and eccentricities—United States—Biography. I. Title.
CT9990.S57 2005 920.073—dc22 [B] 2004062757

Printed in the United States of America

Book design by Robert Overholtzer

MP 10 9 8 7 6 5 4 3 2 1

To my favorite characters —
Jeb, Reid, Timothy, and Paul

Contents

Character Studies

Introduction

Because obsession is regarded, at least in psychotherapeutic circles, as a state of mind in need of melioration, I hesitated before settling on the subtitle of this book. I'm not sure what to make of the analytical consensus. At the moment, for instance, I'm riding a train from Florence to Rome, diverted by the agreeable Tuscan landscape but mildly preoccupied with what the elusive people to whom I entrusted my luggage five days ago might have done with it. If tomorrow morning I'm again forced to befriend the same moldy socks and underwear, I'm going to feel genuinely bothered. Obsessed? Well, a couple more days of this routine and there's no guaranteeing that I wouldn't cross the line. On balance, though, I've found that an aptitude for obsession, rather than being thrust upon unsuspecting souls by external forces like Fortune (in the guise of, say, baggage handlers for Iberia Airlines), upwells from within. Among obsession's virtues (never mind the downside of derangement) is its capacity to generate wonderment and, of course, art.

The countless on-the-job hours I've logged in the company of obsessives have invariably proved rewarding. A lot of what journalists do, I believe, is a form of sublimated voyeurism. (I generalize here from locker-room chats with fellow scribblers; I've never conducted a reliable survey of mental health professionals to confirm this hypothesis.) The genre of journalism that I am inclined toward also resembles, in hybrid form, cultural anthropology. To compose the portraits in this book, I first imposed upon my subjects by requesting permission to shadow them, often for days at a time, usually over some weeks or months. As a reporter, I always know things are going well when it becomes evident that my presence has been taken for granted and that I've managed to fulfill what is both the anthropologist-observer's goal and the voyeur's animating fantasy: to disappear. This is anything but an efficient process, and the longer I've been at this the more slowly I manage to get the job done. My excuse is that the people I write about, having allowed me to scrutinize their lives as they pursue their passions, are entitled to my own obsessive deliberateness.

With the exception of the book collector/gadfly Michael Zinman and the book collector/sleight-of-hand wizard/actor/scholar-of-conjuring-and-unusual-entertainments Ricky Jay, who happen to be close friends, I don't regard the characters in this omnium-gatherum as having much in common, other than their capacity for monomania and my own curiosity about how that is expressed. It has occurred to me that had it not been for my intervention, the rule of six degrees of separation might not apply to the rarely-straying-from-the-farm vegetable-growing virtuosi Tom, Frank, Fred and Kay Chino, of Rancho Santa Fe, California, and the Tom Mix fanatic Richard Seiverling, of Hershey, Pennsylvania. The same thing goes for the superannuated members of the Wednesday Group of El Paso, Texas, and a particular trio of mommies-with-a-vengeance who used to be my neighbors in Pelham, New York. I suppose there have been occasions when Donald Trump and Martin Scorsese have been in the same room. Still, I can imagine at least one of them asking himself why.

All of these stories — which I do regard as stories, because each has a protagonist (or multiple protagonists) who, to some degree, is altered by the events of the narrative — were originally published in *The New Yorker,* over a period of time during which the editor's chair was occupied by Robert Gottlieb, then Tina Brown, then David Remnick. Although I proposed most of the assignments, it was more or less under duress that I agreed to write profiles of Trump and Scorsese. (To Tina Brown and David Remnick, respectively, my retroactive thanks.) My aversion to interviewing and writing about celebrated people is grounded in my expectation that I'm unlikely to ask a question that hasn't previously been asked or to evoke a reply that hasn't already been published elsewhere. There's a lot to be said, however, for the intrinsic value of the process, the challenge of immersing oneself in a sea of facts and impressions until somehow the signifying contours of a given character's story are revealed.

Most of us recognize that we possess multilayered private selves and that we spend our waking hours churning with thoughts and fantasies that we wouldn't dream of sharing with even the most solicitous interviewer. When I first sat down with Scorsese, stacks of books and reams of articles had already been published about his style of filmmaking and its autobiographical underpinnings. I had no idea, at that juncture, what my purpose was or what the result might be. What emerged many months later was not a mini-biography but a travelogue of a journey along Scorsese's rapidly flowing stream of consciousness, an attempt to illustrate how such an extraordinary volume and variety of data could jockey for space inside his capacious brain and eventually get transformed into images on film.

Writing about Trump provided gratification of an entirely different sort. I caught up with him at a time when, by his own account, he was making a "comeback" — in retrospect, the interregnum between the de facto bankruptcy of his real estate enterprise and the formal bankruptcy of his casino operations. It seemed obvious to me that the latter was going down the tubes, but no matter; Trump continued to fly the flag, and I was fittingly awestruck. His specific obsession (with himself) constituted a genus of performance art that was so excruciating to witness it was entertaining, and vice versa. In one-on-one encounters, he could be charming and likable, even intentionally amusing. And it didn't take me long to adjust to his reflexive tendency toward self-serving hyperbole; it wasn't my intelligence per se that was being insulted by the transparent distortions that burbled from his lips, that was just the way the man talked.

It turned out that Trump greatly disliked what I wrote about him — not that he cited any factual errors or even troubled himself to complain to me directly. Rather, in a book called *The Art of the Comeback*, he devoted a couple of pages to impugning my character. Our first encounter: "When [Singer] came into the office I immediately sensed that he was not much of anything, nondescript, with a faint wiseguy sneer and some kind of chip on his shoulder." Which suggests, if nothing else, how effortlessly I managed, in the maestro's presence, to disappear. For some reason, despite these initial misgivings, Trump continued to meet with me. In return, I felt I owed him my best effort.

What ultimately disturbed him, I assume, was the notion that in attempting to ascertain the content of his interior life I'd been forced to grapple with the possibility that he lacked a soul. There was, I realized when I read his complaint, a potentially significant metaphysical implication embedded in that whole proposition, and perhaps I should have dug deeper. But the truth is I didn't subsequently give it much thought. Our obsessions don't choose us. We choose them. And I'd moved on.

Secrets of the Magus

THE PLAYWRIGHT DAVID MAMET and the theater director Gregory Mosher affirm that some years ago, late one night in the bar of the Ritz-Carlton Hotel in Chicago, this happened:

Ricky Jay, who is perhaps the most gifted sleight-of-hand artist alive, was performing magic with a deck of cards. Also present was a friend of Mamet and Mosher's named Christ Nogulich, the director of food and beverage at the hotel. After twenty minutes of disbelief-suspending manipulations, Jay spread the deck face-up on the bar counter and asked Nogulich to concentrate on a specific card but not to reveal it. Jay then assembled the deck face-down, shuffled, cut it into two piles, and asked Nogulich to point to one of the piles and name his card.

"Three of clubs," Nogulich said, and he was then instructed to turn over the top card.

He turned over the three of clubs.

Mosher, in what could be interpreted as a passive-aggressive act, quietly announced, "Ricky, you know, I also concentrated on a card."

After an interval of silence, Jay said, "That's interesting, Gregory, but I only do this for one person at a time."

Mosher persisted: "Well, Ricky, I really was thinking of a card."

Jay paused, frowned, stared at Mosher, and said, "This is a distinct change of procedure." A longer pause. "All right — what was the card?"

"Two of spades."

Jay nodded, and gestured toward the other pile, and Mosher turned over its top card.

The deuce of spades.

A small riot ensued.

Deborah Baron, a screenwriter in Los Angeles, where Jay lives, once invited him to a New Year's Eve dinner party at her home. About a dozen other people attended. Well past midnight, everyone gathered around a coffee table as Jay, at Baron's request, did close-up card magic. When he had performed several dazzling illusions and seemed ready to retire, a guest named Mort said, "Come on, Ricky. Why don't you do something truly amazing?"

Baron recalls that at that moment "the look in Ricky's eyes was, like, 'Mort — you have just fucked with the wrong person.'"

Jay told Mort to name a card, any card. Mort said, "The three of hearts." After shuffling, Jay gripped the deck in the palm of his right hand and sprang it, cascading all fifty-two cards so that they traveled the length of the table and pelted an open wine bottle.

"OK, Mort, what was your card again?"

"The three of hearts."

"Look inside the bottle."

Mort discovered, curled inside the neck, the three of hearts. The party broke up immediately.

ONE MORNING last December, a few days before Christmas, Jay came to see me in my office. He wore a dark-gray suit and a black shirt that was open at the collar, and the colors seemed to match his mood. The most uplifting magic, Jay believes, has a spontaneous, improvisational vigor. Nevertheless, because he happened to be in New York we had made a date to get together, and I, invoking a journalistic imperative, had specifically requested that he come by my office and do some magic while I took notes. He hemmed and hawed and then, reluctantly, consented. Though I had no idea what was in store, I anticipated being completely fooled.

At that point, I had known Jay for two years, during which we had discussed his theories of magic, his relationships with and opinions of other practitioners of the art, his rigid opposition to public revelations of the techniques of magic, and his relentless passion for collecting rare books and manuscripts, art, and other artifacts connected to the history of magic, gambling, unusual entertainments, and frauds and confidence games. He has a skeptically friendly, mildly ironic conversational manner and a droll, filigreed prose style. Jay's collection functions as a working research library. He is the author of dozens of scholarly articles and also of two diverting and richly informative books, *Cards as Weapons* (1977) and *Learned Pigs & Fireproof Women* (1986). For the past several years, he has devoted his energies mainly to scholarship and to acting in and consulting on motion pictures. Though he loves to perform, he is extremely selective about venues and audiences. I've attended lectures and demonstrations by him before gatherings of East Coast undergraduates, West Coast students of the history of magic, and midwestern bunco-squad detectives. Studying videotapes of him and observing at first hand some of his serendipitous microbursts of legerdemain have taught me how inappropriate it is to say that "Ricky Jay does card tricks" — a characterization as inadequate as "Sonny Rollins plays tenor saxophone" or "Darci Kistler dances." None of my scrutinizing has yielded a shred of insight into how he does what he does. Every routine appears seamless, unparsable, simply magical.

Before getting down to business in my office, we chatted about this and that: water spouters and armless origami artists and equestrian bee trainers, all subjects that Jay has written about. As we were talking, an editor friend and two other colleagues dropped by. I had introduced Jay and the editor once before and — presumptuously, it turned out — had mentioned earlier that morning that he would be coming by for a private performance. Politely but firmly, Jay made it plain that an audience of one was what he had in mind. There was an awkward moment after the others left. I apologized for the intrusion, and he apologized for not being more accommodating. He reassured me that he still had something to show me. My cluttered office didn't feel right, however, so we headed upstairs to a lunchroom, found that it was unoccupied, and seated ourselves in a corner booth, facing each other. He unzipped a black leather clutch that he had brought with him and removed a deck of red Bee playing cards imprinted with the logo of Harrah's Casino.

In *Cards as Weapons* Jay refers to Dai Vernon, who died last year, at ninety-eight, as "the greatest living contributor to the magical art," and he quotes Vernon's belief that "cards are like living, breathing human beings and should be treated accordingly." I was reminded of Vernon's dictum as Jay caressed the deck, as gently as if it were a newly hatched chick. He has small hands — just large enough so that a playing card fits within the plane of his palm. There is a slightly raised pad of flesh on the underside of the first joint of each finger. "Not the hands of a man who has done a lot of hard labor," Jay said — a completely disingenuous line, to which he added, "One of the best sleight-of-hand guys I know is a plumber."

. Jay's hands seem out of scale with the rest of him. He is of average height but has a hefty, imposing build. During the seventies, he regularly toured with various rock groups as an opening act and could easily have passed as foreman of the road crew; at the time, he had dark-brown hair that reached the middle of his back, and a dense, flowing beard. He now keeps his hair and beard neatly trimmed. He has a fleshy face, a high forehead, and dark eyes. His eyes light up and then crinkle when he laughs — a burst of what might or might not indicate pleasure, followed by a dry, wise-sounding chuckle that could mean anything. His inflection is New York with a Flatbush edge. In three of Mamet's films — *House of Games, Things Change,* and *Homicide* — Jay has been cast to type as a confidence man, a gangster, and an Israeli terrorist, respectively. In one scene of the play within a play of *House of Games,* he portrays a menacing professional gambler.

"I'm always saying there's no correlation between gambling and magic," Jay said as he shuffle-cut the cards. "But this is a routine of actual gamblers' techniques within the context of a theatrical magic presentation."

He noticed me watching him shuffling, and asked softly, with deadpan sincerity, "Does that look fair?"

When I said it looked fair, he dealt two hands of five-card draw and told me to lay down my cards. Two pair. Then he laid down his. A straight.

"Was that fair?" he said. "I don't think so. Let's discuss the reason why that wasn't fair. Even though I shuffled openly and honestly, I didn't let you cut the cards. So let's do it again, and this time I'll let you cut the cards."

He shuffled again, I cut the cards, he dealt, and this time I had three tens.

"Ready to turn them over?"

My three of a kind compared unfavorably with his diamond flush.

"Is that fair?" he said again. "I don't think so. Let's talk about why that might not be fair. Even though I shuffled the cards" — he was now reshuffling the deck — "and you cut the cards, you saw me pick up the cards after you cut them, and maybe you think there was some way for me to nullify the cut by sleight of hand. So this time I'll shuffle the cards and you shuffle the cards."

Jay shuffled the deck, I riffle-shuffled the deck and handed it back to him, and he said, "And I'll deal six hands of poker — one for myself and five for you. I'll let you choose any one of the five. And I'll beat you."

He dealt six hands. Instead of revealing only one of my five hands, I turned them all face-up.

"Oh, oh," he said. "I see you want to turn them all over. I only intended for you to pick one — but, well, no, that's all right."

The best of my five hands was two pair.

Jay said, "Now, did that seem fair?"

I said yes.

Jay said, "I don't think so," and showed me his cards — four kings.

I rested my elbows on the table and massaged my forehead.

"Now, why might that be unfair?" he continued. "I'll tell you why. Because, even though you shuffled, I dealt the cards. That time, I also shuffled the cards. Now, this time you shuffle the cards and you deal the cards. And you pick the number of players. And you designate any hand for me and any hand for you."

After shuffling, I dealt four hands, arranged as the points of a square. I chose a hand for myself and selected one for him. My cards added up to nothing — king-high nothing.

"Is that fair?" Jay said, picking up his cards, waiting a beat, and returning them to the table, one by one — the coup de grâce. "I. Don't. Think. So." One, two, three, four aces.

JAY HAS an anomalous memory, extraordinarily retentive but riddled with hard-to-account-for gaps. "I'm becoming quite worried about my memory," he said not long ago. "New information doesn't stay. I wonder if it's the NutraSweet." As a child, he read avidly and could summon the title and the author of every book that had passed through his hands. Now he gets lost driving in his own neighborhood, where he has lived for several years — he has no idea how many. He once had a summer job tending bar and doing magic at a place called the Royal Palm, in Ithaca, New York. On a bet, he accepted a mnemonic challenge from a group of friendly patrons. A numbered list of a hundred arbitrary objects was drawn up: no. 3 was "paintbrush," no. 18 was "plush ottoman," no. 25 was "roaring lion," and so on. "Ricky! Sixty-five!" someone would demand, and he had ten seconds to respond correctly or lose a buck. He always won, and, to this day, still would. He is capable of leaving the house wearing his suit jacket but forgetting his pants. He can recite verbatim the rapid-fire spiel he delivered a quarter of a century ago, when he was briefly employed as a carnival barker: "See the magician; the fire 'manipulator'; the girl with the yellow e-e-elastic tissue. See Adam and Eve, boy and girl, brother and sister, all in one, one of the world's three living 'morphrodites.' And the e-e-electrode lady . . ." He can quote verse after verse of nineteenth-century cockney rhyming slang. He says he cannot remember what age he was when his family moved from Brooklyn to the New Jersey suburbs. He cannot recall the year he entered college or the year he left. "If you ask me for specific dates, we're in trouble," he says.

Michael Weber, a fellow magician and close friend, has said, "Basically, Ricky remembers nothing that happened after 1900."

Jay has many loyal friends, a protective circle that includes a lot of people with show-business and antiquarian-book-collecting connections and remarkably few with magic-world connections.

Marcus McCorison, a former president of the American Antiquarian Society, where Jay has lectured and performed, describes him as "a deeply serious scholar — I think he knows more about the history of American conjuring than anyone else."

Nicolas Barker, who recently retired as one of the deputy keepers of the British Library, says, "Ricky would say you can't be a good conjurer without knowing the history of your profession, because there are no new tricks under the sun, only variations. He's a superbly gifted conjurer, and he's an immensely scholarly person whose knowledge in his chosen field is gigantic, in a class by itself. And, like any other scholarly person, he has a very good working knowledge of fields outside his own."

The actor Steve Martin said not long ago, "I sort of think of Ricky as the intellectual elite of magicians. I've had experience with magicians my whole life. He's expertly able to perform and yet he knows the theory, history, literature of the field. Ricky's a master of his craft. You know how there are those teachers of creative writing who can't necessarily write but can teach? Well, Ricky can actually do everything."

A collector named Michael Zinman says, "He's instantly reachable, up to a limit." Those most familiar with his idiosyncrasies realize that there are at least three Ricky Jays: a public persona, a private persona, and a private persona within the private persona. Jay can remember his age — somewhere in his forties — but says that it is irrelevant. It is also irrelevant that Jay was not his surname at birth; it was his middle name. Janus Cercone, who wrote the screenplay for *Leap of Faith,* a recent film that stars Steve Martin as a flimflam faith healer and credits Jay as the "Cons and Frauds Consultant," told me, "I talk to Ricky three times a day. Other than my husband, he's my best friend. I think I know him as well as just about anyone does, and I know less about his background and his childhood than about those of anyone else I know."

Mamet and Jay have been friends for several years — a bond rooted, in part, in their shared fascination with the language, science, and art of cons and frauds.

"I'll call Ricky on the phone," Mamet says. "I'll ask him — say, for something I'm writing — 'A guy's wandering through upstate New York in 1802 and he comes to a tavern and there's some sort of mountebank. What would the mountebank be doing?' And Ricky goes to his library and then sends me an entire description of what the mountebank would be doing. Or I'll tell him I'm having a Fourth of July party and I want to do some sort of disappearance in the middle of the woods. He says, 'That's the most bizarre request I've ever heard. You want to do a disappearing effect in the woods? There's nothing like that in the literature. I mean, there's this one 1760 pamphlet — *Jokes, Tricks, Ghosts and Diversions by Woodland, Stream and Campfire.* But other than that, I can't think of a thing.' He's unbelievably generous. Ricky's one of the world's great people. He's my hero. I've never seen anybody better at what he does."

I once asked Mamet whether Jay had ever shared with him details of his childhood.

Mamet replied, "I can't remember."

I said, "You can't remember whether you discussed it or you can't remember the details?"

He said, "I can't remember whether or not I know a better way to dissuade you from your reiteration of that question without seeming impolite."

Jay's condensed version of his early life goes like this: "I grew up like Athena — covered with playing cards instead of armor — and, at the age of seven, materialized on a TV show, doing magic." Confronted with questions about his parents, he suggests a different topic. Whatever injuries were inflicted, his mother and his father were apparently equally guilty. Any enthusiasm he ever expressed they managed not to share. "I'm probably the only kid in history whose parents made him stop taking music lessons," he says. "They made me stop studying the accordion. And, I suppose, thank God." He loved to play basketball. There was a backboard above the garage of the family house, which had aluminum siding. "Don't dent the house!" his mother routinely warned. His father oiled his hair with Brylcreem and brushed his teeth with Colgate. "He kept his toothpaste in the medicine cabinet and the Brylcreem in a closet about a foot away," Jay recalls. "Once, when I was ten, I switched the tubes. All you need to know about my father is that after he brushed his teeth with Brylcreem he put the toothpaste in his hair."

Though Jay first performed in public at the age of four, he rejects the notion that magic — or, in any case, his mature style of magic — is suitable entertainment for children. Nor does he apologize for his lack of susceptibility to the charms of children themselves. I once drove with him from central Massachusetts to my home, near New York City. We had to catch a plane together the next day, and I had invited him to spend the night in a spare room, on a floor above and beyond earshot of my three sons. While acknowledging that they were Ricky Jay fans, I promised him that they would all be in bed by the time we arrived and off to school before he awoke the next morning. As it turned out, we had no sooner entered the house than I heard one of my six-year-old twins announce, "I think Ricky's here!" Before he could remove his coat, the three of them, all in their pajamas, had him cornered in the kitchen. My eleven-year-old son handed him a deck of cards. The other boys began parroting the monologue from one of his television appearances — patter from a stunt in which he tosses a playing card like a boomerang and during its return flight bisects it with a pair of giant scissors. Jay gave me the same look I imagine he gave Mort, the unfortunate New Year's Eve party guest. I immediately reached for the phone directory and found the number of a nearby motel.

Just as resolutely as he avoids children, Jay declines opportunities to perform for other magicians. This habit has earned him a reputation for aloofness, to which he pleads guilty-with-an-explanation. According to Michael Weber, he has a particular aversion to the "magic lumpen" — hoi polloi who congregate in magic clubs and at conventions, where they unabashedly seek to expropriate each other's secrets, meanwhile failing to grasp the critical distinction between doing tricks and creating a sense of wonder. One guy in a tuxedo producing doves can be magic; ten guys producing doves is a travesty. "Ricky won't perform for magicians at magic shows, because they're interested in things," Weber says. "They don't get it. They won't watch him and be inspired to make magic of their own. They'll be inspired to do that trick that belongs to Ricky. Magic is not about someone else sharing the newest secret. Magic is about working hard to discover a secret and making something out of it. You start with some small principle and you build a theatrical presentation out of it. You do something that's technically artistic that creates a small drama. There are two ways you can expand your knowledge — through books and by gaining the confidence of fellow magicians who will explain these things. Ricky to a large degree gets his information from books — old books — and then when he performs for magicians they want to know, 'Where did that come from?' And he's appalled that they haven't read this stuff. So there's this large body of magic lumpen who really don't understand Ricky's legacy — his contribution to the art, his place in the art, his technical proficiency and creativity. They think he's an elitist and a snob."

Jay does not regard "amateur" as a pejorative. His two most trusted magician confidants are Persi Diaconis, a professor of mathematics at Harvard, and Steve Freeman, a corporate comptroller who lives in Ventura, California. Both are world-class sleight-of-hand artists, and neither ever performs for pay. Jay extols them as "pure amateurs in the best sense." The distinction that matters to Jay is between "good" magic and "bad." Magic "gives me more pleasure and more pain than anything else I've ever dealt with," he says. "The pain is bad magicians ripping off good ones, doing magic badly, and making a mockery of the art." One specific locale that he steers clear of is the Hollywood Magic Castle, a club whose membership consists of both amateur and professional conjurers. On a given night, one can see a great performer at the Magic Castle, but all too often the club is a tepid swamp of gossip, self-congratulation, and artistic larceny — a place where audiences who don't know better are frequently fed a bland diet of purloined ineptitude. Many years ago, Jay had an encounter there that he describes as typical.

"A guy comes up and starts telling me he's a fan," he recalls. "I say thank you, that's nice to hear. He says he used to see me perform in Boulder, Colorado. That's nice, too, I say. Then he starts talking about this wonderful piece I did with a mechanical monkey — really one of the most bizarre routines I ever worked out — and I thank him, and he says, 'Yeah, I get a tremendous response when I do that. Audiences just love it.' And I say, 'Let me ask you something. Suppose I invite you over to my house for dinner. We have a pleasant meal, we talk about magic, it's an enjoyable evening.

Then, as you're about to leave, you walk into my living room and you pick up my television and walk out with it. You steal my television set. Would you do that?' He says, 'Of course not.' And I say, 'But you already did.' He says, 'What are you talking about?' I say, 'You stole my television!' He says, 'How can you say that? I've never even been to your house.' This guy doesn't even know what a metaphor is. People ask me why I don't do lectures at magic conventions, and I say, 'Because I'm still learning.' Meanwhile, you've got people who have been doing magic for ten months and they are actually out there pontificating. It's absurd."

T. A. Waters, a mentalist and writer who is the librarian at the Magic Castle, told me, "Some magicians, once they learn how to do a trick without dropping the prop on their foot, go ahead and perform in public. Ricky will work on a routine a couple of years before even showing anyone. One of the things that I love about Ricky is his continued amazement at how little magicians seem to care about the art. Intellectually, Ricky seems to understand this, but emotionally he can't accept it. He gets as upset about this problem today as he did twenty years ago."

At some point within the past twenty years, Jay asked Dai Vernon — a.k.a. the Professor — how he coped with affronts of this sort, and Vernon replied, "I forced myself not to care."

"Maybe that's how he lived to be ninety-eight years old," Jay says.

Jay's admirers invariably dwell upon his technical mastery — what is known in the trade as "chops." According to Diaconis, he is, "simply put, one of the half-dozen best card handlers in the world. Not maybe; everybody thinks so." Diaconis and Jay were casual acquaintances as kids on the New York magic scene during the fifties, then lost track of each other for several years, in part because Jay deliberately exiled himself from the mainstream magic world. They reestablished contact twenty-odd years ago, after Diaconis caught one of Jay's appearances on the *Tonight Show*. By then, Jay had honed an out-of-left-field brand of gonzo-hip comedy magic, a combination of chops and antic irreverence. Often, he would begin a performance by demonstrating a not easily marketable skill that eventually earned him a listing in the *Guinness Book of World Records:* throwing a playing card for distance. A properly launched card would go ninety miles an hour. Unobstructed, it could travel 190 feet. From ten paces, it could pierce the outer rind of a watermelon. After impaling the flesh of a watermelon with a card, Jay would rifle one card after another into the exact same spot. He also used a plastic chicken and wind-up toys as props and targets, often inflicting disabling injuries. His patter was voluble, embroidered with orotund, baroque locutions; he would describe the watermelon rind, for instance, as the "thick pachydermatous outer melon layer."

In a memorable routine, the "Laughing Card Trick," which involved no words at all, Jay showed his hands empty and then produced cards one at a time, along the way building suspense with cackling laughter. Each time he produced a card — somehow, it was always a jack of spades — he gripped it with his lips. After doing this maneuver four times, he removed the cards from his mouth and revealed that — voilà! — they had become the four aces. Next, he would do spirit writing on a tortilla. Downshifting, he would segue to "The Four Queens," a minuetlike Victorian parable in which the four face cards representing "the feminine portion of the smart set" were "besieged" by "suitors from the lower orders." In other words, each of the four queens was grouped with three numbered cards. "Ladies and gentlemen," he would announce, "as you have seen, I have taken advantage of these tenderly nurtured and unsophisticated young ladies by placing them in positions extremely galling to their aristocratic sensibilities." Somehow, the queens must "find each other's company" — that is, transport themselves so that what remained would be three groups of four numbered cards and a quartet of queens. This Jay accomplished in a manner so simple, natural, and miraculous as to render prestidigitation invisible, thereby raising the strong possibility of divine intervention.

Jules Fisher, the theatrical-lighting designer and a friend of Jay's, told me, "Ricky will look into any effect and find the side of it that is inherently magical. He doesn't present magic as a challenge — as a matter of 'Look, I can make this disappear and you can't.' Rather, he wraps it in a dramatic plot. In many of his tricks, there are stories. In 'The Four Queens,' the cards take on personas, which is much more impressive than the question of how that card disappeared."

Michael Weber has a vivid memory of seeing Jay execute "The Four Queens" fifteen years ago on a network-television special with Doug Henning as host. "It was a transcendent moment in popular magic," he says. "Ricky had attitude, presentation, humor, and chops. Everybody was talking about that show. It was one of those times when all the elements of his talent were so self-evidently on display that even the people who could never before get it finally got it." Dai Vernon once saw Jay perform "The Four Queens" live, during a lecture-demonstration at the William Andrews Clark Memorial Library, at the University of California at Los Angeles. Afterward, the Professor told his disciple that the entire performance "restored dignity to the art of magic."

"The magical aspect of Ricky is very strong," Diaconis says. "It's one thing to see someone who is very skillful with cards and quite another to witness an effect and have just no idea what happens. With Ricky, it's very hard to isolate technique from performance. I can sense when a sleight has happened and how it happened, but I still don't see it. I just feel it intellectually. When Ricky is doing one of his poetical pieces, he's working in his own unique venue. He's mixing disparate things — quirky scholarship, iconoclasm, technique, a good story — into some soup that works. Because he picks good, strong tricks and makes them come to life, in the end there's this basic simplicity about what he does. Before Ricky came along, there had been comedy magicians, but never ones who really fooled people. And you can see the consequence — there are a dozen people now working in nightclubs doing Ricky Jay acts. But none of them are Ricky Jay."

IN *Learned Pigs & Fireproof Women* Jay devotes a chapter to "Max Malini: The Last of the Mountebanks." Malini, who was born in 1873, stood five feet two, had short arms and unusually small hands, dressed like a dandy, spoke English with a comically heavy Eastern European accent, and was celebrated as the most astonishing sleight-of-hand artist of his day. He performed all over the world, for presidents, prime ministers, robber barons, emperors, kings, and Al Capone. Jay quotes Nate Leipzig, "a master exponent of pure magic technique" and a contemporary of Malini's: "I would give up everything I know in magic just to get the reaction Malini does from vanishing a single coin." At a dinner party where Dai Vernon was present, Malini borrowed a female guest's hat, spun a half-dollar on the table, and covered it with the hat, which he then lifted to reveal not the coin but a block of ice. Though Vernon knew ahead of time that this effect would be performed, he later reported that Malini, who had remained at the table throughout the meal, "fooled the hell out of me." Jay recounts this and other Malini anecdotes with a mixture of delight and wistfulness. In a just universe, he seems to imply, he himself would have been in Leipzig's and Vernon's shoes, playing to the same discerning audiences that witnessed Malini's exemplary talents. He writes, "Malini was rarely featured on music hall or theatre stages, even though he performed in the heyday of the great illusionists. Yet far more than Malini's contemporaries, the famous conjurers Herrmann, Kellar, Thurston, and Houdini, Malini was the embodiment of what a magician should be — not a performer who requires a fully equipped stage, elaborate apparatus, elephants, or handcuffs to accomplish his mysteries, but one who can stand a few inches from you and with a borrowed coin, a lemon, a knife, a tumbler, or a pack of cards convince you he performs miracles."

Jay feels connected to Malini not only out of veneration but by a strange coincidence. Malini, who was born in a small town on the Polish-Austrian border, had the given name of Max Katz (or, perhaps, Max Katz-Breit). Max Katz was also the name of Jay's maternal grandfather, a well-to-do accountant and, most important, the one member of the family who loved and appreciated Ricky and for whom Ricky in return felt love and gratitude. "My grandfather was an amateur acquisitor of skill and knowledge," Jay says. "He was interested in a lot of things — pool, chess, checkers, calligraphy, cryptography, origami, magic. His philosophy was to take lessons from the best available people and then proceed on his own. He was really a terrific teacher. And his greatest contribution was to expose me to the best. Because of him, I was able to see on a regular basis the finest close-up-magic people in the world. Unlike me, he actually liked to fraternize with magicians." At one time, Katz was president of the Society of American Magicians. When, at the age of four, Ricky did his first trick in front of an audience — he multiplied paper coffee creamers during a backyard barbecue for the Society of American Magicians — Dai Vernon was a witness.

Jay told me, "When we watched Vernon, my grandfather would say, 'Look at the Professor and study the naturalness with which he handles objects.' He introduced me to Slydini and to Francis Carlyle, two other great close-up illusionists. These were guys who were capable of doing magic — something beyond tricks — and the fact that they were stylistically so different from each other fascinated me. With Slydini, it was important to understand that he was the master of misdirection — drawing the spectator's attention away from the sleight. With Carlyle, the purpose was to absorb what my grandfather called the clarity of instruction — how Carlyle subtly guided the spectator in a way that enhanced the clarity of the effect. There was a period of several years when I took formal lessons with Slydini. In his stage appearances, which were infrequent, he used to perform in a toreador suit, and he made one for me. I wore it with my hair slicked back, and I had these fake sideburns penciled in. I performed with doves. I did a piece called 'The Floating Cane' — stage-illusion work, with no patter, that eventually made me realize I wanted to speak and I preferred close-up. An audition was arranged for me for *The Ed Sullivan Show.* I wore my toreador suit and wanted to pretend I was Spanish, knowing it would increase my chances of getting on the show, but my parents wouldn't let me. By then, I had already done a lot of television. When I was five, I was supposed to appear on *Startime Kids,* with Ed Herlihy, but I dozed during the dress rehearsal and slept through the show. I was on a program called *Time for Pets* when I was seven. I was the youngest magician who had ever been on TV. I was awful. I was a kid. The only thing that's important is that I was very comfortable performing. I was supposed to produce a rabbit, but they couldn't find one, so I had to work with a guinea pig, which took a leak on my father's necktie. My father said, 'Perfect. You get all the glory and I get all the piss.'"

Weekends, Jay often made trips to Manhattan, first in the company of his grandfather and by adolescence often on his own. The cafeteria on the ground floor of the Wurlitzer Building, on West Forty-second Street, was to the magic demimonde what the White Horse Tavern was to literary pretenders. Jay also spent many contented hours at Al Flosso's magic shop, on West Thirty-fourth Street. He preferred Flosso's to the more popular Tannen's, which was then in Times Square, because, above all, he loved Flosso. Also, the marvelous clutter of old posters, handbills, and books appealed to him far more than the antiseptic ambience of Tannen's. "Early on, I knew I didn't want to do the kind of magic other people were doing," he says. "So I started buying old books to look for material." Flosso, in the guise of a sideshow pitchman from Coney Island, did wonderful comedy sleight of hand and had a flourishing career — in the big rooms at Grossinger's and the Concord, on the Sullivan show. When Ricky's parents asked what kind of bar-mitzvah celebration he wanted, he said he wanted Flosso to perform. "The thing that's significant about that event is that it's literally the only warm memory I have of my parents," he has said.

Prodded by Slydini and his grandfather, he entered several performing competitions at magic conventions. "I always won," he says. "But the whole thing soured me on the idea of competitions within an art." By the time he was fifteen, he had had enough of living at home. He moved in with a friend's family, moved back home again, moved to the resort town of Lake George, in upstate New York (where he discovered what it was like to support himself as a pro), and, before he turned eighteen, had left home for good. He either did or did not officially complete high school — another one of those elusive memories. Max Katz died around that time. At the funeral, Flosso ceremonially broke a wand and placed it in the casket — "the single most frightening thing I ever saw," Jay says. His grandfather's death marked the end of his relationship with his parents. (He remains on good terms with his younger sister, whom he says he admires tremendously.) By then, he was living in Illinois, having begun a peripatetic college career. Over a period of ten years, he attended five different colleges and "officially was never anything other than a freshman." At Cornell, he enrolled in the School of Hotel Management. "In case I had my own joint in Vegas, I thought I might be the only guy in the business who would know how to get around in both the casino and the kitchen," he likes to say. He and several friends formed an a-cappella doo-wop group called Chico and the Deaf Tones. The Deaf Tones were five guys named Tony plus a girl named Laura. Their big number was "Tell Laura I Love Her."

To pay tuition and otherwise make ends meet, he briefly sold encyclopedias, traveled with a carnival, worked on Wall Street as an accountant, tended bar, and, of course, did magic. From talking to Jay's friends, I gathered that there was a time when he played cards for a living. Boldly, I once raised this subject with him, and he pretended not to hear me.

"Would anybody play cards with you today?" I asked.

"Sure," he said. "Silly people."

Twice while he was still at Cornell, he appeared on the *Tonight Show*. With Ithaca as his home base, he became nomadic. He performed frequently in Aspen and Lake George, did club and concert dates all over the country with various rock and jazz groups — Ike and Tina Turner, the Chambers Brothers, Leon Redbone, Al Jarreau, Emmylou Harris, Herbie Hancock, the Nitty Gritty Dirt Band. Sometimes he was the opening act, sometimes he was the headliner. Invitations to perform in Europe materialized. In the early seventies, he moved to Los Angeles and found plenty of work, first at a club in Santa Monica called McCabe's Guitar Shop and then at the Magic Castle. Tracy Newman, a television-comedy writer who lived with him for a year, says she went to see him perform "probably seventeen times" before they started dating. Not long ago she told me, "The thing Ricky had that I'd never before seen in a magician was charm. At McCabe's, he was doing improvisational patter. He had his stuff down so well he was just free. He had the guts to bring people onstage and really play with them, instead of having to be so careful that they might see something that would cause him to blow what he was trying to do. He was very casual, but his language had a Shakespearean feel. He was brutal with hecklers — not because it would throw him off. He just didn't like hecklers. He vaporized them."

In those days, Dai Vernon had a sinecure at the Magic Castle that entitled him to living quarters nearby. Vernon's presence was the main thing that had attracted Jay to Los Angeles. When he was not on the road, he sought out the Professor's company virtually every night. Wherever they started the evening — at the Castle or somewhere else — they would invariably wind up at Canter's Deli, on Fairfax Avenue, a shrine of vinyl and Formica and leaden matzo balls. There Vernon would hold forth until five or six in the morning. A few years ago, Jay wrote a magazine article in which he described one such session at Canter's, an occasion when he petitioned for practical counsel rather than the generous praise that Vernon typically dispensed:

> "Professor," I protested, "I really want to know how I can improve my technique and performance. I want to take lessons from you. I really want advice."
>
> Vernon smiled his patented half smile, and with a delicate movement of his eyes beckoned me closer. I leaned forward with anticipation, almost unable to contain my excitement, about to receive my benediction from the master. "You want advice, Ricky," he said. "I'll give you advice. Fuck as many different women as you can. Not the same one. Not the same one. Fuck many different women. Many different women."

Persi Diaconis ran away from his unhappy home at the age of fourteen and spent two years traveling with Vernon — an unsentimental education. "Life with Vernon was a challenge," Diaconis says. "Vernon would use secrecy as a way of torturing you. When he and I were on the road, he woke up one morning and said, 'You know, I've been thinking about sleight of hand my whole life, and I think I now know how to encapsulate it in one sentence.' And then, of course, he refused to tell me." Another friend of Vernon's once said, "I wouldn't have taken a million dollars not to have known him. But I'd give a million not to know another one like him."

Vernon was extroverted, insouciant, a winning combination of gentleman and rake. Though he perfectly fitted the role of guru, he was not the paternal mentor that Jay's grandfather had been. To the extent that anyone could fill that void, Charlie Miller did. *Learned Pigs & Fireproof Women*, which Jay spent ten years writing, is dedicated "to my wonderful friend Charles Earle Miller, a unique, eccentric, and remarkable entertainer." Had Miller not been Vernon's contemporary, Jay believes, he would have been regarded as the greatest sleight-of-hand figure of his time. "For fifty or sixty years, Charlie lived in Vernon's shadow," he says. "And yet Vernon knew that Charlie was the best sleight-of-hand artist he'd ever seen." Vernon once described Miller as "unquestionably the most skillful exponent of the magic art it has ever been my pleasure to know." Miller was a shy, vulnerable man, for whom public performance was a bravura act. As a friend to Jay, Diaconis, Steve Freeman, and another accomplished magician, John Thompson — his four most reverent acolytes — he was emotionally much warmer than Vernon. "Vernon was very comfortable to be around," Freeman says. "But Charlie was your pal, Charlie was your uncle, Charlie cared about you." On the West Coast, he was the premier cruise-ship performer, and this arrangement suited his essentially rootless nature. (Jay himself worked very few cruise ships — a merciful policy, he says, because "the people who went on cruises had saved up their entire lives just to get on a boat and be away from people who looked like me.") For Vernon, Jay says, "making money was only a means of allowing him to sit in a hotel room and think about his art, about cups and balls and coins and cards." Charlie Miller was, if anything, more cerebral, even more obsessive.

"Charlie and Vernon were both magicians for magicians," says Robert Lund, the founder of the American Museum of Magic, in Marshall, Michigan. "Only magicians truly appreciated what Charlie was doing. Charlie knew more about why you do it this way instead of that way than anyone I've ever met in my life, including Ricky Jay. If there were a hundred ways of doing an effect — a card trick or sawing a lady in half — Charlie went through all hundred and analyzed each one, looking for the most natural way of doing it, the approach that would be the most palatable and acceptable to an audience."

More than any other magician Jay has known, Miller had an orthodox devotion to preserving the secrets of the art — a fundamental precept that Jay today shares with Diaconis and Freeman.

To their dismay, Vernon wrote a series of instruction books. When these began to appear in print, Diaconis said to Vernon, "Why did you publish these, Professor? We don't want the animals using tools." As a palliative, they can speculate about the secrets that Miller took to the grave — an absolutism that, while perhaps depriving him of mundane celebrity, at least made the secrets themselves immortal. "Charlie would never tell anything to anybody who wasn't really on the inside," Diaconis says. "There's something called the Sprong shift. Sprong was a night watchman — he did that for a living so that he could spend his days practicing card handling. The Sprong shift is a certain way of reversing the cards so that a card that would be in the middle will end up on top. It's a move that has been passed down only orally. It's never been described or even hinted at in writing that such a thing existed. It got disseminated to three or five of us, and the one who does it beautifully is Ricky. Charlie had the capacity to watch Ricky practice it for several hours nonstop. He'd keep moving around the room to see it from every possible angle."

After both Vernon and Miller died, there were memorial services at the Magic Castle — events that Jay refused to attend, because, he said to Freeman, "most of those people didn't know anything about Vernon and Charlie."

"I now say that keeping secrets is my single most important contribution to magic," Diaconis says. "Listen, I have lots of things I won't tell Ricky about. It's pretty hard for us to fool each other. Several years ago, he borrowed my deck and had me pick a card. Then he told me to reach into my left trousers pocket and there was the card I'd picked. For half an hour, I was as badly fooled as I've ever been. In order for him to bring that about, he had to take dead aim at me. That's a phrase we use in discussing the big con: taking dead aim — deeply researching somebody's habits."

Jay once subjected Freeman to an equally unsettling experience. "I walked into Ricky's apartment one day, and I was wearing a shirt that Charlie Miller had given to Ricky and that Ricky had left at my house," Freeman says. "I was returning it, but, just for fun, I had put it on. I took the shirt off, and Ricky said, 'Oh, just leave it on the back of that chair.' Then we started talking for a while and he said he wanted to show me a new trick. He spread the deck face-up and told me to point to a card. I did, and then I gathered and shuffled and dealt them face-up. There were only fifty-one. I didn't see my card. And he said, 'Oh, well, go over and look in the pocket of that shirt over there.' And the card was in the shirt pocket. It takes a lot of knowledge about people to be able to do something like that. Ricky was enormously satisfied. Did I figure it out? Well, I was very fooled at the time. I felt stupid, but it was nice to be fooled. That's not a feeling we get to have very often anymore."

VICTORIA DAILEY, who, along with her former husband, William Dailey, deals in rare books from a shop on Melrose Avenue in Los Angeles, likes to refer to Jay as "our worst customer." She hastens to point out, "He could be our best customer. He wants everything but can hardly buy anything." Both Daileys regard Jay as "a true eccentric" in the English sense — part Bloomsbury, part Fawlty Towers. More than fifteen years ago, they sold Jay the first book for which he paid more than a hundred dollars. The first time he spent more than a thousand dollars for a book, and, again, when he reached the five-thousand-dollar threshold, the Daileys were also involved. The latter item was Jean Prévost's *Première Partie des Subtiles et Plaisantes Inventions,* the earliest known important conjuring book, printed in Lyons in 1584.

"I bought it unhesitatingly," recalls Jay, for whom possession of the Prévost is a bittersweet memory; uncharacteristically, he parted with it during a fiscal crisis. "I bought it and then, with remarkable rapidity, three particular jobs that I thought I had went sour. One was a Johnny Carson special on practical jokes that didn't pan out because of one of his divorces. Another was a tour of Australia that was canceled by a natural disaster — in other words, by an act of God. This book was so fucking rare that people in the magic world just didn't know about it."

It is the Daileys' impression — a perception shared by other dealers in rare books and incunabula — that Jay spends a higher proportion of his disposable income on rare books and artifacts than anyone else they know. His friend Janus Cercone has described him as "an incunable romantic."

"Probably, no matter how much money he had, he would be overextended bibliomaniacally — or should the word be 'bibliographically'? Anyway, he'd be overextended," William Dailey has said. "The first time I met him, I recognized him as a complete bibliomaniac. He's not a complete monomaniac about books on magic, but within that field he is remarkably focused. His connoisseurship is impeccable, in that he understands the entire context of a book's emergence. He's not just interested in the book's condition. He knows who printed it, and he knows the personal struggle the author went through to get it printed."

In 1971, during Jay's nomadic phase, he spent a lot of time in Boston hanging out with Diaconis, who had begun to assemble a library of rare magic books. Diaconis takes credit for explicating the rudiments of collecting to Jay and animating his academic interest. He now regards Jay as "ten standard deviations out, just the best in the world in his knowledge of the literature of conjuring." Jay's collection — several thousand volumes, plus hundreds of lithographs, playbills, pamphlets, broadsides, and miscellaneous ephemera — reflects his interest not only in magic but also in gambling, cheating, low life, and what he described in the subtitle of *Learned Pigs & Fireproof Women* as "unique, eccentric and amazing entertainers: stone eaters, mind readers, poison resisters, daredevils, singing mice, etc., etc., etc., etc." Though Jay abhors the notion of buying books as investments, his own collection, while it is not for sale and is therefore technically priceless, more or less represents his net worth. There was a time, within the past decade, when he seriously considered becoming a bookdealer himself. The main thing that dissuaded him, he says, is that "I wouldn't want to sell a book to a philistine, which is what every bookseller has to do." Unlike a lot of collectors, he actually reads and rereads the books and other materials he buys, and puts them to scholarly and performing use. Therefore, he has no trouble rationalizing why he, rather than someone else who might turn up at an auction or peruse a dealer's catalog, is more worthy of owning, say, both variant editions of *A Synopsis of the Butchery of the Late Sir Washington Irving Bishop (Kamilimilianalani), a Most Worthy Mason of the Thirty-second Degree, the Mind Reader and Philanthropist, by Eleanor Fletcher Bishop, His Broken Hearted Mother,* Philadelphia, 1889 and 1890.

One day last spring, I got a phone call from Jay, who had just returned to Los Angeles from Florida, where he and Michael Weber spent several months doing "pyromagical effects" on a movie called *Wilder Napalm.*

"There's a pile of mail on my desk," he said.

"I hope there are a few checks in it," I said.

"Yes, actually, there are. But, of course, I just spent it all on a book."

The book in question was Thomas Ady's *Candle in the Dark; or, a Treatise Concerning the Nature of Witches and Witchcraft,* which includes an important seventeenth-century account of an English magic performance. I had once heard Jay allude to *A Candle in the Dark* during a lecture at the Huntington Library, in San Marino, California. The Huntington owned a copy, and so did a few other institutions. Jay described it to me as "exceedingly rare — only one copy has been sold in my collecting lifetime," and said that he had acquired his from a New York dealer "after a long negotiation." On a subsequent visit to New York, he took me to meet the dealer, Steve Weissman, a preternaturally relaxed fellow, who was obviously quite fond of him.

"We have a common interest," Weissman, who does business out of an office on the East Side, said. "We do like the same kinds of books. I don't specialize in Ricky's area of interest — only Ricky does — but I find that I gravitate toward it. My stock is dominantly literary. And I like oddball subjects: slang dictionaries, magic, gambling, con games. The advantage for me with Ricky is that he's an enthusiast for a wide range of subjects. Most customers arrive and they're entering the dealer's world, my world. He walks in and I enter his world. The next customer through the door might be a Byron fanatic and I'll have to enter *his* world. It's not a unique situation, but with Ricky it's particularly gratifying, because of the kind of collector he is — passionate and knowledgeable. Ideally, I would also include rich in that equation, but he doesn't qualify."

Referring to *A Candle in the Dark,* Weissman added, "I don't doubt that I could have sold it for more money to someone else. But it's more fun to sell it to Ricky."

A young man with a ponytail and peach-fuzzy sideburns and wearing a herringbone-tweed topcoat entered the shop. As he closed the door behind him, the doorknob fell off. He picked it up and handed it to Weissman's assistant and said, "I think this is yours."

Sotto voce, Jay said, "Who is that guy?"

"I think he's someone who's trying to swindle us into buying a Visa card, or something," Weissman said.

When the young man was ready to leave, a few minutes later, the doorknob had been reattached but would not turn. Twenty minutes elapsed before we were finally rescued by an upstairs neighbor who was able to open the door from the outside. While we waited, before our liberation seemed certain, Jay gestured at the wall-to-wall, floor-to-ceiling shelves of rare books and said, "To most people this would be hell. But to me it's just a holiday."

Several years ago, Weissman attended an auction at Christie's and, bidding on behalf of Jay and Nicolas Barker, of the British Library, bought a collection of rare engravings whose subject matter was calligraphy. Jay writes in a stylized calligraphic script, and

Barker, having spent much of his professional life cataloging and studying antiquarian manuscripts, confesses to being "passionately interested in the history of handwriting." There were more than thirty items in the auction lot, and Jay and Barker divided them according to a simple formula. "I kept all the images related to armless calligraphers," Jay says, "and Nicolas got all the calligraphers with arms."

In a chapter of *Learned Pigs* entitled "More Than the Sum of Their Parts," Jay recounts the skills and accomplishments of various men and women, all celebrated figures between the sixteenth and the early twentieth centuries, who lacked the usual complement of appendages — arms or legs or digits — and compensated in inspiring ways. He dotes especially on Matthew Buchinger, "The Wonderful Little Man of Nuremberg," who was born in 1674, died around 1740, and, in between, married four times, sired fourteen children, and "played more than a half dozen musical instruments, some of his own invention, and danced the hornpipe . . . amazed audiences with his skills at conjuring . . . was a marksman with the pistol and demonstrated trick shots at nine pins . . . was a fine penman; he drew portraits, landscapes, and coats of arms, and displayed remarkable calligraphic skills." Buchinger managed these transactions without the benefit of feet or thighs, and instead of arms he had "two fin-like excrescences growing from his shoulder blades." He stood, so to speak, only twenty-nine inches high. The Christie's auction enabled Jay to add significantly to his trove of Buchingeriana — playbills, engravings by and of the Wonderful Little Man, self-portraits, specimens of his calligraphy, and accounts of his performances as a conjurer.

Segueing from a passage about Carl Herman Unthan, who was armless, played the violin with his feet, toured in vaudeville as "Unthan, the Pedal Paganini," and "fired the rifle . . . with enough skill and accuracy to be compared with the great trick shot artists Ira Paine and Doc Carver," Jay declares, "Writers, scientists, and medical men have explored the psychologies and physiologies of these prodigies; they and the public alike are intrigued by the relationship between the horrific and miraculous."

This last phrase concisely expresses Jay's central preoccupation as a scholar and a performer. *Learned Pigs* contains only passing references to Houdini, whose tirelessness as a self-promoter was concomitant with his gifts as an illusionist. Jay has attempted to rescue from the margins of history performers who in their day were no less determined than Houdini to please their audiences. Here is an echt-Jay paragraph:

> As the novelty of fire-eating and -handling wore off, those performers not versatile enough to combine their talents into more diversified shows took to the streets. In 1861 Henry Mayhew, in Volume 3 of "London Labour and the London Poor," described one such salamander. After a fascinating and detailed account of a fire king learning his trade and preparing his demonstrations, we find the poor fellow has been reduced to catching rats with his teeth to earn enough money to survive.

The rest of the fire handlers, geeks, acid drinkers, bayonet swallowers, mentalists, contortionists, illiterate savants, faith-healing charlatans, porcine-faced ladies, and noose-wearing high divers who populate *Learned Pigs* routinely sacrifice their dignity, but they never lose their humanity. "I don't want to be seen as somebody who just writes about freaks," Jay says. "A lot of the people I write about were very famous in their day, and they were a great source of entertainment. Today, audiences are just as curious, just as willing to be amazed. But look at everything we're barraged with — it just doesn't lodge in the imagination the same way." His mission, in sum, is to reignite our collective sense of wonder.

Jay's fruitful combination of autodidacticism and freelance scholarship is itself a wonderful phenomenon. Reviewing *Learned Pigs* in the *Times,* John Gross wrote, "One effect of Mr. Jay's scholarship is to make it clear that even among freaks and prodigies there is very little new under the sun. Show him a stone-eater or a human volcano or an enterologist and he will show you the same thing being done before, often hundreds of years earlier." In the *Philadelphia Inquirer* Carlin Romano wrote, "'Learned Pigs & Fireproof Women' is a book so magnificently entertaining that if a promoter booked it into theaters and simply distributed a copy to each patron to read, he'd have the hit of the season." A blurb on the jacket from Penn and Teller says, "It's the coolest book . . . and probably the most brilliantly weird book ever." Jay wrote much of *Learned Pigs* while occupying a carrel in the rare-book stacks of the Clark Library at UCLA. At one point, Thomas Wright, a librarian at the Clark and a former professor of English literature, tried to persuade him to apply for a postdoctoral research fellowship. When Jay explained that he didn't have a doctorate, Wright said, "Maybe a master's degree would be sufficient."

"Thomas, I don't even have a B.A."

Wright replied, "Well, you know, Ricky, a Ph.D. is just a sign of docility."

AS JAY WAS COMPLETING the writing of *Learned Pigs,* he received an offer, unexpected and irresistible, to become the curator of the Mulholland Library of Conjuring and the Allied Arts. John Mulholland, who died in 1970, was a distinguished magician, historian, and writer. He was also a close friend of Houdini, whom he befriended in his capacity as editor of *The Sphinx,* the leading magic journal of its time. Above all, he was an obsessively thorough collector of printed materials and artifacts relating to magic and other unusual performing arts. In other words, if Jay and Mulholland had gotten to know each other they would have become soul mates. Mulholland's collection comprised some ten thousand volumes, in twenty languages. In 1966, he moved it to the Players Club, on Gramercy Park, and until his death he remained its curator. In 1984, the club put it up for sale. The auction gallery that was handling the sale enlisted Jay to help catalog the collection and advise on its dispersal. Jay feared that it would be broken up or sold overseas, and either outcome seemed perilously likely. At a late hour, however, a young Los Angeles attorney, businessman, and novice magician named Carl Rheuban — someone Jay had never heard of — turned up and bought the library intact, for $575,000.

Like a lot of promoters who floated extravagant fantasies during the profligate eighties, Rheuban knew friendly and indulgent bankers. As it happened, the friendliest of these bankers was Rheuban himself. In 1983, he founded the First Network Savings Bank, leased office space in Century City, offered high interest rates to attract deposits from all over the country, and started investing the funds in complex and wishful real-estate ventures. By the spring of 1985, Jay had an office on the bank premises, where the collection was housed. Soon, he also had a steady salary, a staff of three assistants, a healthy acquisitions allowance, friendlier-than-ever relationships with dealers all over the world, and control of a superb research library. Plans were drafted for what Jay anticipated would be "a dream come true": the collection would be moved to a building in downtown Los Angeles, which would also accommodate a museum and a small theater where he would regularly perform, as would other artists who appealed to his sensibilities. Edwin Dawes, a British historian of magic and a professor of biochemistry, who visited the library and regularly corresponded with Jay, has said, "It just seemed as if Ricky's fairy godmother had appeared to provide the environment in which to work and all the facilities to do the job." Even from the perspective of Jay, the inveterate skeptic, it was a nearly ideal situation. And, clearly, Rheuban, who was occupied with diverse enterprises, regarded him as the ideal overseer.

In April of 1990, however, First Network was abruptly closed by California banking regulators, and the Resolution Trust Corporation (RTC), the federal agency created to cope with the nationwide savings-and-loan crisis, moved in to liquidate its assets. Rheuban soon filed for personal bankruptcy, and was reported to be the subject of a criminal-fraud investigation. With no forewarning, Jay discovered that he could not even gain access to his own office without first receiving permission from self-important bureaucrats who didn't know Malini from minestrone. The irony of this was unbearable. Had Ricky Jay, of all people, been victimized by a high-stakes con game?

If Rheuban did commit crimes, the government has yet to persuade a grand jury that they were transgressions worthy of an indictment. Nor does Jay at this point have a desire to know how, precisely, First Network came undone. Regardless of what was going on inside the bank, Jay had felt that his working arrangement with Rheuban was basically satisfactory. Though they have not spoken in almost two years, he expresses no bitterness toward his former employer and benefactor. For the functionaries of the RTC, however, he harbors deep contempt. Because Rheuban's personal insolvency was enmeshed with the bank's insolvency, the fate of the Mulholland Library was for many months suspended in legal limbo. Brian Walton, an attorney and friend of Jay's who advised him during the fiasco, has said, "When you look at the question of the ownership of the library, the moral ownership was clearly in Ricky's hands. The financial ownership was obviously elsewhere. But, of course, artists will often become divorced from what they create. Every day, there would be one yahoo or another messing with what were, in a moral sense, Ricky's treasures. One day, Ricky came by the library and there were some government people videotaping the collection for inventory purposes. And they'd just placed their equipment wherever they felt like it. Ricky looked at one guy and said, 'Get your stuff off those posters.' And the guy said, 'I'm So-and-So, from the FBI.' And Ricky said, 'I don't care who the fuck you are. Get your crap off those posters.'"

The outlandishness of the situation was compounded by the fact that the Mulholland Library proved to be a splendid investment — the only asset in the First Network bankruptcy that had appreciated significantly. After a year and a half of what Jay regarded as neglect and mismanagement, the RTC finally put it up for sale at auction. The day before the auction, which was to be presided over by a bankruptcy judge in a downtown courtroom, Jay gave me my first and last glimpse of the collection, which was still in Century City. In the building lobby, on our way to what had been First Network's offices, on the fifth floor, Jay pointed out that the bank's small retail operation was now occupied by a custom tailor shop. Upstairs, we walked through an empty anteroom that had once been lined with vitrines, then headed down a long beige-carpeted corridor. James Rust, a young RTC employee, emerged from a corner office — formerly Rheuban's — and greeted us.

Our first stop was a large storage room filled with material from the collection of a German physician named Peter Hackhofer. "I bought different parts of this collection from Hackhofer in several crazy transactions," Jay said. "He used to lead me on incredible goose chases all over Germany. We'd end up doing business at three in the morning on the autobahn, halfway between Cologne and Frankfurt. We'd be pulled over to the side of the road with theatrical posters spread out on the roof of his car. Once, I went all the way to Germany to buy a collection that Hackhofer was going to broker, only to find out that the owner refused to sell. Months later, in New York, I met Hackhofer at a hotel. He'd brought with him a hundred posters, which, because his room was so small, he spread out in the hallway. He had to restrain me from attacking a bellboy who rolled over some of them with a luggage cart." The storage room contained hundreds of books, in German and French, as well as a silk pistol, a billiard-ball stand, a vanishing and appearing alarm clock, a cube-shaped metal carrying case for a spirit bell, and a paper box with a ribbon on it, which was about the size of a lady's handbag, and which Jay said was "a Victorian production reticule." I knew that I could have happily occupied myself there for several hours, but he seemed eager to move on. We walked down another long corridor, past the erstwhile loan-servicing and accounting departments, and came to a locked door. As

Rust unlocked it, Jay looked at me with a wry, I-will-now-have-my-liver-eaten-by-vultures sort of smile.

We stepped into a square room, perhaps thirty by thirty. Bookshelves and glass-enclosed cabinets lined the walls, and tables and flat files filled the interior. Separated from this room by a glass partition was a ten-by-twelve cubicle that had been Jay's office. It contained a desk, a wall of bookshelves, and a side table. Two automatons stood on the table. One, called "The Singing Lesson," was the creation of Jean-Eugène Robert-Houdin, the nineteenth-century watchmaker-turned-conjurer who is considered the father of modern magic. The other was a Chinese cups-and-balls conjurer built by Robert-Houdin's father-in-law, Jacques Houdin. A large, framed color poster of Malini, advertising his "Round the World Tour," hung on the wall to the left of Jay's desk.

"I heard that that poster holds some sort of special significance for you, Ricky," James Rust said.

Jay responded with an opaque, querulous stare that said, in effect, "Hey, pal, everything in this place holds special significance for me."

Along the back wall of the main room were shelved bound volumes of *The Sphinx, The Wizard, The Conjurer's Monthly, The Linking Ring, The Magic Circular, Das Programm, La Prestidigitation, Ghost, The Magic Wand, The Gen, Mahatma*, and other periodicals. I spent an hour and a half in the main room, exploring the contents of the file drawers, staring into the glass display cases, pulling books from shelves, admiring framed lithographs, and listening to Jay. Ultimately, the experience was disquieting. Connected to virtually every item was a piquant vignette — a comic oddity, a compilation of historical or biographical arcana — but each digression inevitably led to a plaintive anticlimax, because the tangible artifacts had now passed from Jay's care. I paged through the scrapbook of Edward Maro, "a Chautauqua-circuit magician who played the mandolin and did hand shadows." A Barnum and Bailey poster trumpeting automotive daredevils — "L'Auto Bolide

Thrilling Dip of Death" — had been used by Jay when he was "writing a piece about crazy car acts for an automotive magazine." There was a lithograph of Emil Naucke, a corpulent charmer in a flesh-colored tutu, of whom Jay said, "He was a German wrestler in drag, he was a famous strongman, he had a theater of varieties, and as part of his act he danced with a midget." A lithograph of Martini-Szeny depicted "a Hungarian Houdini imitator who wore chaps and a Mexican hat and used to have himself strapped to a cactus," Jay said. "I was going to write a book on Houdini imitators that I would call 'Houdini: Howdini, Oudini, Martini-Szeny, and Zucchini, Pretenders to the Throne.' And with these reference books over here I could look up and see exactly where Martini-Szeny performed in, say, February of 1918. I bought this entire collection from an old circus artist in Atlanta who did a barrel act."

We wandered back into Jay's former office at one point. To his obvious annoyance, Rust wound up the "Singing Lesson" automaton. While it was playing, Jay turned his attention to a book that had been sitting on his desk, a seventeenth-century copy of the first book on magic to be printed in Dutch. The front cover had become separated from the binding.

"That's nice," he said with sarcasm. "This was not detached."

Rust nodded in acknowledgment.

"That's creepy," Jay continued. "This was a really solid vellum binding. That's why I don't want people in here who don't know how to handle books."

"Do you know how many hands have been here, Ricky?"

"Yes, and it's really creepy."

When Rust left the room, Jay said to me, "You know, I never had any agreement with Carl. At the outset, he asked me, 'What do you want?' And I said, 'I want access to this collection for the rest of my life.' And he said, 'Fine.' After we moved in here, I unpacked every single book. We cataloged what we could, but, as with any active collection, you can never really catch up. In the five years I was here, I almost doubled the size of the collection. This was the only thing I ever did that I spoke of myself as doing into the indefinite future."

Shortly after eight o'clock the next morning, I picked Jay up in front of his apartment building, and we drove downtown to the courthouse, where the auction would take place. A couple of days earlier, he had said to me, "I've talked to a lot of people who say they might be bidding, and I can tell you that, without a single exception, they're utterly soulless. No one gets it, no one has a clue to what the collection is really about. There actually are people who are knowledgeable about this, but they're not the ones who are able to buy it." As it was, the disposition of the Mulholland Library now seemed a foregone conclusion. David Copperfield, the workaholic stage illusionist who spends several weeks each year performing in Las Vegas and the other weeks touring the world, had agreed to pay $2.2 million for it. The only thing that could alter this outcome would be a competing bidder — bids would be allowed in minimum increments of fifty thousand dollars — and none had materialized.

At the courthouse, we discovered that the bankruptcy-court clerk had altered the docket and we were more than an hour early. Jay and I retreated to a cafeteria, where we were soon joined by William Dailey, the bookdealer, and by Steve Freeman, Michael Weber, and Brian Walton. When we finally entered the courtroom, Copperfield was already seated in the front row of the spectator gallery, along with two attorneys, a personal assistant, and a couple of advisers, who were also acquaintances of Jay's. Twenty or so other people, among them several lawyers representing creditors in the Rheuban bankruptcy, were also present. Copperfield is a slender, almost gaunt man in his mid-thirties with thick black eyebrows, brown eyes, aquiline features, and leonine dark hair. He was dressed all in black: double-breasted suit, Comme des Garçons T-shirt, suede cowboy boots.

John Gaughan, a designer of stage illusions, who was seated with Copperfield, said to Jay, "Did you bring some cards?"

"Oh, yes," Jay replied. "When you feel your life threatened, you're always prepared." Then he asked Copperfield, "Where have you come from?"

"Atlantic City."

"Ah — from one gambling arena to another."

The judge, the Honorable Vincent P. Zurzolo, appeared briefly, only to learn that Katherine Warwick, the main lawyer for the RTC, had not yet arrived. Ten minutes later, she breezed in and, in a friendly, casual manner, distributed to the other lawyers present her reply to a motion objecting to the allocation of the proceeds. About half an hour of legalistic colloquy ensued — a debate over whether the auction could even take place and, if so, when. At last, the judge asked a fifty-thousand-dollar question: "Is there anyone who is here to overbid the bidder who has made the initial offer?"

There was a minute of silence, broken in my corner of the spectator section by Jay muttering, "Unbelievable. Unbelievable."

And, with that, David Copperfield — a man who owned neither a home nor an automobile but was reported to be looking for a warehouse; a man whose stage presentations were once described to me as "resembling entertainment the way Velveeta resembles cheese" — had bought the Mulholland Library for $2.2 million. Katherine Warwick reminded Copperfield's attorneys that he had fifteen days — until the end of the month — to remove the collection from Century City, because the RTC was shutting down its operation there. There were handshakes among the Copperfield entourage, and then Copperfield approached Jay.

"Thank you for everything," he said, extending his hand.

"You'll enjoy it," Jay said. "I did."

"You know you'll be welcome anytime."

"We'll speak again in the future, I'm sure," Jay said.

A friend of Jay's who also knew Copperfield said to me later, "David Copperfield buying the Mulholland Library is like an Elvis impersonator winding up with Graceland."

A few weeks ago, Copperfield arranged for Jay to be flown to Las Vegas to discuss the collection. A driver met Jay at the airport and delivered him to a warehouse. In front was an enormous neon sign advertising bras and girdles. It was Copperfield's conceit that the ideal way for a visitor to view the Mulholland Library would be to pass first through a storefront filled with lingerie-clad mannequins and display cases of intimate feminine apparel. With enthusiasm, Copperfield escorted Jay around the premises, insisting that he read each of the single-entendre slogans posted on the walls — "We Support Our Customers" and "Our Bras Will Never Let You Down" — and also the punning tributes inscribed on celebrity photographs from the likes of Debbie Reynolds, Jerry Lewis, and Buddy Hackett. When Copperfield pressed one of the red-nippled breasts of a nude mannequin, the electronic lock on a mirrored door deactivated, and he and Jay stepped into the main warehouse space. Construction work had recently been completed on an upper level. Jay followed Copperfield up a stairway and into a suite of rooms that included several offices, a bedroom, and a marble-tiled bathroom. The bathroom had two doors, one of which led to an unpartitioned expanse where the contents of the Mulholland Library — much of it shelved exactly as it had been in Century City, some of it on tables, some of it not yet unpacked — had been deposited.

Jay stayed an hour — long enough to register pleasure at seeing the collection once again and dismay at the context in which he was seeing it. When Copperfield asked whether he would be willing to work as a consultant on an occasional basis — "In effect, he wanted to know whether, whenever he needs me, I would drop whatever I'm doing and tell him what he'd bought" — Jay recognized an offer that he could easily resist.

After Jay returned to Los Angeles, he said, "As much as I love this collection, I didn't think I could handle going through Copperfield's bra-and-girdle emporium every time I went to see it."

*　　*　　*

CLEARLY, Jay has been more interested in the craft of magic than in the practical exigencies of promoting himself as a performer. His friend T. A. Waters has said, "Ricky has turned down far more work than most magicians get in a lifetime." Though he earns high fees whenever he does work, a devotion to art rather than a devotion to popular success places him from time to time in tenuous circumstances. At the moment, he is mobilizing a project that should reward him both artistically and financially. What he has in mind is a one-man show, on a stage somewhere in New York, to be billed as "Ricky Jay and His 52 Assistants" — an evening's entertainment with a deck of cards. He envisions an intimate setting.

"All I value as a performer is for people to want to see me," Jay says. "I mean people who have come just to see me — they're not going out to hear music, they're not out to get drunk or to pick up women. I'd much rather perform in a small theater in front of a few people than in an enormous Las Vegas nightclub."

Provided that the right theater and the right situation materialize, David Mamet has agreed to direct such a production. "I'm very honored to be asked," Mamet told me. "I regard Ricky as an example of the 'superior man,' according to the I Ching definition. He's the paradigm of what a philosopher should be: someone who's devoted his life to both the study and the practice of his chosen field."

Having directed Jay now in three films — and they are collaborating on the screenplay of another — Mamet holds him in high esteem as an actor. "Ricky's terrific," Mamet said. "He doesn't make anything up. He knows the difference between doing things and not doing things. The magician performs a task and the illusion is created in the mind of the audience. And that's what acting is about."

Jay now spends the greater part of his typical workdays alone in his Old Spanish–style Hollywood apartment. It is the repository of his collection, the research facility for his scholarly pursuits. Overloaded bookshelves line the living-room and bedroom walls, and stacks of books on the floors make navigation a challenge. Posters, playbills, and engravings decorate any available wall space — several Buchingers, Toby the Learned Pig (the most gifted of the sapient swine), Madame Girardelli (the fireproof woman), Houdini suspended upside down in a water-torture cell, Erno Acosta balancing a piano on his head, a three-sheet poster of Cinquevalli (the most famous juggler at the turn of the century). Jay sleeps beneath a huge color lithograph of an Asian-looking man billed as Okito, whom he described to me as "the fifth of six generations or the fourth of five generations — depending on whose story you want to believe — of a family of Dutch Jewish magicians, a twentieth-century performer whose real name was Theodore Bamberg." Between two books on a shelf in the corner of his kitchen is a photograph of Steve Martin, inscribed "To Ricky, Without you there would be no Flydini. Think about it. Steve." This refers to a comedy magic routine that Jay helped Martin develop a few years ago, a dumb-show piece that he has performed at charity events and on television. As the Great Flydini, Martin appears onstage dressed in tails, unzips his trousers, and smiles uncomfortably as an egg emerges from his fly, followed by another egg, a third egg, a lighted cigarette, a puff of smoke, two more eggs, a ringing telephone, a bouquet of flowers, a glass of wine, a silk handkerchief that a pretty girl walks off with and drops, whereupon it flies back inside his trousers, a Pavarotti hand puppet, and soap bubbles.

The last time I visited Jay in his apartment, he was working simultaneously on more than half a dozen projects. Within the past year, he has begun to do his writing on a computer, rather than in longhand on a legal pad with a calligraphic pen. This has evidently not made the process any less daunting. "Writing is the only thing in my life that hasn't gotten easier," he said. "I can say that categorically. Right now, I'm finishing a magazine article that was supposed to be about human ingenuity, but somehow I've ended up writing about child prodigies. Here's my lead sentence: 'Solomon Stone, the midget lightning calculator, was an overachiever.' I go from Solomon Stone to the Infant Salambo. This was a child who was from a turn-of-the-century show-biz family. She was abandoned by them for several years, and when they turned up again they realized she had been neglected, had had absolutely no education. But within a year she was appearing onstage, having been reinvented as Salambo, the Infant Historian — get this — 'absolutely the most clever and best-informed child the world has ever seen.'"

He showed me a prospectus for *Jay's Journal of Anomalies*, a letterpress-printed broadside for "a periodical devoted to the investigation of conjurers, cheats, hustlers, hoaxers, pranksters . . . arcana, esoterica, curiosa, varia . . . scholarly and entertaining . . . amusing and elucidating . . . iconographically stimulating."

"I just finished a piece for *Jay's Journal* on performing dogs who stole the acts of other dogs," he said. "Next, I want to do a piece about crucifixion acts — you know, real crucifixions that were done as entertainment. The idea for this came to me one Easter Sunday. Bob Lund, from the American Museum of Magic, had just sent me a little book on Billy Rose's theater that contained one sentence he knew would interest me — about a woman who swung nude from a cross to the strains of Ravel's *Boléro*. Her name was Faith Bacon. This was in the thirties. Unlike some of the other performers I've turned up, in her act she only simulated crucifixion. Anyway, I'm playing around with that."

Over the past few years, Jay has given a number of lectures on the origins of the confidence game, which he hopes to expand into a book-length history of cheating and deception. For the Whitney Museum's Artists and Writers series, he is writing a book to be illustrated by William Wegman and others. It is a history of trick magic books, which were first produced in the sixteenth century. "I'm really intrigued with the concept of the book as both a subject and an object of mystery," he said.

Most afternoons, Jay spends a couple of hours in his office, on Sunset Boulevard, in a building owned by Andrew Solt, a television producer who three years ago collaborated with him on an hour-long CBS special entitled *Learned Pigs & Fireproof Women*, which is the only prime-time network special ever hosted by a sleight-of-hand artist. He decided now to drop by the office, where he had to attend to some business involving a new venture that he has begun with Michael Weber — a consulting company called Deceptive Practices, Ltd., and offering "Arcane Knowledge on a Need to Know Basis." They are currently working on the new Mike Nichols film, *Wolf,* starring Jack Nicholson. When Jay arrived at his office, he discovered that a parcel from a British dealer had been delivered in that day's mail.

"Oh my. Oh my. This is wonderful," he said as he examined an early-nineteenth-century chapbook that included a hand-colored engraving of its subject — Claude Seurat, the Living Skeleton. "Look," he said, pointing to some scratched numerals on the verso of the title page. "This shelf mark means this was in the library of Thomas Phillips, the most obsessive book-and-manuscript collector of the nineteenth century."

The mail had also brought a catalog from another British dealer, who was offering, for £150, an engraving and broadside of Ann Moore, the Fasting Woman of Tutbury. By the time we left the office, an idea for an issue of *Jay's Journal* had begun to percolate.

"I could do fasting impostors and living skeletons," Jay said. "Or what might really be interesting would be to do living skeletons and fat men. For instance, I could write about Seurat and Edward Bright, the Fat Man. Except I might prefer a contemporary of Seurat's, Daniel Lambert. He was even fatter than Bright, but he's been written about more. With Bright, the pleasure would be writing about the wager involving his waistcoat. When he died, the wager was that five men twenty-one years of age could fit into his waistcoat. As it happened, seven grown men could fit inside. I have an exquisite black-and-white engraving of Bright, from 1751. And I have a great hand-colored engraving of Bright and Lambert, from 1815, which has an inset of the seven men in the waistcoat."

Back at the apartment, Jay examined the Seurat book and brought out for comparison an 1827 eight-page French pamphlet on Seurat. I asked what other Seurat material he had, and he removed his shoes, stood on the arm of a sofa, and brought down from a shelf one of four volumes of the 1835 edition of *Hone's Every Day Book, and Table Book; or, Everlasting Calendar of Popular Amusements, Sports, Pastimes, Ceremonies, Manners, Customs, and Events, Incident to Each of the Three Hundred and Sixty-five Days, in Past and Present Times; Forming a Complete History of the Year, Months, and Seasons, and a Perpetual Key to the Almanac.* In it he immediately found two engravings of Seurat, alongside one of which he had written in pencil a page reference to a competing living skeleton. "Oh, yes, I remember this," he said. "I have stuff on other living skeletons, too. I've got to show you this George Anderson poster I bought at an auction in London in 1983."

We moved into the dining room, where there was a flat-file cabinet. He opened the bottom drawer, which was filled to capacity with lithographs and engravings, each one a Ricky Jay divagation: "T. Nelson Downs, the King of Koins . . . Samri S. Baldwin, the White Mahatma . . . Holton the Cannonball Catcher. I have a lot of stuff on cannonball catchers . . . The Freeze Brothers, blackface tambourine jugglers . . . Sylvester Schaffer, a great variety artist . . . Josefa and Rosa Blazek, the Bohemian violin-playing Siamese twins. And here are Daisy and Violet Hilton, the saxophone-playing Siamese twins from San Antonio . . . And here's Rastelli, perhaps the greatest juggler who ever lived . . . What's that? Oh, a poster for *House of Games.* . . . I'm just trying to get to the George Anderson piece that's sticking out at the end . . . Oh, this is the Chevalier D'Eon, a male fencer in drag. He used to be the French ambassador to the Court of St. James's. It's a great story but it takes too long."

Jay had reached and placed on the dining-room table the George Anderson poster, a postbellum piece printed in New Hampshire using wooden type and a large woodblock image of Anderson, who had made an art and livelihood of attenuation. He appeared to be five and a half feet tall and to weigh about sixty-five pounds.

"I know some people find this strange and weird," Jay said. "Actually, after this life I've lived, I have no idea what is strange and weird and what isn't. I don't know who else waxes poetic about the virtues of skeleton men, fasting impostors, and cannonball catchers. And, to be honest, I don't really care. I just think they're wonderful. I really do."

— 1993

Trump Solo

ONE MORNING LAST WEEK, Donald Trump, who under routine circumstances tolerates publicity no more grudgingly than an infant tolerates a few daily feedings, sat in his office on the twenty-sixth floor of Trump Tower, his mood rather subdued. As could be expected, given the fact that his three-and-a-half-year-old marriage to Marla Maples was ending, paparazzi were staking out the exits of Trump Tower, while all weekend helicopters had been hovering over Mar-a-Lago, his private club in Palm Beach. And what would come of it? "I think the thing I'm worst at is managing the press," he said. "The thing I'm best at is business and conceiving. The press portrays me as a wild flamethrower. In actuality, I think I'm much different from that. I think I'm totally inaccurately portrayed."

So, though he'd agreed to a conversation at this decisive moment, it called for wariness, the usual quota of prefatory "off-the-record"s and then some. He wore a navy-blue suit, white shirt, black-onyx-and-gold links, and a crimson print necktie. Every strand of his interesting hair — its gravity-defying ducktails and dry pompadour, its telltale absence of gray — was where he wanted it to be. He was working his way through his daily gallon of Diet Coke and trying out a few diversionary maneuvers. Yes, it was true, the end of a marriage was a sad thing. Meanwhile, was I aware of what a success he'd had with the Nation's Parade, the Veterans Day celebration he'd been very supportive of back in 1995? Well, here was a little something he wanted to show me, a nice certificate signed by both Joseph Orlando, president, and Harry Feinberg, secretary-treasurer, of the New York chapter of the Fourth Armored Division Association, acknowledging Trump's participation as an associate grand marshal. A million four hundred thousand people had turned out for the celebration, he said, handing me some press clippings. "OK, I see this story says a half-million spectators. But, trust me, I heard a million four." Here was another clipping, from the *Times*, just the other day, confirming that rents on Fifth Avenue were the highest in the world. "And who owns more of Fifth Avenue than I do?" Or how about the new building across from the United Nations Secretariat, where he planned a "very luxurious hotel-condominium project, a major project." Who would finance it? "Any one of twenty-five different groups. They all want to finance it."

Months earlier, I'd asked Trump whom he customarily confided in during moments of tribulation. "Nobody," he said. "It's just not my thing" — a reply that didn't surprise me a bit. Salesmen — and Trump is nothing if not a brilliant salesman — specialize in simulated intimacy rather than the real thing. His modus operandi had a sharp focus: fly the flag, never budge from the premise that the universe revolves around you, and, above all, stay in character. The Trump tour de force — his evolution from rough-edged rich kid with Brooklyn and Queens political-clubhouse connections to an international name-brand commodity — remains, unmistakably, the most rewarding accomplishment of his ingenious career. The patented Trump palaver, a gaseous blather of "fantastic"s and "amazing"s and "terrific"s and "incredible"s and various synonyms for "biggest," is an indispensable ingredient of the name brand. In addition to connoting a certain quality of construction, service, and security — perhaps only Trump can explicate the meaningful distinctions between "super luxury" and "super super luxury" — his eponym subliminally suggests that a building *belongs* to him even after it's been sold off as condominiums.

Everywhere inside the Trump Organization headquarters, the walls were lined with framed magazine covers, each a shot of Trump or someone who looked an awful lot like him. The profusion of these images — of a man who possessed unusual skills, though not, evidently, a gene for irony — seemed the sum of his appetite for self-reflection. His unique talent — being "Trump" or, as he often referred to himself, "the Trumpster," looming ubiquitous by reducing himself to a persona — exempted him from introspection.

If the gossips hinted that he'd been cuckolded, they had it all wrong; untying the marital knot was based upon straightforward economics. He had a prenuptial agreement, because "if you're a person of wealth you have to have one." In the words of his attorney, Jay Goldberg, the agreement was "as solid as concrete." It would reportedly pay Marla a million dollars, plus some form of child support and alimony, and the time to do a deal was sooner rather than later. A year from now, she would become entitled to a percentage of his net worth. And, as a source *very close* to Trump made plain, "If it goes from a fixed amount to what could be a very enormous amount — even a small percentage of two and a half billion dollars or whatever is a lot of money — we're talking about very huge things. The numbers are much bigger than people understand."

The long-term matrimonial odds had never been terrifically auspicious. What was Marla Maples, after all, but a tabloid cartoon of the Other Woman, an alliteration you could throw the cliché manual at: a leggy, curvaceous blond-bombshell beauty-pageant-winning actress-model-whatever? After a couple of years of deftly choreographed love spats, Donald and Marla produced a love child, whom they could not resist naming Tiffany. A few months before they went legit, Marla told a television interviewer that the contemplation of marriage tended to induce in Donald the occasional "little freak-out" or visit from the "fear monster." Her role, she explained, was "to work with him and help him get over that fear monster." Whenever they traveled, she said, she took along her wedding dress. ("Might as well. You've got to be prepared.") The ceremony, at the Plaza Hotel, right before Christmas 1993, drew an audience of a thousand but, judging by the heavy turnout of Atlantic City high rollers, one not deemed A-list. The Trump Taj Mahal casino commemorated the occasion by issuing a Donald-and-Marla five-dollar gambling chip.

The last time around, splitting with Ivana, he'd lost the PR battle from the get-go. After falling an entire news cycle behind Ivana's spinmeisters, he never managed to catch up. In one ill-advised eruption, he told Liz Smith that his wife reminded him of his bête noire Leona Helmsley, and the columnist chided, "Shame on you, Donald! How dare you say that about the mother of your children?" His only moment of unadulterated, so to speak, gratification occurred when an acquaintance of Marla's blabbed about his swordsmanship. The screamer BEST SEX I'VE EVER HAD — an instant classic — is widely regarded as the most libel-proof headline ever published by the *Post*. On the surface, the coincidence of his first marital breakup with the fact that he owed a few billion he couldn't exactly pay back seemed extraordinarily unpropitious. In retrospect, his timing was *excellent*. Ivana had hoped to nullify a postnuptial agreement whose provenance could be traced to Donald's late friend and preceptor the lawyer-fixer and humanitarian Roy Cohn. Though the agreement entitled her to fourteen million dollars plus a forty-six-room house in Connecticut, she and her counsel decided to ask for half of everything Trump owned; extrapolating from Donald's blustery pronouncements over the years, they pegged her share at two and a half billion. In the end, she was forced to settle for the terms stipulated in the agreement because Donald, at that juncture, conveniently appeared to be broke.

Now, of course, according to Trump, things were much different. Business was stronger than ever. And, of course, he wanted to be fair to Marla. Only a million bucks? Hey, a deal was a deal. He meant "fair" in a larger sense: "I think it's very unfair to Marla, or, for that matter, anyone — while there are many positive things, like lifestyle, which is at the highest level — I think it's unfair to Marla always to be subjected to somebody who enjoys his business and does it at a very high level and does it on a big scale. There are lots of compensating balances. You live in the Mar-a-Lagos of the world, you live in the best apartment. But, I think you understand, I don't have very much time. I just don't have very much time. There's nothing I can do about what I do other than stopping. And I just don't want to stop."

A SECURITIES ANALYST who has studied Trump's peregrinations for many years believes, "Deep down, he wants to be Madonna." In other words, to ask how the gods could have permitted Trump's resurrection is to mistake profound superficiality for profundity, performance art for serious drama. A prime example of superficiality at its most rewarding: the Trump International Hotel and Tower, a fifty-two-story hotel-condominium conversion of the former Gulf and Western Building, on Columbus Circle, which opened last January. The Trump name on the skyscraper belies the fact that his ownership is limited to his penthouse apartment and a stake in the hotel's restaurant and garage, which he received as part of his development fee. During the grand-opening ceremonies, however, such details seemed not to matter as he gave this assessment: "One of the great buildings anywhere in New York, anywhere in the world."

The festivities that day included a feng-shui ritual in the lobby, a gesture of respect to the building's high proportion of Asian buyers, who regard a Trump property as a good place to sink flight capital. An efficient schmoozer, Trump worked the room quickly — a backslap and a wink, a finger on the lapels, no more than a minute with anyone who wasn't a police commissioner, a district attorney, or a mayoral candidate — and then he was ready to go. His executive assistant, Norma Foerderer, and two other Trump Organization executives were waiting in a car to return to the office. Before it pulled away, he experienced a tug of noblesse oblige. "Hold on, just lemme say hello to these Kinney guys," he said, jumping out to greet a group of parking attendants. "Good job, fellas. You're gonna be working here for years to come." It was a quintessential Trumpian gesture, of the sort that explains his popularity among people who barely dare to dream of living in one of his creations.

Back at the office, a *Times* reporter, Michael Gordon, was on the line, calling from Moscow. Gordon had just interviewed a Russian artist named Zurab Tsereteli, a man with a sense of grandiosity familiar to Trump. Was it true, Gordon asked, that Tsereteli and Trump had discussed erecting on the Hudson River a statue of Christopher Columbus that was six feet taller than the Statue of Liberty?

"Yes, it's already been made, from what I understand," said Trump, who had met Tsereteli a couple of months earlier, in Moscow. "It's got forty million dollars' worth of bronze in it, and Zurab would like it to be at my West Side Yards development" — a seventy-five-acre tract called Riverside South — "and we are working toward that end."

According to Trump, the head had arrived in America, the rest of the body was still in Moscow, and the whole thing was being donated by the Russian government. "The mayor of Moscow has written a letter to Rudy Giuliani stating that they would like to make a gift of this great work by Zurab. It would be my honor if we could work it out with the city of New York. I am absolutely favorably disposed toward it. Zurab is a very unusual guy. This man is major and legit."

Trump hung up and said to me, "See what I do? All this bullshit. Know what? After shaking five thousand hands, I think I'll go wash mine."

Norma Foerderer, however, had some pressing business. A lecture agency in Canada was offering Trump a chance to give three speeches over three consecutive days, for $75,000 a pop. "Plus," she said, "they provide a private jet, secretarial services, and a weekend at a ski resort."

How did Trump feel about it?

"My attitude is if somebody's willing to pay me two hundred and twenty-five thousand dollars to make a speech, it seems stupid not to show up. You know why I'll do it? Because I don't think anyone's ever been paid that much."

Would it be fresh material?

"It'll be fresh to them."

Next item: Norma had drafted a letter to Mar-a-Lago members, inviting them to a dinner featuring a speech by George Pataki and entertainment by Marvin Hamlisch. "Oh, and speaking of the governor, I just got a call. They're shooting a new 'I Love New York' video and they'd like Libby Pataki to go up and down our escalator. I said fine."

A Mar-a-Lago entertainment booker named Jim Grau called about a Carly Simon concert. Trump switched on his speakerphone: "Is she gonna do it?"

"Well, two things have to be done, Donald. Number one, she'd like to hear from you. And, number two, she'd like to turn it in some degree into a benefit for Christopher Reeve."

"That's not a bad idea," said Trump. "Is Christopher Reeve gonna come? He can come down on my plane. So what do I have to do, call her?"

"I want to tell you how we got Carly on this because some of your friends are involved."

"Jim, I don't give a shit. Who the hell cares?"

"Please, Donald. Remember when you had your yacht up there? You had Rose Styron aboard. And her husband wrote *Sophie's Choice*. And it's through her good offices —"

"OK. Good. So thank 'em and maybe invite 'em."

Click.

"Part of my problem," Trump said to me, "is that I have to do a lot of things myself. It takes so much time. Julio Iglesias is coming to Mar-a-Lago, but I have to *call* Julio, I have to have *lunch* with Julio. I have Pavarotti coming. Pavarotti doesn't perform for anybody. He's the highest-paid performer in the world. A million dollars a performance. The hardest guy to get. If I call him, he'll do it — for a *huge* amount less. Why? Because they like me, they respect me, I don't know."

DURING TRUMP'S ASCENDANCY, in the 1980s, the essence of his performance art — an opera-buffa parody of wealth — accounted for his populist appeal as well as for the opprobrium of those who regard with distaste the spectacle of an unbridled id. Delineating his commercial aesthetic, he once told an interviewer, "I have glitzy casinos because people expect it . . . Glitz works in Atlantic City . . . And in my residential buildings I sometimes use flash, which is a level below glitz." His first monument to himself, Trump Tower, on Fifth Avenue at Fifty-sixth Street, which opened its doors in 1984, possessed many genuinely impressive elements — a sixty-eight-story saw-toothed silhouette, a salmon-colored Italian-marble atrium equipped with an eighty-foot waterfall — and became an instant tourist attraction. In Atlantic City, the idea was to slather on as much ornamentation as possible, the goal being (a) to titillate with the fantasy that a Trump-like life was a lifelike life and (b) to distract from the fact that he'd lured you inside to pick your pocket.

At times, neither glitz nor flash could disguise financial reality. A story in the *Times* three months ago contained a reference to his past "brush with bankruptcy," and Trump, though gratified that the *Times* gave him play on the front page, took umbrage at that phrase. He "never went bankrupt," he wrote in a letter to the editor, nor did he "ever, at any time, come close." Having triumphed over adversity, Trump assumes the prerogative to write history.

In fact, by 1990, he was not only at risk, he was, by any rational standard, hugely in the red. Excessively friendly bankers infected with the promiscuous optimism that made the eighties so memorable and so forgettable had financed Trump's acquisitive impulses to the tune of $3.75 billion. The personally guaranteed portion — almost a billion — represented the value of Trump's goodwill, putative creditworthiness, and capacity for shame. A debt restructuring began in the spring of 1990 and continued for several years. In the process, six hundred or seven hundred or perhaps eight hundred million of his creditors' dollars vaporized and drifted wherever lost money goes. In America, there is no such thing as a debtors' prison, nor is there a tidy moral to this story.

Several of Trump's trophies — the Plaza Hotel and all three Atlantic City casinos — were subjected to "prepackaged bankruptcy," an efficiency maneuver that is less costly than the full-blown thing. Because the New Jersey Casino Control Act requires "financial stability" for a gaming license, it seems hard to avoid the inference that Trump's Atlantic City holdings were in serious jeopardy. Nevertheless, "blip" is the alternative "b" word he prefers, as in "So the market, as you know, turns lousy and I have this blip."

Trump began plotting his comeback before the rest of the world — or, perhaps, even he — fully grasped the direness of his situation. In April of 1990, he announced to the *Wall Street Journal* a plan to sell certain assets and become the "king of cash," a stratagem that would supposedly set the stage for a shrewd campaign of bargain hunting. That same month, he drew down the final $25 million of an unsecured $100-million personal line of credit from Bankers Trust. Within seven weeks, he failed to deliver a $43-million payment due to bondholders of the Trump Castle Casino, and he also missed a $30-million interest payment to one of the estimated 150 banks that were concerned about his well-being. An army of bankruptcy lawyers began camping out in various boardrooms.

Making the blip go away entailed, among other sacrifices, forfeiting management control of the Plaza and handing over the titles to the Trump Shuttle (the old Eastern Airlines Boston–New York–Washington route) and a twin-towered thirty-two-story condominium building near West Palm Beach, Florida. He also said goodbye to his 282-foot yacht, the *Trump Princess*, and to his Boeing 727. Appraisers inventoried the contents of his Trump Tower homestead. Liens were attached to just about everything but his Brioni suits. Perhaps the ultimate indignity was having to agree to a personal spending cap of $450,000 a month.

IT WOULD HAVE BEEN tactically wise, to say nothing of tactful, if, as Trump's creditors wrote off large chunks of their portfolios, he could have curbed his breathtaking propensity for self-aggrandizement. The bravado diminished somewhat for a couple of years — largely because the press stopped paying attention — but by 1993 he was proclaiming, "This year has been the most successful year I've had in business." Every year since, he's issued the same news flash. A spate of Trump-comeback articles appeared in 1996, including several timed to coincide with his fiftieth birthday.

Then, last October, Trump came into possession of what a normal person would regard as real money. For $142 million, he sold his half interest in the Grand Hyatt Hotel, on Forty-second Street, to the Pritzker family, of Chicago, his longtime, and long-estranged, partners in the property. Most of the proceeds weren't his to keep, but he walked away with more than $25 million. The chief significance of the Grand Hyatt sale was that it enabled Trump to extinguish the remnants of his once monstrous personally guaranteed debt. When *Forbes* published its annual list of the four hundred richest Americans, he sneaked on (373rd position) with an estimated net worth of $450 million. Trump, meanwhile, had compiled his own unaudited appraisal, one he was willing to share along with the amusing caveat "I've never shown this to a reporter before." According to his calculations, he was actually worth

$2.25 billion — *Forbes* had low-balled him by 80 percent. Still, he had officially rejoined the plutocracy, his first appearance since the blip.

Jay Goldberg, who in addition to handling Trump's matrimonial legal matters also represented him in the Grand Hyatt deal, told me that, after it closed, his client confessed that the novelty of being unencumbered had him lying awake nights. When I asked Trump about this, he said, "Leverage is an amazing phenomenon. I love leverage. Plus, I've never been a huge sleeper." Trump doesn't drink or smoke, claims he's never even had a cup of coffee. He functions, evidently, according to inverse logic and metabolism. What most people would find unpleasantly stimulating — owing vastly more than you should to lenders who, figuratively, at least, can carve you into small pieces — somehow engenders in him a soothing narcotic effect. That, in any event, is the impression Trump seeks to convey, though the point is now moot. Bankers, typically not the most perspicacious species on earth, from time to time get religion, and there aren't many who will soon be lining up to thrust fresh bazillions at him.

WHEN I MET with Trump for the first time, several months ago, he set out to acquaint me with facts that, to his consternation, had remained stubbornly hidden from the public. Several times, he uttered the phrase "off the record, but you can use it." I understood the implication — I was his tool — but failed to see the purpose. "If you have me saying these things, even though they're true, I sound like a schmuck," he explained. How to account, then, for the bombast of the previous two decades? Alair Townsend, a former deputy mayor in the Koch administration, once quipped, "I wouldn't believe Donald Trump if his tongue were notarized." In time, this bon mot became misattributed to Leona Helmsley, who was only too happy to claim authorship. Last fall, after Evander Holyfield upset Mike Tyson in a heavyweight title fight, Trump snookered the *News* into reporting that he'd collected twenty million bucks by betting a million on the underdog. This prompted the *Post* to make calls to some Las Vegas bookies, who confirmed — shockingly! — that nobody had been handling that kind of action or laying odds close to 20–1. Trump never blinked, just moved on to the next bright idea.

"I don't think people know how big my business is," Trump told me. "Somehow, they know Trump the celebrity. But I'm the biggest developer in New York. And I'm the biggest there is in the casino business. And that's pretty good to be the biggest in both. So that's a lot of stuff." He talked about 40 Wall Street — "truly one of the most beautiful buildings in New York" — a seventy-two-story landmark that he was renovating. He said he owned the new Niketown store, tucked under Trump Tower; there was a deal to convert the Mayfair Hotel, at Sixty-fifth and Park, into "super-super-luxury apartments . . . but that's like a small one." He owned the land under the Ritz-Carlton, on Central Park South. ("That's a little thing. Nobody knows that I own that. In that way, I'm not really understood.") With CBS, he now owned the Miss USA, Miss Teen USA, and Miss Universe beauty pageants. He pointed to a stack of papers on his desk, closing documents for the Trump International Hotel and Tower. "Look at these contracts. I get these to sign every day. I've signed hundreds of these. Here's a contract for two-point-two million dollars. It's a building that isn't even opened yet. It's eighty-three percent sold, and nobody even knows it's there. For each contract, I need to sign twenty-two times, and if you think that's easy . . . You know, all the buyers want my signature. I had someone else who works for me signing, and at the closings the buyers got angry. I told myself, 'You know, these people are paying a million eight, a million seven, two million nine, four million one — for those kinds of numbers, I'll sign the fucking contract.' I understand. Fuck it. It's just more work."

As a real-estate impresario, Trump certainly has no peer. His assertion that he is the biggest real-estate *developer* in New York, however, presumes an elastic definition of that term. Several active developers — among them the Rudins, the Roses, the Milsteins — have added more residential and commercial space to the Manhattan market and have historically held on to what they built. When the outer boroughs figure in the tally — and if Donald isn't allowed to claim credit for the middle-income high-rise rental projects that generated the fortune amassed by his ninety-one-year-old father, Fred — he slips further in the rankings. But if one's standard of comparison is simply the number of buildings that bear the developer's name, Donald dominates the field. Trump's vaunted art of the deal has given way to the art of "image ownership." By appearing to exert control over assets that aren't necessarily his — at least not in ways that his pronouncements suggest — he exercises his real talent: using his name as a form of leverage. "It's German in derivation," he has said. "Nobody really knows where it came from. It's very unusual, but it just is a good name to have."

In the Trump International Hotel and Tower makeover, his role is, in effect, that of broker-promoter rather than risktaker. In 1993, the General Electric Pension Trust, which took over the building in a foreclosure, hired the Galbreath Company, an international real-estate management firm, to recommend how to salvage its mortgage on a nearly empty skyscraper that had an annoying tendency to sway in the wind. Along came Trump, proposing a three-way joint venture. GE would put up all the money — $275 million — and Trump and Galbreath would provide expertise. The market timing proved remarkably favorable. When Trump totted up the profits and calculated that his share came to more than forty million bucks, self-restraint eluded him, and he took out advertisements announcing "The Most Successful Condominium Tower Ever Built in the United States."

A minor specimen of his image ownership is his ballyhooed "half interest" in the Empire State Building, which he acquired in 1994. Trump's initial investment — not a dime — matches his apparent return thus far. His partners, the illegitimate daughter and disreputable son-in-law of an even more disreputable Japanese billionaire named Hideki Yokoi, seem to have paid forty million dollars for the building, though their title, even on a sunny day, is somewhat clouded. Under the terms of leases executed in 1961, the building is operated by a partnership controlled by Peter Malkin and the estate of the late Harry Helmsley. The lessees receive almost $90 million a year from the building's tenants but are required to pay the lessors (Trump's partners) only about $1.9 million. Trump himself doesn't share in these proceeds, and the leases don't expire until 2076. Only if he can devise a way to break the leases will his "ownership" acquire any value. His strategy — suing the Malkin-Helmsley group for a hundred million dollars, alleging, among other things, that they've violated the leases by allowing the building to become a "rodent infested" commercial slum — has proved fruitless. In February, when an armed madman on the eighty-sixth-floor observation deck killed a sightseer and wounded six others before shooting himself, it seemed a foregone conclusion that Trump, ever vigilant, would exploit the tragedy, and he did not disappoint. "Leona Helmsley should be ashamed of herself," he told the *Post*.

One day when I was in Trump's office, he took a phone call from an investment banker, an opaque conversation that, after he hung up, I asked him to elucidate.

"Whatever complicates the world more I do," he said.

Come again?

"It's always good to do things nice and complicated so that nobody can figure it out."

Case in point: The widely held perception is that Trump is the sole visionary and master builder of Riverside South, the megadevelopment planned for the former Penn Central Yards, on the West Side. Trump began pawing at the property in 1974, obtained a formal option in 1977, allowed it to lapse in 1979, and reentered the picture in 1984, when Chase Manhattan lent him eighty-four million dollars for land-purchase and development expenses. In the years that followed, he trotted out several elephantine proposals, diverse and invariably overdense residential and commercial mixtures. "Zoning for me is a life process," Trump told me. "Zoning is something I have done and ultimately always get because people appreciate what I'm asking for and they know it's going to be the highest quality." In fact, the consensus among the West Side neighbors who studied Trump's designs was that they did not appreciate what he was asking for. An exotically banal hundred-and-fifty-story phallus — "The World's Tallest Building" — provided the centerpiece of his most vilified scheme.

The oddest passage in this byzantine history began in the late eighties, when an assortment of high-minded civic groups united to oppose Trump, enlisted their own architects, and drafted a greatly scaled-back alternative plan. The civic groups hoped to persuade Chase Manhattan, which held Trump's mortgage, to help them entice a developer who could wrest the property from their nemesis. To their dismay, and sheepish amazement, they discovered that one developer was willing to pursue their design: Trump. Over time, the so-called civic alternative has become, in the public mind, thanks to Trump's drumbeating, *his* proposal; he has appropriated conceptual ownership.

Three years ago, a syndicate of Asian investors, led by Henry Cheng, of Hong Kong's New World Development Company, assumed the task of arranging construction financing. This transaction altered Trump's involvement to a glorified form of sweat equity; for a fee paid by the investment syndicate, Trump Organization staff people would collaborate with a team from New World, monitoring the construction already under way and working on designs, zoning, and planning for the phases to come. Only when New World has recovered its investment, plus interest, will Trump begin to see any real profit — twenty-five years, at least, after he first cast his covetous eye at the Penn Central rail yards. According to Trump's unaudited net-worth statement, which identifies Riverside South as "Trump Boulevard," he "owns 30–50% of the project, depending on performance." This "ownership," however, is a potential profit share rather than actual equity. Six hundred million dollars is the value Trump imputes to this highly provisional asset.

OF COURSE, the "comeback" Trump is much the same as the Trump of the eighties; there is no "new" Trump, just as there was never a "new" Nixon. Rather, all along there have been several Trumps: the hyperbole addict who prevaricates for fun and profit; the knowledgeable builder whose associates profess awe at his attention to detail; the narcissist whose self-absorption doesn't account for his dead-on ability to exploit other people's weaknesses; the perpetual seventeen-year-old who lives in a zero-sum world of winners and "total losers," loyal friends and "complete scumbags"; the insatiable publicity hound who courts the press on a daily basis and, when he doesn't like what he reads, attacks the messengers as "human garbage"; the chairman and largest stockholder of a billion-dollar public corporation who seems unable to resist heralding overly optimistic earnings projections, which then fail to materialize, thereby eroding the value of his investment — in sum, a fellow both slippery and naive, artfully calculating and recklessly heedless of consequences.

Trump's most caustic detractors in New York real-estate circles disparage him as "a casino operator in New Jersey," as if to say, "He's not really even one of us." Such derision is rooted in resentment that his rescue from oblivion — his strategy for remaining the marketable real-estate commodity "Trump" — hinged upon his ability to pump cash out of Atlantic City. The Trump image is nowhere more concentrated than in Atlantic City, and it is there, of late, that the Trump alchemy — transforming other people's money into his own wealth — has been most strenuously tested.

To bail himself out with the banks, Trump converted his casinos to public ownership, despite the fact that the constraints inherent in answering to shareholders do not come to him naturally. Inside the Trump Organization, for instance, there is talk of "the Donald factor," the three to five dollars per share that Wall Street presumably discounts Trump Hotels and Casino Resorts by allowing for his braggadocio and unpredictability. The initial public offering, in June 1995, raised $140 million, at $14 a share. Less than a year later, a secondary offering, at $31 per share, brought in an additional $380 million. Trump's personal stake in the company now stands at close to 40 percent. As chairman, Donald had an excellent year in 1996, drawing a million-dollar salary, another million for miscellaneous "services," and a bonus of five million. As a shareholder, however, he did considerably less well. A year ago, the stock traded at thirty-five dollars; it now sells for around ten.

Notwithstanding Trump's insistence that things have never been better, Trump Hotels and Casino Resorts has to cope with several thorny liabilities, starting with a junk-bond debt load of $1.7 billion. In 1996, the company's losses amounted to $3.27 per share — attributable, in part, to extraordinary expenses but also to the fact that the Atlantic City gaming industry has all but stopped growing. And, most glaringly, there was the burden of the Trump Castle, which experienced a 10 percent revenue decline, the worst of any casino in Atlantic City.

Last October, the Castle, a heavily leveraged consistent money loser that had been wholly owned by Trump, was bought into Trump Hotels, a transaction that gave him 5,837,000 shares of stock. Within two weeks — helped along by a reduced earnings estimate from a leading analyst — the stock price, which had been eroding since the spring, began to slide more precipitously, triggering a shareholder lawsuit that accused Trump of self-dealing and a "gross breach of his fiduciary duties." At which point he began looking for a partner. The deal Trump came up with called for Colony Capital, a sharp real-estate outfit from Los Angeles, to buy 51 percent of the Castle for a price that seemed to vindicate the terms under which he'd unloaded it on the public company. Closer inspection revealed, however, that Colony's capital injection would give it high-yield preferred, rather than common, stock — in other words, less an investment than a loan. Trump-l'oeil: Instead of trying to persuade the world that he owned something that wasn't his, he was trying to convey the impression that he would part with an onerous asset that, as a practical matter, he would still be stuck with. In any event, in March the entire deal fell apart. Trump, in character, claimed that he, not Colony, had called it off.

The short-term attempt to solve the Castle's problems is a four-million-dollar cosmetic overhaul. This so-called re-theming will culminate in June, when the casino acquires a new name: Trump Marina. One day this winter, I accompanied Trump when he buzzed into Atlantic City for a re-theming meeting with Nicholas Ribis, the president and chief executive officer of Trump Hotels, and several Castle executives. The discussion ranged from the size of the lettering on the outside of the building to the sparkling gray granite in the lobby to potential future renderings, including a version with an as yet unbuilt hotel tower and a permanently docked yacht to be called *Miss Universe*. Why the boat? "It's just an attraction," Trump said. "You understand, this would be part of a phase-two or phase-three expansion. It's going to be the largest yacht in the world."

From the re-theming meeting, we headed for the casino, and along the way Trump received warm salutations. A white-haired woman wearing a pink warm-up suit and carrying a bucket of quarters said, "Mr. Trump, I just love you, darling." He replied, "Thank you. I love you, too," then turned to me and said, "You see, they're good people. And I like people. You've gotta be nice. They're like friends."

The Castle had 2,239 slot machines, including, in a far corner, 13 brand-new and slightly terrifying *Wheel of Fortune*-theme contraptions, which were about to be officially unveiled. On hand were representatives of International Game Technology (the machines' manufacturer), a press entourage worthy of a military briefing in the wake of a Grenada-caliber invasion, and a couple of hundred onlookers — all drawn by the prospect of a personal appearance by Vanna White, the doyenne of *Wheel of Fortune*. Trump's arrival generated satisfying expressions of awe from the rubberneckers, though not the spontaneous burst of applause that greeted Vanna, who had been conscripted for what was described as "the ceremonial first pull."

When Trump spoke, he told the gathering, "This is the beginning of a new generation of machine." Vanna pulled the crank, but the crush of reporters made it impossible to tell what was going on or even what denomination of currency had been sacrificed. The demographics of the crowd suggested that the most efficient machine would be one that permitted direct deposit of a Social Security check. After a delay that featured a digital musical cacophony, the machine spat back a few coins. Trump said, "Ladies and gentlemen, it took a little while. We hope it doesn't take you as long. And we just want to thank you for being our friends." And then we were out of there. "This is what we do. What can I tell you?" Trump said, as we made our way through the casino.

Vanna White was scheduled to join us for the helicopter flight back to New York, and later, as we swung over Long Island City, heading for a heliport on the East Side, Trump gave Vanna a little hug and, not for the first time, praised her star turn at the Castle. "For the opening of thirteen slot machines, I'd say we did all right today," he said, and then they slapped high fives.

IN A 1990 *Playboy* interview, Trump said that the yacht, the glitzy casinos, the gleaming bronze of Trump Tower were all "props for the show," adding that "the show is 'Trump' and it is sold-out performances everywhere." In 1985, the show moved to Palm Beach. For $10 million, Trump bought Mar-a-Lago, a 118-room Hispano-Moorish-Venetian castle built in the twenties by Marjorie Merriweather Post and E. F. Hutton, set on 17.5 acres extending from the ocean to Lake Worth. Ever since, his meticulous restoration and literal regilding of the property have been a work in progress. The winter of 1995–96 was Mar-a-Lago's first full season as a commercial venture, a private club with a twenty-five-thousand-dollar initiation fee (which later rose to fifty thousand and is now quoted at seventy-five thousand). The combination of the Post-Hutton pedigree and Trump's stewardship offered a paradigm of how an aggressively enterprising devotion to Good Taste inevitably transmutes to Bad Taste — but might nevertheless pay for itself.

Only Trump and certain of his minions know who among Mar-a-Lago's more than three hundred listed members has actually forked over initiation fees and who's paid how much for the privilege. Across the years, there have been routine leaks by a mysterious unnamed spokesman within the Trump Organization to the effect that this or that member of the British royal family was planning to buy a pied-à-terre in Trump Tower. It therefore came as no surprise when, during early recruiting efforts at Mar-a-Lago, Trump announced that the Prince and Princess of Wales, their mutual antipathy notwithstanding, had signed up. Was there any documentation? Well, um, Chuck and Di were *honorary* members. Among the honorary members who have yet to pass through Mar-a-Lago's portals are Henry Kissinger and Elizabeth Taylor.

The most direct but not exactly most serene way to travel to Mar-a-Lago, I discovered one weekend not long ago, is aboard Trump's 727, the same aircraft he gave up during the blip and, after an almost decent interval, bought back. My fellow passengers included Eric Javits, a lawyer and nephew of the late Senator Jacob Javits, bumming a ride; Ghislaine Maxwell, the daughter of the late publishing tycoon and inadequate swimmer Robert Maxwell, also bumming a ride; Matthew Calamari, a telephone-booth-size bodyguard who is the head of security for the entire Trump Organization; and Eric Trump, Donald's thirteen-year-old son.

The solid-gold fixtures and hardware (sinks, seat-belt clasps, door hinges, screws), well-stocked bar and larder, queen-size bed, and bidet (thoughtfully outfitted with a leather-cushioned cover in case of sudden turbulence) implied hedonistic possibilities — the plane often ferried high rollers to Atlantic City — but I witnessed only good clean fun. We hadn't been airborne long when Trump decided to watch a movie. He'd brought along *Michael,* a recent release, but twenty minutes after popping it into the VCR he got bored and switched to an old favorite, a Jean Claude Van Damme slugfest called *Bloodsport,* which he pronounced "an incredible, fantastic movie." By assigning to his son the task of fast-forwarding through all the plot exposition — Trump's goal being "to get this two-hour movie down to forty-five minutes" — he eliminated any lulls between the nose hammering, kidney tenderizing, and shin whacking. When a beefy bad guy who was about to squish a normal-size good guy received a crippling blow to the scrotum, I laughed. "Admit it, you're laughing!" Trump shouted. "You want to write that Donald Trump was loving this ridiculous Jean Claude Van Damme movie, but are you willing to put in there that you were loving it, too?"

A small convoy of limousines greeted us on the runway in Palm Beach, and during the ten-minute drive to Mar-a-Lago Trump waxed enthusiastic about a "spectacular, world-class" golf course he was planning to build on county-owned land directly opposite the airport. Trump, by the way, is a skilled golfer. A source extremely close to him — by which I mean off the record, but I can use it — told me that Claude Harmon, a former winner of the Masters tournament and for thirty-three years the club pro at Winged Foot, in Mamaroneck, New York, once described Donald as "the best weekend player" he'd ever seen.

The only formal event on Trump's agenda had already gotten under way. Annually, the publisher of *Forbes* invites eleven corporate potentates to Florida, where they spend a couple of nights aboard the company yacht, the *Highlander,* and, during the day, adroitly palpate each other's brains and size up each other's short games. A supplementary group of capital-gains-tax skeptics had been invited to a Friday-night banquet in the Mar-a-Lago ballroom. Trump arrived between the roast-duck appetizer and the roasted-portabello-mushroom salad and took his seat next to

Malcolm S. (Steve) Forbes, Jr., the erstwhile presidential candidate and the chief executive of Forbes, at a table that also included *les grands fromages* of Hertz, Merrill Lynch, the CIT Group, and Countrywide Credit Industries. At an adjacent table, Marla Maples Trump, who had just returned from Shreveport, Louisiana, where she was rehearsing her role as cohost of the Miss USA pageant, discussed global politics and the sleeping habits of three-year-old Tiffany with the corporate chiefs and chief spouses of AT&T, Sprint, and Office Depot. During coffee, Donald assured everyone present that they were "very special" to him, that he wanted them to think of Mar-a-Lago as home, and that they were all welcome to drop by the spa the next day for a freebie.

Tony Senecal, a former mayor of Martinsburg, West Virginia, who now doubles as Trump's butler and Mar-a-Lago's resident historian, told me, "Some of the restoration work that's being done here is so subtle it's almost not Trump-like." Subtlety, however, is not the dominant motif. Weary from handling Trump's legal work, Jay Goldberg used to retreat with his wife to Mar-a-Lago for a week each year. Never mind the tapestries, murals, frescoes, winged statuary, life-size portrait of Trump (titled *The Visionary*), bathtub-size flower-filled samovars, vaulted Corinthian colonnade, thirty-four-foot ceilings, blinding chandeliers, marquetry, overstuffed and gold-leaf-stamped everything else, Goldberg told me; what nudged him around the bend was a small piece of fruit.

"We were surrounded by a staff of twenty people," he said, "including a footman. I didn't even know what that was. I thought maybe a chiropodist. Anyway, wherever I turned there was always a bowl of fresh fruit. So there I am, in our room, and I decide to step into the bathroom to take a leak. And on the way I grab a kumquat and eat it. Well, by the time I come out of the bathroom the *kumquat has been replaced.*"

As for the Mar-a-Lago spa, aerobic exercise is an activity Trump indulges in "as little as possible," and he's therefore chosen not to micromanage its daily affairs. Instead, he brought in a Texas outfit called the Greenhouse Spa, proven specialists in mud wraps, manual lymphatic drainage, reflexology, shiatsu and Hawaiian hot-rock massage, loofah polishes, sea-salt rubs, aromatherapy, acupuncture, peat baths, and Japanese steeping-tub protocol. Evidently, Trump's philosophy of wellness is rooted in a belief that prolonged exposure to exceptionally attractive young female spa attendants will instill in the male clientele a will to live. Accordingly, he limits his role to a pocket veto of key hiring decisions. While giving me a tour of the main exercise room, where Tony Bennett, who does a couple of gigs at Mar-a-Lago each season and has been designated an "artist-in-residence," was taking a brisk walk on a treadmill, Trump introduced me to "our resident physician, Dr. Ginger Lea Southall" — a recent chiropractic-college graduate. As Dr. Ginger, out of earshot, manipulated the sore back of a grateful member, I asked Trump where she had done her training. "I'm not sure," he said. "Baywatch Medical School? Does that sound right? I'll tell you the truth. Once I saw Dr. Ginger's photograph, I didn't really need to look at her résumé or anyone else's. Are you asking, 'Did we hire her because she'd trained at Mount Sinai for fifteen years?' The answer is no. And I'll tell you why: because by the time she's spent fifteen years at Mount Sinai, we don't want to look at her."

MY VISIT happened to coincide with the coldest weather of the winter, and this gave me a convenient excuse, at frequent intervals, to retreat to my thousand-dollar-a-night suite and huddle under the bedcovers in fetal position. Which is where I was around ten-thirty Saturday night when I got a call from Tony Senecal, summoning me to the ballroom. The furnishings had been altered since the *Forbes* banquet the previous evening. Now there was just a row of armchairs in the center of the room and a couple of low tables, an arrangement that meant Donald and Marla were getting ready for a late dinner in front of the TV. They'd already been out to a movie with Eric and Tiffany and some friends and bodyguards, and now a theater-size screen had descended from the ceiling so that they could watch a pay-per-view telecast of a junior-welterweight-championship boxing match between Oscar de la Hoya and Miguel Angel Gonzalez.

Marla was eating something green, while Donald had ordered his favorite, meat loaf and mashed potatoes. "We have a chef who makes the greatest meat loaf in the world," he said. "It's so great I told him to put it on the menu. So whenever we have it, half the people order it. But then afterward, if you ask them what they ate, they always deny it."

Trump is not only a boxing fan but an occasional promoter, and big bouts are regularly staged at his hotels in Atlantic City. Whenever he shows up in person, he drops by to wish the fighters luck beforehand and is always accorded a warm welcome, with the exception of a chilly reception not long ago from the idiosyncratic Polish head-butter and rabbit-puncher Andrew Golota. This was just before Golota went out and pounded Riddick Bowe into retirement, only to get himself disqualified for a series of low blows that would've been perfectly legal in *Bloodsport*.

"Golota's a killer," Trump said admiringly. "A stone-cold killer."

When I asked Marla how she felt about boxing, she said, "I enjoy it a lot, just as long as nobody gets hurt."

WHEN A CALL CAME a while back from Aleksandr Ivanovich Lebed, the retired general, amateur boxer, and restless pretender to the presidency of Russia, explaining that he was headed to New York and wanted to arrange a meeting, Trump was pleased but not surprised. The list of superpower leaders and geopolitical strategists with whom Trump has engaged in frank and fruitful exchanges of viewpoints includes Mikhail Gorbachev, Richard Nixon, Jimmy Carter, Ronald Reagan, George Bush, former Secretary of Defense William Perry, and the entire Joint Chiefs of Staff. (He's also pals with Sylvester Stallone and Clint Eastwood, men's men who enjoy international reputations for racking up massive body counts.) In 1987, fresh from his grandest public-relations coup — repairing in three and a half months, under budget and for no fee, the Wollman skating rink, in Central Park, a job that the city of New York had spent six years and $12 million bungling — Trump contemplated how, in a larger sphere, he could advertise himself as a doer and dealmaker. One stunt involved orchestrating an "invitation" from the federal government to examine the Williamsburg Bridge, which was falling apart. Trump had no real interest in the job, but by putting on a hard hat and taking a stroll on the bridge for the cameras he stoked the fantasy that he could rebuild the city's entire infrastructure. From there it was only a short leap to saving the planet. What if, say, a troublemaker like Muammar al-Qaddafi got his hands on a nuclear arsenal? Well, Trump declared, he stood ready to work with the leaders of the then Soviet Union to coordinate a formula for coping with Armageddon-minded lunatics.

The clear purpose of Lebed's trip to America, an unofficial visit that coincided with the second Clinton inaugural, was to add some reassuring human texture to his image as a plainspoken tough guy. Simultaneously, his domestic political prospects could be enhanced if voters back home got the message that Western capitalists felt comfortable with him. Somewhere in Lebed's calculations was the understanding that, to the nouveau entrepreneurs of the freebooter's paradise that is now Russia, Trump looked and smelled like very old money.

Their rendezvous was scheduled for midmorning. Having enlisted as an interpreter Inga Bogutska, a receptionist whose father, by coincidence, was a Russian general, Trump decided to greet his visitor in the lobby. When it turned out that Lebed, en route from an audience with a group of *Times* editors and reporters, was running late, Trump occupied himself by practicing his golf swing and surveying the female pedestrians in the atrium. Finally, Lebed arrived, a middle-aged but ageless fellow with a weathered, fleshy face and hooded eyes, wearing a gray business suit and an impassive expression. After posing for a *Times* photographer, they rode an elevator to the twenty-sixth floor, and along the way Trump asked, "So, how is everything in New York?"

"Well, it's hard to give an assessment, but I think it is brilliant," Lebed replied. He had a deep, bullfroggy voice, and his entourage of a half-dozen men included an interpreter, who rendered Inga Bogutska superfluous.

"Yes, it's been doing very well," Trump agreed. "New York is on a very strong up. And we've been reading a lot of great things about this gentleman and his country."

Inside his office, Trump immediately began sharing with Lebed some of his treasured possessions. "This is a shoe that was given to me by Shaquille O'Neal," he said. "Basketball. *Shaquille O'Neal.* Seven feet three inches, I guess. This is his sneaker, the actual sneaker. In fact, he gave this to me after a game."

"I've always said," Lebed sagely observed, "that after size forty-five, which I wear, then you start wearing trunks on your feet."

"That's true," said Trump. He moved on to a replica of a Mike Tyson heavyweight-championship belt, followed by an Evander Holyfield glove. "He gave me this on my fiftieth birthday. And then he beat Tyson. I didn't know who to root for. And then, again, here is Shaquille O'Neal's shirt. Here, you might want to see this. This was part of an advertisement for Versace, the fashion designer. These are photographs of Madonna on the stairs at Mar-a-Lago, my house in Florida. And this photograph shows something that we just finished and are very proud of. It's a big hotel called Trump International. And it's been very successful. So we've had a lot of fun."

Trump introduced Lebed to Howard Lorber, who had accompanied him a few months earlier on his journey to Moscow, where they looked at properties to which the Trump moniker might be appended. "Howard has major investments in Russia," he told Lebed, but when Lorber itemized various ventures none seemed to ring a bell.

"See, they don't know you," Trump told Lorber. "With all that investment, they don't know you. Trump they know."

Some "poisonous people" at the *Times*, Lebed informed Trump, were "spreading some funny rumors that you are going to cram Moscow with casinos."

Laughing, Trump said, "Is that right?"

"I told them that I know you build skyscrapers in New York. High-quality skyscrapers."

"We are actually looking at something in Moscow right now, and it would be skyscrapers and hotels, not casinos. Only quality stuff. But thank you for defending me. I'll soon be going again to Moscow. We're looking at the Moskva Hotel. We're also looking at the Rossiya. That's a very big project; I think it's the largest hotel in the world. And we're working with the local government, the mayor of Moscow and the mayor's people. So far, they've been very responsive."

LEBED: You must be a very confident person. You are building straight into the center.

TRUMP: I always go into the center.

LEBED: I hope I'm not offending by saying this, but I think you are a litmus testing paper. You are at the end of the edge. If Trump goes to Moscow, I think America will follow. So I consider these projects of yours to be very important. And I'd like to help you as best I can in putting your projects into life. I want to create a canal or riverbed for capital flow. I want to minimize the risks and get rid of situations where the entrepreneur has to try to hide his head between his shoulders. I told the *New York Times* I was talking to you because you are a professional — a high-level professional — and if you invest, you invest in real stuff. Serious, high-quality projects. And you deal with serious people. And I deem you to be a very serious person. That's why I'm meeting you.

TRUMP: Well, that's very nice. Thank you very much. I have something for you. This is a little token of my respect. I hope you like it.

This is a book called *The Art of the Deal*, which a lot of people have read. And if you read this book you'll know the art of the deal better than I do.

The conversation turned to Lebed's lunch arrangements and travel logistics — "It's very tiring to meet so many people," he confessed — and the dialogue began to feel stilted, as if Trump's limitations as a Kremlinologist had exhausted the potential topics. There was, however, one more subject he wanted to cover.

"Now, you were a boxer, right?" he said. "We have a lot of big matches at my hotels. We just had a match between Riddick Bowe and Andrew Golota, from Poland, who won the fight but was disqualified. He's actually a great fighter if he can ever get through a match without being disqualified. And, to me, you look tougher than Andrew Golota."

In response, Lebed pressed an index finger to his nose, or what was left of it, and flattened it against his face.

"You do look seriously tough," Trump continued. "Were you an Olympic boxer?"

"No, I had a rather modest career."

"Really? The newspapers said you had a great career."

"At a certain point, my company leader put the question straight: either you do the sports or you do the military service. And I selected the military."

"You made the right decision," Trump agreed, as if putting to rest any notion he might have entertained about promoting a Lebed exhibition bout in Atlantic City.

Norma Foerderer came in with a camera to snap a few shots for the Trump archives and to congratulate the general for his fancy footwork in Chechnya. Phone numbers were exchanged, and Lebed, before departing, offered Trump a benediction: "You leave on the earth a very good trace for centuries. We're all mortal, but the things you build will stay forever. You've already proven wrong the assertion that the higher the attic, the more trash there is."

When Trump returned from escorting Lebed to the elevator, I asked him his impressions.

"First of all, you wouldn't want to play nuclear weapons with this fucker," he said. "Does he look as tough and cold as you've ever seen? This is not like your average real-estate guy who's rough and mean. This guy's beyond that. You see it in the eyes. This guy is a killer. How about when I asked, 'Were you a boxer?' Whoa — that nose is a piece of rubber. But me he liked. When we went out to the elevator, he was grabbing me, holding me, he felt very good. And he liked what I do. You know what? I think I did a good job for the country today."

The phone rang — Jesse Jackson calling about some office space Trump had promised to help the Rainbow Coalition lease at 40 Wall Street. ("Hello, Jesse. How ya doin'? You were on Rosie's show? She's terrific, right? Yeah, I think she is . . . Okay-y-y, how are *you?*") Trump hung up, sat forward, his eyebrows arched, smiling a smile that contained equal measures of surprise and self-satisfaction. "You gotta say, I cover the gamut. Does the kid cover the gamut? Boy, it never ends. I mean, people have no idea. Cool life. You know, it's sort of a cool life."

ONE SATURDAY THIS WINTER, Trump and I had an appointment at Trump Tower. After I'd waited ten minutes, the concierge directed me to the penthouse. When I emerged from the elevator, there Donald stood, wearing a black cashmere topcoat, navy suit, blue-and-white-pinstriped shirt, and maroon necktie. "I thought you might like to see my apartment," he said, and as I squinted against the glare of gilt and mirrors in the entrance corridor he added, "I don't really do this." That we both knew this to be a transparent fib — photo spreads of the fifty-three-room triplex and its rooftop park had appeared in several magazines, and it had been featured on *Lifestyles of the Rich and Famous* — in no way undermined my enjoyment of the visual and aural assault that followed: the twenty-nine-foot-high living room with its erupting fountain and vaulted ceiling decorated with neo-Romantic frescoes; the two-story dining room with its carved ivory frieze ("I admit that the ivory's kind of a no-no"); the onyx columns with marble capitals that had come from "a castle in Italy"; the chandelier that originally hung in "a castle in Austria"; the African blue-onyx lavatory. As we admired the view of Central Park, to the north, he said, "This is the greatest apartment ever built. There's never been anything like it. There's no apartment like this anywhere. It was harder to build this apartment than the rest of the building. A lot of it I did just to see if it could be done. All the very wealthy people who think they know great apartments come here and they say, 'Donald, forget it. This is the greatest.'" Very few touches suggested that real people actually lived there — where was it, exactly, that Trump sat around in his boxers, eating roast-beef sandwiches, channel surfing, and scratching where it itched? Where was it that Marla threw her jogging clothes? — but no matter. "Come here, I'll show you how life works," he said, and we turned a couple of corners and wound up in a sitting room that had a Renoir on one wall and a view that extended beyond the Statue of Liberty. "My apartments that face the park go for twice as much as the apartments that face south. But I consider *this* view to be more beautiful than *that* view, especially at night. As a cityscape, it can't be beat."

We then drove down to 40 Wall Street, where members of a German television crew were waiting for Trump to show them around. ("This will be the finest office building anywhere in New York. Not just downtown — anywhere in New York.") Along the way, we stopped for a light at Forty-second Street and First Avenue. The driver of a panel truck in the next lane began waving, then rolled down his window and burbled, "I never see you in person!" He was fortyish, wore a watch cap, and spoke with a Hispanic inflection. "But I see you a lot on TV."

"Good," said Trump. "Thank you. I think."

"Where's Marla?"

"She's in Louisiana, getting ready to host the Miss USA pageant. You better watch it. OK?"

"OK, I promise," said the man in the truck. "Have a nice day, Mr. Trump. And have a *profitable* day."

"Always."

Later, Trump said to me, "You want to know what total recognition is? I'll tell you how you know you've got it. When the Nigerians on the street corners who don't speak a word of English, who have no clue, who're selling watches for some guy in New Jersey — when you walk by and those guys say, 'Trump! Trump!' That's total recognition."

Next, we headed north, to Mount Kisco, in Westchester County — specifically to Seven Springs, a fifty-five-room limestone-and-granite Georgian splendor completed in 1917 by Eugene Meyer, the father of Katharine Graham. If things proceeded according to plan, within a year and a half the house would become the centerpiece of the Trump Mansion at Seven Springs, a golf club where anyone willing to part with $250,000 could tee up. As we approached, Trump made certain I paid attention to the walls lining the driveway. "Look at the quality of this granite. Because I'm like, you know, into quality. Look at the quality of that wall. Hand-carved granite, and the same with the house." Entering a room where two men were replastering a ceiling, Trump exulted, "We've got the pros here! You don't see too many plasterers anymore. I take a union plasterer from New York and bring him up here. You know why? Because he's the best." We canvassed the upper floors and then the basement, where Trump sized up the bowling alley as a potential spa. "This is very much Mar-a-Lago all over again," he said. "A great building, great land, great location. Then the question is what to do with it."

From the rear terrace, Trump mapped out some holes of the golf course: an elevated tee above a par three, across a ravine filled with laurel and dogwood; a couple of parallel par fours above the slope that led to a reservoir. Then he turned to me and said, "I bought this whole thing for seven and a half million dollars. People ask, 'How'd you do that?' I said, 'I don't know.' Does that make sense?" Not really, nor did his next utterance: "You know, nobody's ever seen a granite house before."

Granite? Nobody? Never? In the history of humankind? Impressive.

A few months ago, Marla Maples Trump, with a straight face, told an interviewer about life with hubby: "He really has the desire to have me be more of the traditional wife. He definitely wants his dinner promptly served at seven. And if he's home at six-thirty it should be ready by six-thirty." Oh well, so much for that.

In Trump's office the other morning, I asked whether, in light of his domestic shuffle, he planned to change his living arrangements. He smiled for the first time that day and said, "Where am I going to live? That might be the most difficult question you've asked so far. I want to finish the work on my apartment at Trump International. That should take a few months, maybe two, maybe six. And then I think I'll live there for maybe six months. Let's just say, for a period of time. The buildings always work better when I'm living there."

What about the Trump Tower apartment? Would that sit empty?

"Well, I wouldn't sell that. And, of course, there's no one who would ever build an apartment like that. The penthouse at Trump International isn't nearly as big. It's maybe seven thousand square feet. But it's got a living room that is the most spectacular residential room in New York. A twenty-five-foot ceiling. I'm telling you, the best room anywhere. Do you understand?"

I think I did: the only apartment with a better view than the best apartment in the world was the same apartment. Except for the one across the park, which had the most spectacular living room in the world. No one had ever seen a granite house before. And, most important, every square inch belonged to Trump, who had aspired to and achieved the ultimate luxury, an existence unmolested by the rumbling of a soul. "Trump" — a fellow with universal recognition but with a suspicion that an interior life was an intolerable inconvenience, a creature everywhere and nowhere, uniquely capable of inhabiting it all at once, all alone.

— 1997

Joe Mitchell's Secret

ONLY THE MOST mule-headed writer, or maybe only the luckiest and least distractible, willingly pursues wire to wire a single theme. Joseph Mitchell grew up a cotton and tobacco grower's son in Fairmont, a small town in southeastern North Carolina. His father had hoped he'd join the family enterprise but gave up when it became plain that his oldest child, though an otherwise fine student, could never get the hang of multiplication and long division. He arrived in New York in the fall of 1929, when he was twenty-one, and found work as a newspaper reporter. A couple of years later, briefly "sick of the whole business," he went to sea aboard a Russia-bound freighter, then returned to reporting. For another sixty-five years he stayed at it, until the spring of 1996, when he died and created an unfillable hole in the city and at *The New Yorker*, where he'd joined the staff in 1938. Death meant repatriation, figurative and literal — to a specific spot in the sandy soil beneath a slight rise in a treeless field bordered on one side by a swamp, on another by sweet gums, pines, and oaks, and on another by farmland planted with rotating crops of soybeans, corn, and winter wheat. This was a destination he'd contemplated since 1964, when his mother died and his father invested in a family burial plot. Mitchell was a connoisseur of graveyards, a pensive but not necessarily gloomy necropolitan tourist, and a virtuoso of

what he called "graveyard humor." In one of his most arresting reporting pieces, "Mr. Hunter's Grave," he described the pleasure of
wandering with "a wild-flower book and a couple of sandwiches in
my pockets" among the old graveyards on the south shore of
Staten Island. Such constitutionals consistently had a tonic effect:
"For some reason I don't know and don't want to know, after I
have spent an hour or so in one of these cemeteries, looking at
gravestone designs and reading inscriptions and identifying wild
flowers and scaring rabbits out of the weeds and reflecting on the
end that awaits me and awaits us all, my spirits lift, I become quite
cheerful, and then I go for a long walk."

Staten Island, especially its faded oystering and truck-farming
settlements, must have reminded Mitchell of the Carolina coastal
plains. Leaving home, he shouldered the classic burden — a mixture of resolve and regret — and this ambivalence was implicit in
the elegiac rustle of his prose. "The rats of New York are quicker-
witted than those on farms, and they can outthink any man who
has not made a study of their habits," he wrote in a 1944 story.
"Even so, they spend most of their lives in a state of extreme anxiety, the black rats dreading the brown and both species dreading
human beings. Away from their nests, they are usually on the edge
of hysteria." From "Obituary of a Gin Mill," which was published
in 1939: "Dick's old place was dirty and it smelled like the zoo, but
it was genuine; his new place is as shiny and undistinguished as a
two-dollar alarm clock. The bar-equipment salesman was so relentless that Dick, who merely wanted a bigger kitchen, ended up
by keeping nothing but the big, greasy, iron safe and a framed and
fly-specked photograph of Gallant Fox. He even threw away all his
photographs of Lupe Velez, his favorite movie actress." Mitchell accepted New York City and its citizens as he found them. Even when
he witnessed human spectacles that saddened or disgusted him,
he maintained a compulsive curiosity and an evergreen sense of
wonder. His preferred reporting subjects, he once explained, were
"visionaries, obsessives, impostors, fanatics, lost souls, the-end-

is-near street preachers, old Gypsy kings and old Gypsy queens, and out-and-out freak-show freaks." Without playing dumb, he had a country fellow's deadly ability to sniff out pretentiousness three avenues away. And he possessed extraordinary courtesy and patience as a listener, an aptitude nurtured during a childhood spent among folk who never tired of telling stories about themselves.

His reward was that, to the end of his life, people wanted to talk to him — a convenient bargain, given Mitchell's determination to render precisely the contents and cadences of the variegated New York vernacular. Of an encounter with the eponymous curator of Captain Charley's Private Museum for Intelligent People, he observed, "The last time I went to see him I took a notebook along, and while he rummaged through the museum — he was searching for a bone which he said he hacked off an Arab around 9 P.M. one full-moon night in 1907 after the Arab had been murdered for signing a treaty — I wrote down everything he said." In all five boroughs, he discovered "ear-benders" worthy of his perfectionism, but the greatest concentrations materialized on the Bowery, in Times Square, Harlem, and the Irish saloons of the East Side, and, above all, along the waterfront: "The only people I do not care to listen to are society women, industrial leaders, distinguished authors, ministers, explorers, moving picture actors (except W. C. Fields and Stepin Fetchit), and any actress under the age of thirty-five."

Mitchell's urban peregrinations per se were not his theme. Rather, they delineated a romantic quest, the trajectory of a polite but persistent intimate affection. New York City wasn't exactly what he thought of when the word "home" came to mind, but — in the same way that his avatar James Joyce responded to Dublin — it provoked and inspired him to write in a style no one previously had, and he loved it for what it was. There was, though, this important distinction: Joyce's early memories were rooted in Dublin, and Mitchell landed in New York already grown, so that it must have appeared to him no less strange than Mars. With a novelist's eye, he quickly made it familiar by mapping his own geography — transforming into landmarks an ordinary Greek coffee shop or a "big, roomy, jukeboxy" diner.

He had plenty of soft spots, but he was tough to fool. He never cheapened his stories with moist nostalgia or maudlin sentiment. Reporting in and about New York — recounting its inhabitants' daily adventures and dreamy follies, their resilience and their fragility — enabled Mitchell to sustain and reiterate his overarching conviction that the past, marinated in human memory and recollected in everyday speech, yields an elixir that can fortify against all manner of indignities inflicted in the name of progress.

DEPENDING UPON who's remembering what, however, the past can also, of course, haunt and shackle; this became an unintended theme of Mitchell's later years. In 1938, he published his first book, *My Ears Are Bent*, a collection of feature stories from the *New York Herald Tribune* and the *World-Telegram*. His second book, *McSorley's Wonderful Saloon* (1943), broadened and solidified his reputation as a matchless chronicler of Gotham exotica. The richly textured portraits include, among others, the owners and clientele of the ancient Cooper Square alehouse of the title story; Mazie P. Gordon, the brassy blond ticket seller at a dime movie theater who, when she wasn't threatening obnoxious patrons ("Outa here on a stretcher! Knock your eyeballs out! . . . Big baboon! Every tooth in your head! Bone in your body!"), doled out daily fistfuls of small change to Bowery vagrants; Arthur Samuel Colborne, the founder and head of the Anti-Profanity League ("You start out with 'hell,' 'devil take it,' 'Dad burn it,' 'Gee whizz,' and the like of that, and by and by you won't be able to open your trap without letting loose an awful, awful, blasphemous oath. It's like the cocaine dope habit"); and Joseph Ferdinand Gould, AKA Professor Sea Gull, a homeless Harvard-graduate Greenwich Village fixture, a mimic of seagulls who claimed to have "translated a number of Henry

Wadsworth Longfellow's poems into sea gull," and the author of "An Oral History of Our Time," which Gould, in expansive moments, would compare to Gibbon's *Decline and Fall of the Roman Empire.* During several early encounters, Mitchell stayed up half the night with Gould, buying him drinks and recording his verbal incontinence. But Gould wasn't a solo self-promoter; a number of serious writers — Ezra Pound, E. E. Cummings, William Saroyan, Marianne Moore — took him seriously. The "Oral History," then twenty-six years in the works, had grown to an estimated nine million words, Mitchell wrote, and "may well be the lengthiest unpublished work in existence."

The pace of Mitchell's own word output, meanwhile, decelerated. Legging around town for newspapers, he had often reported and written three stories a day, an enervating regimen that made an assignment to file a daily dispatch from the trial of Bruno Hauptmann, the Lindbergh kidnapper, feel like a holiday. ("After a reporter has covered features for a while there is nothing like a fast murder trial to get the lead out of his pants. It discourages him from trying to make literature out of every little two by four news story.") In 1939, his most prolific year at *The New Yorker,* he had thirteen bylines, each one appended to an artifact of literature. However, in 1942, when "Professor Sea Gull" appeared, he published only one other piece, and the following year but a single Profile. For the next two decades, a Joseph Mitchell story ran in the magazine roughly every two years; almost all these small masterpieces were collected in two books, *Old Mr. Flood* and *The Bottom of the Harbor.*

In the early sixties, Mitchell decided to revisit the life and legend of Joe Gould — "an odd and penniless and unemployable little man who came to the city in 1916 and ducked and dodged and held on as hard as he could for over thirty-five years." The result was a more melancholy than funny, full-of-surprises account of an elaborate but benign deception, as well as, indirectly, a deft psychological study of both the author and his subject. In the years after he first wrote about Gould, Mitchell gradually came to realize that — apart from several autobiographical chapters that weren't really oral history — "An Oral History of Our Time" didn't exist on paper. To tell the tale of his unnerving discovery, he felt obliged to interject his feelings about a reporter's duty to the people he writes about. Gould could be quite entertaining, and for the most part he elicited Mitchell's sympathy. But he was also an obsessive, an impostor, and a lost soul in one tidy bundle — not to mention neurotic, alcoholic, narcissistic, opportunistic, and prone to remind Mitchell, at critical moments, that he had, after all, invited himself into Gould's life. "Joe Gould's Secret" was serialized in two consecutive issues of *The New Yorker* in September 1964, seven years after Gould's death, at sixty-eight, in a mental hospital. The following year, when Mitchell turned fifty-seven, it was published as a book. Whereupon the bylines ceased.

MITCHELL WAS a creature of steadfast habits. Each year he bought four Irish Sweepstakes tickets and displayed them on the mantelpiece in the apartment on West Tenth Street, between Fifth and Sixth avenues, where he and his wife, Therese, raised their daughters, Nora and Elizabeth. He lived there fifty-six years — alone after Therese's death, in 1980. Every December 24, he delighted the family with his reading of "'Twas the Night Before Christmas." Every summer, they spent about six weeks at the Mitchell homestead in North Carolina. He rose early each day and gargled for a full minute before his breakfast of orange juice, toast with marmalade or strawberry jam, and eggs (until his eighties, when some salmonella-tainted eggs made him sick). In New York, when he headed out the door he was dressed in Brooks Brothers clothing down to his underwear, socks, and wingtips. On the farm, he dressed in worn-out Brooks Brothers clothing. He wore gabardine or flannel suits and a felt fedora in winter, seersucker or poplin suits and a coconut-straw fedora in summer. In the seventies, when he deviated and bought a tweed sports jacket, Nora asked,

"What's next, Daddy, muttonchop sideburns?" In his inside breast pocket he always carried a sheet of plain 8½-by-11 typing paper, folded horizontally in half and then in thirds, and a soft-leaded pencil. Throughout the day, he wrote things down.

Which is to say he never stopped being a reporter. He filed his daily jottings in folders, presumably because he felt they were relevant to something — an article, a memoir — that he would someday publish. He showed up for work at his *New Yorker* office — not every single day, but regularly — and his neighbors often heard the sound of a typewriter from behind his closed door. Visitors noticed that the desktop and other surfaces were uncluttered; if he was accumulating a fat manuscript, he kept it hidden. This endured for more than thirty years.

None of us — revering Mitchell and flattering ourselves in thinking of him as a "colleague" — knew what to make of it. Calvin Trillin recalls that a particularly bold and insouciant receptionist once asked Mitchell why he'd stopped writing and he solicitously replied, "Well, they said that those people I wrote about were crazy. And they might have been. But they weren't dangerous-crazy, like the people who get written about now." I'm willing to believe this anecdote up to a point, but who's to say that he in fact stopped writing? Propriety inclined the rest of us to reciprocate Mitchell's silence by avoiding the topic. Did his silence possess an eloquent majesty? Or did we fear that it could happen to any of us, like being struck with a piece of falling masonry? Anyway, there were so many other things to talk about with Joe Mitchell, who easily became animated and who stammered with a marvelous coherence, editing each sentence as he uttered it, so that it never quite got completed before the next interesting thought tumbled from his brain. Was his diction a manifestation of some transaction that occurred — or stopped occurring — when he confronted a blank page? Was he constantly writing and rewriting in his mind but nowhere else?

✶ ✶ ✶

FOR DECADES, though his books had gone out of print and were selling at steep premiums in secondhand bookstores, Mitchell resisted urgings from readers and publishers to reissue them. He wasn't much impressed by a revival of interest, during the seventies and eighties, in his soul mate A. J. Liebling — in their prime at *The New Yorker,* Mitchell's only true peer as both a reporter and a stylist. Several Liebling titles, including a two-volume compendium, came out in paperback, but Mitchell felt that paperbacks were ephemeral. A Mitchell omnibus, if he were to allow one, would have to be in hardcover. With a diffident vagueness, he also explained that he was working on "something else" — a major new piece of writing, it seemed — that he would want to include.

In the mid-eighties, Dan Frank, then an editor at Viking, which was the original publisher of *Joe Gould's Secret,* began gently and patiently wooing him. Frank moved to Pantheon in early 1991, and soon thereafter Mitchell agreed to the publication of *Up in the Old Hotel,* a single volume that comprised *McSorley's, Old Mr. Flood, The Bottom of the Harbor,* and *Joe Gould's Secret,* plus seven previously uncollected stories from the thirties, forties, and fifties. Whatever became of the new piece of writing that Mitchell had alluded to, Frank never laid eyes on it. With typical meticulousness, Mitchell made microsurgical changes in his old pieces. One day, Sheila McGrath, a former *New Yorker* office manager who was Mitchell's companion during his final decade, asked him what he was up to as he scrutinized one of his stories. A semicolon had found its way into the published version, and he changed it back to a comma, as it had been in his original manuscript. "Don't worry, honey," he explained. "I'm just taking out the improvements." McGrath helped him proofread galleys and provided general logistical assistance and encouragement, and he dedicated the book to her. When *Up in the Old Hotel* was published, in the summer of 1992, it became a unanimous critical success and, at eighty-four, Mitchell had his first bestseller — three weeks on the *Times* hardcover nonfiction list. It still sells about seven thousand copies a year in a not-so-ephemeral Vintage paperback.

Up in the Old Hotel enabled a new generation of readers to discover Mitchell — acolytes of the sort who turned the now departed Books and Company, on upper Madison Avenue, into a highbrow mosh pit, spilling out of the front door and onto the street, when, three months before his death, he gave a reading to mark the Modern Library's publication of *Joe Gould's Secret*. (A Modern Library edition of *The Bottom of the Harbor* had come out in 1994.) It was inevitable that Hollywood — best possible scenario: the Hollywood that actually reads books — would come knocking. This indeed happened while Mitchell was still alive. Because it's a byzantine show-biz story, I will skip the details, other than to say that its scariest moment occurred when *Joe Gould's Secret* was pursued by Tom Cruise's production company.

Instead, shooting begins next month on a movie version of *Joe Gould's Secret* that will be directed by Stanley Tucci and will feature Tucci as Mitchell, Ian Holm as Gould, Hope Davis as Therese Mitchell, Isabella Rossellini as an art-gallery owner who befriended Gould, and Glenn Close as the artist Alice Neel, whose drawings and paintings of Gould included a nude portrait in which he was equipped with more than the usual allotment of male genitalia. ("Anatomically, the painting was fanciful and grotesque but not particularly shocking," Mitchell wrote. "Except for the plethora of sexual organs, it was a strict and sober study of an undernourished middle-aged man.")

Tucci — judging from his two previous directorial efforts, the elegantly wistful comedies *Big Night* and *The Impostors* — seems poised to eclipse Woody Allen as the filmmaker with the most unabashedly indulgent romantic attachment to the New York cityscape. He plans to shoot in about forty locations around town, and the result will be, he hopes, "a celebration of New York in a lot of ways." One day recently, when I joined him during a location-scouting expedition in Manhattan and Queens, we started out at the Minetta Tavern, near Washington Square, where caricatures of Gould have been hanging on the walls for more than fifty years. After "Professor Sea Gull" was published, Gould enjoyed a temporary surge of not quite respectability, perhaps, but acceptability, and he secured a position as the Minetta Tavern's "house bohemian." Mitchell used to track him down there to forward letters, some of which included cash contributions to the "Joe Gould Fund," that had been sent care of *The New Yorker*. Gould's job was to occupy a booth in the restaurant's front room and attract tourists, and in exchange he was entitled to a nightly plate of spaghetti and whatever free drinks he could cadge. As Tucci conferred with his production designer about possible camera placements, he glimpsed through the MacDougal Street window a spooky sight, one that gave us all pause: a wild-haired, gray-bearded passerby, a specimen of old Greenwich Village fauna capable of causing a busload of out-of-towners to gawk. The phrase "Joe Gould's ghost" crossed my mind.

The screenplay for *Joe Gould's Secret*, which was originally adapted by Howard A. Rodman, has been revised by Tucci. As the script now reads, before the credits roll at the end of the movie a black screen will appear with white letters saying:

JOE GOULD DIED IN 1957.

JOSEPH MITCHELL PUBLISHED "JOE GOULD'S SECRET" IN 1964.

FOR THE NEXT THIRTY-TWO YEARS OF HIS LIFE HE CAME TO HIS OFFICE EVERY DAY . . .

. . . AND NEVER PUBLISHED ANOTHER WRITTEN WORD.

An evocative and "literary" coda, I suppose — but, to be punctilious, a not precisely accurate statement. By my count, Mitchell published close to two thousand words from 1992 to 1996 — the five-page prefatory "Author's Note" in *Up in the Old Hotel* and, as Dan Frank pointed out to me, the flap copy for that book's dust jacket and the biographical notes and dust-jacket copy for the Modern Library reprints.

I've already mentioned Mitchell's scribbled notes to himself, the equivalent of journal entries. Other unpublished material exists, in a variety of forms. During the eighties, when his siblings and in-laws began dying off, he wrote epitaphs for their gravestones. After his own death, the writer Marie Winn, who had become a close friend during Mitchell's first years as a widower, received from his daughters a file folder that contained drafts, filigreed with corrections, of the many post cards and letters he had sent her. Winn also showed me her copy of *The Bottom of the Harbor*, which bore an inscription from Mitchell that ran to four pages — filling the blanks in the front and back of the book — a single sentence, a syntactic high-wire walk, a flow of blue ink with a mesmerizing rhythm reminiscent of Molly Bloom's soliloquy. How many drafts must he have gone through to get to that?

Both Winn and McGrath say that Mitchell showed them pages from a number of works in progress. Winn believes that some of the material she read was "of a piece" with autobiographical passages that found their way into the *Up in the Old Hotel* preface. McGrath, who is the literary executor of Mitchell's estate, sat in my office one day not long ago and spoke coyly of "a shopping bag with various sections of stories." With Mitchell's consent, she said, she began transcribing these texts and storing them on a computer disk. "And that's where they are," she said. "I haven't been able to look at them since he died, so I couldn't say they're publishable as they stand, or with a little minor editing . . ." She never completed this sentence.

MITCHELL HAD no trouble finding ways to occupy himself that didn't involve sitting in front of a typewriter. For thirty years, he attended meetings of the James Joyce Society, at the Gotham Book Mart. He was also a board member of the Gypsy Lore Society and helped found the South Street Seaport Museum. A backcountry

Baptist who in New York embraced Episcopalianism and modernism, he became a vestryman of Grace Church. (Mitchell's stories provide ample evidence that he strongly believed in Hell; Heaven seems a more problematic and remote prospect.) During the eighties, he spent five years as a commissioner of the New York City Landmarks Preservation Commission. This public service enabled him, in an official capacity, to do something to keep at bay the dark forces he lumped under the general heading "goddamn sons of bitches" — bill collectors with stupid computers, smug politicians and plutocrats, designers and promoters of noisy or ugly machines and buildings. He walked all over the city, often with binoculars, admiring architecture — he was a charter member of the Friends of Cast-Iron Architecture — and he lavished special attention upon ruins. When he came across an old building in the early stages of demolition, he would wander inside — a natty gent in a well-pressed business suit, usually carrying a shopping bag — and drag out whatever he could carry that looked interesting: bricks, shards of marble cornices, elevator pulleys.

"My father would collect entire skyscrapers and stick them under the bed," Nora Mitchell Sanborn told me when I paid her a visit not long ago. Now widowed, she lives in central New Jersey, in a house brimming with her father's odd treasures — glass bottlenecks, New York hotel spoons, brass hinges. Two of Mitchell's siblings and a sister-in-law died within three months of him, she said, "and my sister and I noticed that our cousins ended up dividing diamonds and stock certificates, and we wondered how we had ended up dividing doorknobs and drawer pulls."

At one point, she led me to an upstairs room where she kept boxes filled with old jam and marmalade jars that now contained objects her father had picked up or dug up as he walked the family fields in North Carolina. For an hour, I opened jars and tried to puzzle out what I was looking at: arrowheads, pottery fragments, quartzes, flints, pieces of rusty hardware. Inside each was a dated scrap of paper, in Mitchell's scrawl, a hybrid prose-poem catalog of the contents: "The large broken projectile point was found in a rut in a gully in the road between our house and Miss Dinabel's that had been filled with sand from a pit somewhere near Adam Davis's. I found the purple bottle throat on the site of the Cephus blue house at the Butler place between the road and the ditch — at the edge of the soybeans." As I sifted through these relics — bits of the past that Mitchell had sifted from the soil of his birthplace, a past that gave him far more comfort than the present — I understood that an ordinary object, held up to the light in a certain way, could possess for Mitchell the same fascination as a Gypsy king, a bearded lady, or a street preacher with a "frantic voice." When Mitchell wrote, he made the exotic seem companionable and the everyday seem strange. As long as he stayed attached to these relics, it meant that he hadn't stopped trying.

NO DOUBT Mitchell was aware that, among other writers, his failure to publish incited speculations about what he was up to, including the speculation that he wasn't up to anything. Mitchell himself was probably the source of the hypothesis that quitting smoking, when he turned fifty — almost four decades before cancer caught up with him — made it more difficult to concentrate. Another theory I've come across — one I don't give much credence to — is that the death of Liebling, in 1963, deprived him of his ideal reader. (When I ran this by the writer and editor William Maxwell, he smiled and said, "If I had an ideal reader who died, I'd go and find another ideal reader." My own guess is that Mitchell, in his bones, knew that he was his own ideal reader.) Despite the reticence on this general topic that prevailed within the precincts of *The New Yorker,* it seems that when thoughtful inquisitors brought it up, Mitchell, with his characteristic courtliness, tried to accommodate. Reviewing *Up in the Old Hotel* in *The American Scholar,* William Zinsser — who, as it happens, introduced me to Mitchell's work when he taught an undergraduate writing seminar at Yale, during the seventies — postulated a fatal combination of Gould's endless monologues and excessive neediness and Mitchell's excessive forbearance: "Gould just plumb wore Mitchell out." In reply, Mitchell inscribed a copy of *The Bottom of the Harbor,* thanking Zinsser "for your deeply understanding review of 'Up in the Old Hotel.'"

I think Zinsser is half right: Mitchell's experience with Gould deromanticized the reporter's life, at least the part that involved sitting up until four in the morning in a smoky bar listening to the prattle of a long-winded dipsomaniac. But there were other stories, conducive to more leisurely approaches, that Mitchell wanted to write, and evidently tried to write, before, for reasons known only to him, he abandoned them. He contemplated writing about his family (but decided he couldn't proceed while certain people were still alive); a sequel to "Mr. Hunter's Grave" (same inhibition); a memoir centered upon Ann Honeycutt, a fellow southern exile, whom he'd befriended during their early years in New York; another piece about the McSorley family (which would have given him a convenient excuse to spend time in Ireland, where he was happy to breathe the air on even the dreariest of days).

The pivotal passage in *Joe Gould's Secret* occurs when Mitchell, thoroughly exasperated, confronts Gould with his knowledge that the "Oral History" is a phantasm. "It exists in your mind, I guess," he says angrily. "But you've always been too lazy to write it down." Gould replies so softly that Mitchell can't quite make it out: "If I heard him right — and I have often wondered if I did hear him right — he said, 'It's not a question of laziness.' Then, evidently deciding not to say any more, he turned his back on me again."

After Gould departs, Mitchell is immediately filled with remorse: "I have always deeply disliked seeing anyone shown up or found out or caught in a lie or caught red-handed doing anything, and now, with time to think things over, I began to feel ashamed of myself for the way I had lost my temper and pounced on Gould." After musing about how he thinks Gould got himself into this fix, he writes of the "Oral History," "The oral part of it might not exactly be down on paper, but he had it all in his head, and any day now he was going to start getting it down."

When Robert Gottlieb was the editor of *The New Yorker*, from 1987 to 1992, every so often he would drop by Mitchell's office and they would have, as Gottlieb recalls, "a very pleasant chat about the progress he was making." Mitchell never mentioned the specifics of what he was writing about and Gottlieb didn't press him to deliver. "He'd say, 'Oh, I hope to be able to show you something within the year.' I liked him, liked his work, and I wanted to be respectful without being demanding. I just showed, I hoped, a continuing affectionate interest without being exigent. It quickly became apparent to me that we were going through some ritual."

Tina Brown, who was the editor during the last four years of Mitchell's life, tried a rather different approach: "When there was a big fire at the Fulton Fish Market, I called and asked him to do a piece. He said he'd try. The subtext of the conversation was he wished he could but he no longer could. He was a newsman who had a certain energy level and, left to his own devices, became more and more trapped by his own myth."

On the dust-jacket flap of *Joe Gould's Secret*, Mitchell, writing in the third person, quotes himself: "When I found out Gould's secret . . . I was appalled, but I soon regained my respect for him, and through the years my respect has grown, though I must confess that he is still an enigma to me. Nowadays, in fact, when his name comes into my mind, it is followed instantly by another name — the name of Bartleby the Scrivener — and then I invariably recall Bartleby's haunting, horrifyingly self-sufficient remark 'I would prefer not to.'"

This allusion to Melville's antihero suggests that what bedeviled Mitchell wasn't an excess of craftsmanship — the perfectionist writing himself into a corner — but an existential unease. Instead of "I would prefer not to," Mitchell routinely demurred, "It does not speak to my condition."

Still, I think — because he knew as well as anyone the stoic beauty and mystique of the thing left unsaid — Mitchell deliberately and misleadingly overplayed the parallel between Gould and himself. It was all right to toy with the paradox that he was some sort of Joe Gould manqué — to see, in effect, if he could make his shadow dance. But Mitchell was, in the end, a wise, proud, fastidious Carolina gentleman who regularly used to vacuum the rows and stacks of thousands of books that filled his apartment. And Gould was a flea-bitten, lice-ridden, rheumy-eyed, toothless, intermittently diverting flophouse denizen whose native Yankee pride had been subverted by deep psychological wounds that never healed. What they had in common, above all, was a fascination with the way people presented themselves when they talked about what most mattered to them. For most of his life, only Mitchell got it down on paper.

Philip Hamburger, who was a *New Yorker* contemporary and a devoted friend of Mitchell's, told me recently that, in his estimation, questions about Mitchell's long silence struck him as not merely gauche but also "prurient."

"I equate them with questions about the president's sex life," he said. "Joe and I had lunch together regularly for sixty years. During that entire period, I can swear he never once asked me what I was doing and I never asked him what he was doing. All these people are asking a sort of tabloid question: Why didn't he write more? I've always felt it was a completely unnecessary question. If Joe had died at seventy, nobody would have raised it. Why didn't he write more? Well, he wrote enough."

On his deathbed, Mitchell said, "There was so much I still wanted to do." Of course he wrote enough. Except that certain varieties of greed aren't really sinful — they're an expression of sensual appetite. Rereading him, we couldn't help ourselves. Like Joe Mitchell himself, thinking about heading home one last time, we wanted more.

— 1999

La Cabeza de Villa

NONE OF THE CURRENT MEMBERS of the Wednesday Group can say precisely when it was founded. They know that the original Wednesday Group — a weekly luncheon gathering of self-selected representatives of the intelligentsia of El Paso, Texas — got started more than twenty-five years ago, and that Pablo Bush Romero, who goes back almost twenty years, is the senior active member. They know that solidarity is a Wednesday Group tradition. In other words, whatever Pablo Bush Romero ultimately decides to do about Pancho Villa's skull — even if circumstances force him to drag the Wednesday Group into a high-profile geopolitical controversy — the other members are a good bet to back him up 100 percent, more or less.

Pablo Bush Romero, a tall and imposing bald man with a pencil-thin mustache, who is now in his mid-eighties, reads a lot. A couple of years ago, he came across *Let the Tail Go with the Hide,* a cowhide-bound vanity-press as-told-to memoir that was published in 1984 by an Arizona rancher and businessman named Ben F. Williams and his daughter-amanuensis, Teresa Williams Irvin. "I read this book by accident," Bush Romero said later, meaning that the general subject matter lay outside his usual areas of interest, which include underwater archaeology, big-game hunting, and Mexican history. What did arouse his interest was two passages that seemed to explain the fate of Pancho Villa's skull — *la cabeza de Villa* — which became separated from the rest of his bones in 1926 and has been missing ever since. Villa, the fabled Mexican Centaur — peon hero, scourge of the landowner, part-time *bandido*, brilliant military strategist — was assassinated and buried in Parral, a town south of Chihuahua, in 1923. According to *Let the Tail Go with the Hide,* Ben Williams happened to turn up in Parral in February of 1926, a few days after an acquaintance of his, an American soldier of fortune named Emil Holmdahl, was jailed as a suspect in the desecration of Villa's tomb. Williams described visiting Holmdahl in the Parral jail, receiving assurances that he had had nothing to do with robbing the tomb, and arranging for his release. When Williams next encountered Holmdahl, about six weeks later in El Paso, the soldier of fortune confessed not only that he had robbed the tomb and disposed of the head but also that he had collected twenty-five thousand dollars for his trouble and wished to express his gratitude. An apparent capacity for recalling punchy dialogue verbatim was one of Williams's remarkable skills:

> "Half the money is yours, because you got me out of that damned jail. I have it in my pocket."
>
> I looked at him and said, "Emil, if I had known then what you're telling me now, you'd still be in that jail. I'm not interested in your goddamn money!"
>
> He said, "What difference does it make, whether that head is in the hole where it was or where it is now?"
>
> I got up from the table and left. That was the last time I ever saw Major Emil Holmdahl.

Forty-five years and 185 pages later, in Phoenix, Williams visited a friend, Frank Brophy. On Brophy's wall he saw "a plaque of the Skull and Bones Society." When Brophy acknowledged that he was a member of Skull and Bones and remarked that "we have Pancho

Villa's skull in our house at Yale," Williams proceeded to tell him the tale of Holmdahl, the jail in Parral, and the twenty-five thousand dollars. Brophy replied, "By God, that's right! Five of us put up five thousand dollars apiece. The other members of Skull and Bones covered his expenses."

It is a simple fact that Frank Brophy graduated from Yale College but was never a member of Skull and Bones, the most myth-shrouded of Yale's undergraduate senior societies. Whatever hung on Brophy's wall would therefore not have been "a plaque of the Skull and Bones Society." This strongly implies, of course, that if Frank Brophy (who died in 1978) told Ben Williams (who died in 1985) that he and four Bones accomplices had paid twenty-five thousand dollars for Pancho Villa's cranium his object was to embroider an anecdote that sounded to him more colorful than truthful. It also implies that Brophy was the sort of person who would have enjoyed knowing that a casual, innocent prevarication of his could resurface and cause a stir in El Paso many years later. Above all, it implies that Frank Brophy and Ben Williams would have fitted right in with the Wednesday Group. In El Paso — along the blurry border, where the truth can often become as cloudy as the water in the Rio Grande, where history has immediacy and mythology counts for a lot — simple facts tend to ferment awhile before they're allowed to imply much at all.

BEING DEAD for sixty-six years has not seriously diminished Pancho Villa's topicality in El Paso. Newspaper editors there have long assumed that interchangeable stories marking the anniversary of Villa's assassination or one of his military skirmishes — with headlines like PANCHO VILLA RIDES AGAIN IN MEMORY — make good if not necessarily fresh copy. If no anniversary is convenient, it's always OK to send a feature writer over to Juárez to interview one of Villa's widows. In downtown El Paso, the hotel concierge can still point you to buildings that bear alleged bullet scars left by Villa's troops. Knowledgeable natives can offer directions to the of-

fice of the doctor who periodically treated Villa for chronic gonor-
rhea. A man in El Paso told me not long ago, with obvious pride,
that his mother once danced with General John (Black Jack) Per-
shing, Villa's nemesis. Any self-respecting nightspot in Juárez, it is
said, comes equipped with a mariachi group capable of rendering
at least half a dozen *corridos,* or ballads, about Villa — including, of
course, the popular standard "La Decapitación de Pancho Villa."

In 1960, Haldeen Braddy, a professor at what was then Texas
Western College and is now the University of Texas at El Paso, or
UTEP, published an article in the journal *Western Folklore* titled
"The Head of Pancho Villa." Braddy cataloged all the extant theories concerning the missing skull: the tomb was violated by Villa's
enemies, among them one of his assassins and a Mexican Army
general; the skull ended up in the hands of American scientists
who thought studying it would reveal the source of Villa's bat-
tlefield genius; the culprits were treasure hunters attracted by the
legend that tattooed on Villa's scalp was a map showing where he
had buried gold ingots in the Sierra Madre. Braddy also discussed
Emil Holmdahl but offered an account of his capture, interroga-
tion, and release not at all consistent with what Ben Williams recorded in his memoirs a quarter of a century later. Other sources
suggested that Holmdahl had once tried to buy the head — from
the Mexican general — but had failed to come up with the money.
Braddy, however, turned up no evidence of this. "The head of
Pancho Villa, in the absence of proof to the contrary, is still in
Mexico," Braddy concluded.

Current events have been a staple of Wednesday Group conversations, along with history, archaeology, and anthropology. Haldeen Braddy's scholarship notwithstanding, however, until Pablo
Bush Romero introduced *la cabeza de Villa* as a discussion topic
none of the other members had given it much thought. "As a matter of fact, we didn't even know the son of a bitch was missing,"
Frank Hunter told me. Hunter started hanging out with the Wednesday Group around the time he stopped practicing law full-

time, seven years ago, and he doesn't deny that his eagerness to pursue *la cabeza de Villa* has dovetailed with his wife's eagerness to get him out of the house more often. Three afternoons a week, Hunter puts in regular hours on the golf course, but golf alone cannot nourish an inquisitive mind. It was the former American consul general in Juárez, now a lapsed member, who originally invited Hunter to join the Wednesday Group. As now constituted, the group reflects a catholic range of interests. Pablo Bush Romero, the exemplar, has had several lucrative careers — automobile dealer (the largest Ford agencies in Mexico City and Juárez), resort developer (on the Yucatán Peninsula), and movie producer (he once showed me a picture of himself with Lupita Topar, "the Mexican Mary Pickford"). Alex Apostolides is an archaeologist, a museum curator, a freelance folklorist, cohost (with his wife) of a weekly southwestern-history program on the local National Public Radio affiliate, and a weekly columnist for the *El Paso Herald-Post*. Oscar González has a ranch near Juárez and occasionally promotes bullfights and prizefights. Eugene Finke is a retired navy captain and electrical engineer who has taught political science at UTEP. Bob Massey has taught studio-art courses at the university. John Bockoven, who happens to be Frank Hunter's brother-in-law, was stationed in El Paso, at Fort Bliss, during the Second World War but devoted his civilian career to the insurance business in Wisconsin until five years ago; then he retired to El Paso and immediately joined the Wednesday Group. A couple of retired army generals, among them a commanding officer of Fort Bliss, have drifted in and out. So have a rabbi and an FBI agent. Donald Rathbun, an active member, is a physician who once trekked part of the way up Mt. Everest. He is also an accomplished photographer and geologist who carries two business cards — one for his medical practice and one that says "Meteorite Recovery El Paso." Along with Apostolides, he has organized extracurricular Wednesday Group excursions to Mexico. Because his avocations demand as much time as his vocation, Dr. Rathbun says, it is a convenient coincidence that his medical specialty is neurology and that the missing part of Pancho Villa is the skull.

I once asked Frank Hunter to explain the protocols of the Wednesday Group, and he said, "No officers, no rules, no nothin.'" As Hunter recalls the scene, Bush Romero showed up at lunch one Wednesday in the spring of 1987 with a copy of *Let the Tail Go with the Hide,* read the passages relating to Villa and Skull and Bones, and said, "Who wants to help me get this thing back?" No one at the table that day had any grasp of the rather more refined protocols of Bones: that fifteen male Yale seniors are selected each year to join the society, thereby entering a brotherhood whose bonds are supposed to offer ineffable but enduring spiritual sustenance; that no one who is not a member or an employee is ever supposed to enter Bones' so-called tomb, a nearly windowless sandstone monolith in the center of the Yale campus; that it was once customary for a member who happened to be outside the tomb and heard the phrase "skull and bones" uttered to excuse himself, more or less in the manner of Clark Kent abruptly heading off to be Superman for a while. The Wednesday Group merely had a sense that Skull and Bones was old (it was founded in 1832), eastern, and elitist. And the name, of course, suggested the potential for shadowy activities — say, plundering gravesites in the Mexican outback.

"Pablo's immediate suggestion was that he would pay for tickets for us to go up to Connecticut and get the skull out of the Skull and Bones tomb up there at Yale," Hunter said. "The thing that squashed that idea was that we would have to get some sort of admission into the place and we knew we didn't have it. There was no sense all of us just wandering around New Haven."

Instead, Hunter put in a call to Benno Schmidt, then recently installed as president of Yale. Without much difficulty, he got through and was able to explain why the Wednesday Group was interested in Villa's skull. Schmidt replied that the subject was brand-new to him but that he would check it out. A few days later, Hunter received a call from Endicott Peabody Davison, Bones

Class of '48, a partner in the white-shoe Wall Street law firm Win-throp, Stimson, Putnam and Roberts, a former officer of Yale University, and at the time the designated spokesman for the Russell Trust Association, the governing body of Bones. Both Hunter and Davison, who is known to his familiars as Cottie, recall their first conversation as friendly. After stating with confidence that Skull and Bones didn't have *la cabeza de Villa,* Cottie Davison said, "But if you're looking for a skull we can probably get you one from the Yale Medical School." Hunter demurred. What he and his friends had in mind, after all, was a *particular* skull.

I once heard a Bonesman from the 1930s brag that there was a time when all senior societies collected relics, and that Bonesies, being naturally superior in every respect, could not avoid excelling at this sport. He quickly added, however, that this institutional interest in relics "was of course generic rather than specific." (According to this logic, there is no obvious explanation of how Wolf's Head, the only other remaining all-male senior society, came to possess a set of Hitler's silverware.) A Bonesman who was an undergraduate in the early seventies, and who has difficulty discerning the humor in this subject, said, "We're not in the business of buying human remains." A journalist and Yale alumnus who once investigated Skull and Bones says he is disinclined to believe the *cabeza de Villa* story, "because those old Wasps are so cheap it's very unlikely they'd pay twenty-five thousand dollars for it."

If Davison expected Hunter simply to go away after their first conversation, he failed to take account of several factors, not the least of which was that Hunter, a lifelong resident of El Paso, relished the challenge of corresponding with a New England Brahmin named Endicott Peabody Davison. What motivated the members of the Wednesday Group above all was the knowledge that, no matter how slight might be their reason to believe that Pancho Villa's skull reposed within the Bones tomb, they had plenty of free time to search for corroborating evidence. And so what if they couldn't *prove* that Bones had *la cabeza de Villa*? Merely by stating their suspicion, they had burdened the trustees of Skull and Bones with the logically impossible task of proving that Bones *didn't* have it.

SOME MONTHS AGO, I sat in Dr. Rathbun's office, in a quiet neighborhood near downtown El Paso, in a room lined with glass display cases full of archaeological and geological specimens and bookshelves stacked with medical literature. A square brown metal file box with an orange label that said "Villa's Head" rested at our feet. *La cabeza de Villa* — or, for that matter, the head of an adult gorilla — would have fitted neatly inside. In fact, however, the box contained copies of Dr. Rathbun's voluminous avocational correspondence. During the past two years, he had written more than two hundred letters on behalf of the Wednesday Group. He wrote to the American Medical Association asking whether its archives might contain information about Villa's head injuries. He also wrote to the AMA requesting information about Holmdahl, who seems to have last been heard of in Arizona in the fifties. He had been in touch with a forensic archaeologist at the University of Wyoming who had developed a computer technique that made it possible to regenerate from a skull the image of a human face. From the director of research of the Institute of Texas Cultures he requested photographs showing Villa with his mouth open. In El Paso, Dr. Rathbun tracked down the daughter of a dentist who treated Villa on several occasions, but it turned out that the dentist had been dead for more than a decade and the daughter had burned all his records. In a letter to the National Academy of History and Geography in Mexico City he sought, among other things, information about a dentist whose first name was Roberto (but whose last name he could not recall), who might have treated Villa. The Armed Forces Institute of Pathology, in Washington, sent Dr. Rathbun 8-by-10 glossy photographs, taken July 22, 1923, of the fresh corpse of Villa. A publisher in Parral sent photocopies of similar images, newspaper accounts of the assassination, excerpts from a book that recounted the assassination and the robbing of the grave, and a transcription of excerpts from Villa's autopsy. In a letter to a Latin-American-studies expert at New Mexico State University — a possible source of dental records, x-rays, or pathology reports — Dr. Rathbun discussed suing Skull and Bones to force their representatives to swear under oath that they didn't have the skull.

"Our only goal in this whole thing is to improve relations between the United States and Mexico," Dr. Rathbun said as he leafed through his files. "I think Mexico is embarrassed that the head of one of its national heroes is missing, and the Mexicans feel paranoid. Our roads are better, our schools are better, they owe our banks billions of dollars. At a gut level, when they come to the realization that the head of one of their heroes is residing in a club in a rich man's school this is a thorn in their side. I think some people would be very pissed off about this. As citizens of a Catholic country, the Mexicans have a greater respect for the dead — reverence for the afterlife — than we do."

During the time that Dr. Rathbun was accumulating his files, his Wednesday Group colleagues were not idle. Suing Skull and Bones, and Yale as well, was originally Hunter's idea. The prerequisite for this strategy was a plaintiff with recognizable grounds for complaint — with what is known in the law as "standing." The Wednesday Group's curiosity and sincere intentions did not, as a legal technicality, amount to standing. Hunter also looked into the 1970 Treaty of Cooperation between the United States and Mexico, and the Convention on Cultural Property Implementation Act. The latter, in particular, seemed to offer a basis for a lawsuit, but the sticking point remained: no plaintiff. Then it occurred to Hunter, a regular reader of the El Paso newspapers, that somewhere in Mexico there must be a widow of Villa. "Pancho Villa had a unique method of courtship," Hunter told me. "Whenever he saw a chick he wanted to spend the night with, he would marry her. He did this something like twenty-nine times. At the time we showed up, the Mexican government had decided that his legitimate widow was Soledad Seanez la Viuda de Villa. So I prepared an authorization for the lawsuit to be brought in her name."

Oscar González, who was once described to me as "one of those people about whom it's said 'They mean well,'" was dispatched to Juárez to recruit Soledad Seanez to the cause. He carried a document that authorized him and Pablo Bush Romero, the Wednesday Group's only Mexican citizens, "to bring such action as may be necessary to recover the head of my late husband, and have it returned to Mexico, to be buried with his remains." Unfortunately, negotiations between Oscar and the incumbent Mrs. Villa did not proceed smoothly.

Hunter: "Oscar took it to her to sign and she refused."

Dr. Rathbun: "At times, Oscar tends to be a little bombastic."

Asked to account for what went wrong in Juárez, González expressed strong suspicion that Soledad Seanez, at ninety-two, no longer possessed a full complement of marbles. Bush Romero, after one conversation with her, reached a similar conclusion. With what seemed like almost ideological fervor, the widow insisted that Villa's skull was not missing from his grave.

Hunter's correspondence with Davison, meanwhile, failed to maintain a tone of unalloyed affability: "Very frankly, Mr. Davidson [sic], we are convinced . . . that the skull of Pancho Villa is held by the Skull and Bones Society of Yale University. If you would be so kind as to contact the governing body of that Society and inform them of the contents of this letter, we would be most appreciative. We feel they would be only too happy to return the skull to the proper authorities, rather than have us proceed under the applicable law with its attendant publicity."

To which Davison replied, "Dear Mr. Hunter: . . . Your letter does not help your cause in finding the skull of Pancho Villa."

Not long after Bush Romero first mentioned *Let the Tail Go with the Hide,* Alex Apostolides wrote about it, rather elliptically, in his weekly column in the *Herald-Post.* Apostolides invited readers to send along any intelligence they might have about the skull, but he never returned to the subject in his subsequent columns. Therefore, when, more than a year later, a *Herald-Post* reporter named Tom Tolan wrote a story about *la cabeza de Villa* — a story that, in the fourth paragraph, invoked George Bush, Bones '48 — he appeared to have come up with a scoop. The *Herald-Post* played it across the top of the front page, and the wire services picked it up. That happened just as the 1988 Republican National Convention was about to get under way. Previously, the Wednesday Group's sphere of political influence had been limited to El Paso: a former mayor was a lapsed member. By seeming to link the Republican nominee for president of the United States, however loosely, to the theft of the head of a Mexican national hero, the Wednesday Group was, for the first time, meddling directly with issues of geopolitical import. According to Tolan, going public with the accusations against Skull and Bones was a last resort. The most telling quotation came from Hunter: "We've come to the conclusion that the main thing they don't want is publicity."

Hunter's analysis was accurate. Tolan discovered this for himself when he tried to interview Davison. "When I explained why I was calling, he sounded *so sad*," Tolan told me. "He said, 'But I've just spent two years putting to rest the Geronimo story.'"

The Geronimo story, a first cousin of the *cabeza de Villa* story, had floated around for years, and is not enormously popular with Cottie Davison. According to Skull and Bones' accusers in this instance — principally Ned Anderson, a former chairman of the San Carlos Apache tribe, of Arizona — the grave of Geronimo, the Apache chief, was violated in 1918 by a six-man raiding party that included the young Prescott Bush, father of George. This depredation was described in a 1933 typewritten manuscript titled "Continuation of the History of Our Order for the Century Celebration," and a copy of it somehow found its way into Anderson's hands. Davison and other Bonesies agreed that the document was authentic, but insisted that the events it described — the prying open of the iron doors of Geronimo's tomb, the use of carbolic acid to clean the skull — were purely apocryphal. Nevertheless, fire or no fire, a tinge of smoke hung in the air. Several generations of Bonesies were familiar with the contents of a glass display case inside the New Haven tomb: a skull that everyone referred to as Geronimo. Whose skull it truly was and how it wound up in the display case were less clearly established. The Apaches had to be dealt with respectfully, and Davison made an effort. In 1986, in New York City, he and other representatives of Skull and Bones — among them George Bush's brother Jonathan — met with Anderson. They brought a skull, and offered it to Anderson, but he declined it because it seemed not to be the same one he had seen in photographs surreptitiously provided by an anonymous dissident member of Bones. The nose and eye cavities didn't match. Also, Anderson took offense at a document that Davison wanted him to sign, which stipulated that neither the Apaches nor Skull and Bones would publicly discuss the whole business. Following this encounter, the dispute, though it remained unresolved, became more or less dormant. Anderson has from time to time petitioned public officials for help, but he still lacks proof that Geronimo's grave was ever robbed. The chief is buried on an army base in southwestern Oklahoma, and his descendants there oppose disturbing his remains.

PABLO BUSH ROMERO, meanwhile, feels ill served by the president of the United States. When Tom Tolan broke the story in the *Herald-Post,* Bush Romero and Dr. Rathbun, both of whom strongly support the agenda of the Republican party, felt apprehensive — for the same reason that Hunter and Apostolides, who are loyal Democrats, did not mind a bit seeing George Bush accused in print of being soft on grave robbers. Dr. Rathbun still marvels at the failure of the Democrats to exploit the issue during the presidential campaign. "Because I'm a Bush enthusiast, I was worried that this was going to become a big controversy," Dr.

Rathbun has said. "I never understood why Dukakis didn't make a fuss about it. He could have made hay out of the fact that Bush was a member of a Yale secret society that collected heads and that his father had done the same thing. He could have hurt Bush more with Pancho Villa's head than Bush hurt him with the Pledge of Allegiance. The only thing I can think of is that there must have been Democrats who were members of Skull and Bones and who prevented Dukakis from bringing this up."

Although Pablo Bush Romero and George Bush share no blood ties, in jocular moments Bush Romero refers to the president as "my poor relative," and it gives him no pleasure to speculate that he and the Wednesday Group might yet be forced to escalate the matter of *la cabeza de Villa* into an international incident. Each time the president's handlers abandon modesty and enumerate his accomplishments since he took office, Bush Romero notes with regret that the repatriation of Villa's headbone is not on the list, and he feels his self-restraint weakening. His poor relative, he believes, owes him one — a sentiment that he readily conveys to anybody fortunate enough to be invited to a meeting of the Wednesday Group. For more than a year now, the Wednesday Group has gathered at the Pinetum, an ostensibly Chinese restaurant on the west side of El Paso, which is part of a commercial strip also populated by floor-covering stores, automotive-service centers, and what seems to be every franchise restaurant known to man. The Pinetum, sui generis, comes equipped with bamboo-print wallpaper and Masonite in the seating area and someone in the kitchen who is not afraid to be generous with the monosodium glutamate. Its main attraction is that it has less ambient noise than other places where the Wednesday Group has convened, among them the Juárez country club and a kosher butcher shop. Hunter has said of the Pinetum, "The reason we're here is that they have a very limited clientele and they have a room that's just right for us. We can meet and speak in plain language and no one ever objects."

The first time I dined with the Wednesday Group, Ben Williams's daughter, Terry Irvin, was also a guest. The conversation that day naturally centered on *la cabeza de Villa,* and at one point I polled the crowd. On a scale of one to ten, how strongly did they believe that Skull and Bones had the head? "Ten-plus," Mrs. Irvin said. "I know my dad did not make that story up. There is no reason in the world for this subject even to have come up when we were writing that book if it wasn't true. I'm convinced in my own mind that they did it and they paid Emil Holmdahl to do it."

While waiting for *la cabeza de Villa* to resurface, she has written a screenplay about it. She has also enlisted as an ally Garry Trudeau, the cartoonist, who has published two series of "Doonesbury" strips satirizing Skull and Bones. When I polled the other members, Bush Romero was a solid ten, and Hunter turned up at the low end, with a seven (demonstrating, hardly for the first time, that for the pleasure of an argument most lawyers will advocate anything). Oscar González, the finest hairsplitter in the crowd, came in at 9.85. Something in González's manner — a naturally antic quality — brought to mind a joke I had heard, about the man who was offered (in this version) two authentic Villa skulls: one of Villa as a boy and one as an adult. González still holds out hope that one of Villa's sons, Hippólito, who now lives in Mexico City, will agree to become the plaintiff in a lawsuit. The notion that anyone would regard such a lawsuit as frivolous offends González. "This is an international group — we go all over," he said. "We're men. We're not kids. We know what we're doing." González had to leave early that day, and he made a ceremonious exit. He put on a black cowboy hat, which made him appear at least five and a half feet tall, gave Bush Romero a brotherly hug, and bade farewell to his other compadres with a "Viva Villa!" The last thing he said to me was "If you have Villa's skull and you bring it back to Mexico, that would be one hell of an act of international friendship."

Pablo Bush Romero, wishing to make approximately the same point, was more specific. He told me that Villa's body was buried in the Monument of the Revolution, in Mexico City, and that if I could arrange for *la cabeza de Villa* to once again repose with it he would see to it that I received the Aztec Eagle, the highest honor that Mexico can give to a foreigner. At the time of this tempting offer, we were seated in a room in his house that he uses as a study, and he had just shown me Villa's death mask — a bronze casting taken from a plaster-of-Paris impression of Villa's face made shortly after his assassination.

Without wishing to seem immodest, Bush Romero said he assumed that he had read more about Villa than anyone else in the Wednesday Group. His library contains about twenty-five books on the subject, among them *Pancho Villa en la Intimidad,* by Luz Corral Vda. de Villa, Soledad Seanez's predecessor as Villa's officially recognized widow, and *Pancho Villa's Shadow: The True Story of Mexico's Robin Hood, As Told by His Interpreter,* by Ernest Otto Schuster. The latter book, one of Bush Romero's favorites, features a dust-jacket photograph of a diminutive man wearing a dark suit and a straw boater and cavorting with a German shepherd. The caption says, "The author and his pal, Lobo." Bush Romero also showed me a photograph of Villa taken in 1913, at the battle of Ojinaga; a photograph of Villa and Emiliano Zapata sitting in a chair that they had looted from the presidential palace in Mexico City; a Villa autograph; and a bronze statue of Villa. These artifacts shared the room with photographs of Bush Romero and J. Edgar Hoover, Bush Romero and Marshal Tito, Bush Romero and Ronald Reagan, and Bush Romero and some Pygmies, in what is now Zaire, posing with the largest privately owned ivory tusks in the world (at the time, Bush Romero owned them); with many big-game trophies (an Alaskan black bear, a wolf from Chihuahua, a wolf from Canada, a tiger from India, a lion from Africa, a Mexican fox and wildcat, a table with an elephant foot for a base and a surface covered with an elephant ear, on which sat a lamp made from an elk's foot); and with a couple of shrunken human heads, from Colombia, one of which had been in better shape before "rats got to it."

Bush Romero said he had shown the death mask of Villa and the relevant passages from *Let the Tail Go with the Hide* to the Mexican consul general in El Paso, who was impressed and sympathetic. He added that he had thus far avoided getting the Mexican government directly involved, however, because that would involve excessive red tape. "I could have gone to the governor of Chihuahua or the president of Mexico," he said. "I wrote a letter to the president of Mexico today. But I didn't go into this. I have other things I'm dealing with him on." Rather, Bush Romero favored a strategy of direct appeal to George Bush. "I think that eventually we're going to get something. President Bush wants good relations with Mexico, and that would be one of the best things he could do — influence his club to return the head."

I mentioned a conversation I had had with a Bonesman who spent many years working in Washington and was of the opinion that "the demand for the return of the head of Pancho Villa is not a White House matter."

Bush Romero seemed unfazed. "I'm looking at this from the international point of view," he said.

The last time I happened to be in El Paso, I discovered that there were no recent developments. The local press, for instance, had not been on top of the story. When I spoke with Tom Tolan, of the *Herald-Post*, he said that other than extending himself a while back to check out "a misleading rumor that Villa's head was buried under a G-string at the Naked Harem," a southeast El Paso interpretive-dance laboratory, he had been preoccupied with other matters. The contingent at the Pinetum for that week's Wednesday Club gathering was rather modest: Bush Romero, Hunter, Apostolides, Dr. Rathbun, John Bockoven, and Bob Massey. Of course, we talked about *la cabeza de Villa*. I felt somewhat sheepish accepting their hospitality, because I had come to lunch to report my growing suspicion that hounding Skull and Bones was a fruitless endeavor — not because the Bonesies would refuse to come clean about the skull but because they really didn't have it. I warmed up to this by recounting a conversation with one Bonesman who told me he recalled during the early seventies seeing perhaps thirty skulls, not all of them human, scattered about the tomb.

"The fact that they have thirty or more skulls proves that they *might* have the skull of Villa," Bush Romero said. "It can't be proved. It's just a matter of goodwill — Bush prevailing on his fellow club members. They collected heads. Why?" He turned his palms up and shrugged. "But they have a few. They've consulted with their lawyers and they've come to the conclusion that they're not going to admit anything. And we're trying to convince them that if they'll return the head that'll be it. We'll bury the whole thing. Or they can leave the head somewhere where we'll find it. One of the things we were going to discuss here was whether we should write another letter to Bush, my poor relative. You tell him, Frank."

Bush Romero deferred to Hunter, who extemporaneously paraphrased the text of a proposed letter to Skull and Bones, a copy of which would go to the president. Its concluding sentiment was "So now it's time to put up or shut up."

"If the letter goes unnoticed, then we'll have to make it an international affair," Bush Romero said. "It's vital to Mexico's history to get that head back with the body. I would make enough fuss that if the Mexican government even *thinks* not to act they'll hear plenty about it. I'll just take the whole thing to Mexico City. I know I can get Channel Two and Channel Eleven interested. If the president of Mexico or the secretary of foreign affairs gets involved, then Bush will have to get involved."

"The skull has got to be in New Haven," Apostolides said. "By golly, we'll take any skull that has a hole in the brain."

"Villa is news," Bush Romero said. "And Villa is international news. He is the man most known in the Mexican Revolution worldwide. And anything that concerns Villa is news worldwide. And we're banking on keeping that alive. Because it's news."

— 1989

The Chinos' Artful Harvest

THE WOMAN ARRIVED in a metallic-blue Chevy van with all the options. She wanted corn. She parked under a Torrey pine next to an irrigation pump, walked toward the wooden roadside vegetable stand, and said, *"Corn."*

"No," said the man behind the counter. She was wearing Gucci sweatclothes; he was wearing a red-white-and-black plaid flannel shirt and faded Levi's. Between them stretched a vinyl countertop twenty-five feet long and three feet wide, covered with stainless-steel trays of neatly arranged beets (yellow, golden, red, white with red stripes), carrots (white, orange, yellow, red, long-and-tapered, thumb-size, in-between), turnips (white, golden, red, black, white-and-purple, round, long), radishes (white, red, red-and-white, purple, pink, daikon, red-fleshed Chinese, green-fleshed Chinese), celeriac, fennel, escarole, white endive, red endive, white cauliflower, Romanesque cauliflower (pale green with a stegosauroid architecture), mibuna, mizuna, bok choy, choi sun, cilantro, French thyme, winter savory, lemon balm, rappini, garlic chives, nasturtiums, basil (lemon, cinnamon, Thai, French, piccolo fino), Vietnamese coriander, Chinese spinach, Chinese long beans, French green beans as slender as candlewicks, purple cabbage, green cabbage, flat black cabbage, two dozen varieties of lettuce, a plastic tray of mixed lettuce hearts — and that's not all.

"How soon?" she asked, as if she might wait.

"May."

There would be corn in late May, in three months. As she drove away, the man said, "People have no conception of what's in season anymore. At the supermarket, everything is in season all the time. And everything tastes out of season all the time."

A black Chrysler Le Baron arrived, and a crisply tailored red-haired woman stepped out: crimson linen skirt and blazer, white silk blouse, and an American-flag brooch of rubies, sapphires, and diamonds. She had a forced smile that suggested an unsureness of the protocol. She was also unsure which of the variegated root crops were carrots, beets, radishes, or turnips.

Tom Haruya Chino, the man in the flannel shirt and Levi's, could have put her at ease, but he said nothing. Forty-three years ago, he was born fifty yards west of here. The roadside stand of-ficially does business as the Vegetable Shop, but regulars call it the Chinos'. It sits on the periphery of a fifty-six-acre farm twenty-one miles north of San Diego and five miles from the Pacific. Tom, who was born in 1949 and has spent all but four years of his life on the farm, is the youngest of nine children, all Nisei-second-generation Japanese-Americans. His active business partners are a sister, Kazumi, and two brothers, Koo and Fumio. The world outside the family knows Kazumi as Kay, Koo as Frank, and Fumio as Fred.

Though the Vegetable Shop's mailing address is Del Mar, the nearest post office is actually in Rancho Santa Fe. Given that the Chinos are devoting their lives to an obsessive and luxurious endeavor — producing vegetables far too special to be treated the way venders typically treat vegetables — they could not have picked a more rewarding neighborhood for a roadside retail oper-ation. When economic recession grips Rancho Santa Fe, the real-estate listings in the local newspaper say "Priced for Quick Sale — $1,650,000" and "Escape from Mediocrity — $1,895,000." The Veg-etable Shop has the approximate dimensions of a recreational ve-hicle, four doors, four plywood shutters that are unlatched during business hours, plenty of counter space and shelf space, a concrete floor, and a pale-yellow paint job with white trim. A mulberry, a mimosa, and a Chinese umbrella tree provide shade. A hand-lettered sign above one of the shutters indicates the hours: open at 10:00 A.M. six days a week, closed Mondays. On this particular day, a Sunday, closing time was noon, half an hour away.

The red-haired woman contemplated the beets, carrots, and turnips for a full three minutes, in awkward silence. Finally, she tried what she hoped would be an effective conversation starter: "So which one of these would be best just for snacking?"

Next came a petite white-haired woman wearing a red Ralph Lauren cardigan, white slacks, and a belt with a gold buckle about the size of the one the world heavyweight boxing champion poses in. "Cucumbers?" she asked. She used her hands to describe what one looked like — a gesture implying that Tom Chino probably didn't speak much English.

"No. There are no cucumbers left." Within the month, the Chinos would plant five varieties of cucumbers in the field, and in mid-April they'd begin harvesting them.

The woman saw leafy greens in a plastic bin and asked what they were.

"Lettuce hearts."

"Oh, they look so clean. You mean I don't have to do anything? Just pour dressing on them?"

"You might dry them first," Tom said.

"Just dry them in the air?"

Tom explained the concept of salad spinners and volunteered that paper towels were also an option.

"What about fruit?"

There were strawberries earlier in the day, he said, and there would be more on Tuesday.

"*Your* strawberries?"

If the Chinos sell it, the Chinos have raised it and, that very day, picked it.

"Yes." He turned down the corners of his mouth, as if reminding himself of the virtue of tact. "*Our* strawberries."

Watching him bag eight dollars' worth of lettuce hearts, I experienced a surge of pride. Four hours earlier, in the lettuce field of the Chino farm, he had given me explicit instructions: "Only the hearts." I had a twelve-inch carbon-steel kitchen knife. We were surrounded by rigorously straight lines of crops. I bent over a head of rosalita, a red romaine, severed its roots, extracted it, and peeled the outer leaves until I was down to a dozen pristine lime-and-pink petals, the longest about four inches.

"Is this small enough?" I asked.

"Not by my standards," Tom said.

He has a soft-edged, often barely audible voice.

I ate four of the outer leaves, tossed the heart of the heart into a rectangular plastic tray, and went about harvesting and stripping another and another.

"We've got so much of this lettuce," he said. "So we can sell the hearts. Only the hearts."

As a percentage of California's gross agricultural revenue, what the Chinos produce is infinitesimal. If their farm were to cease to exist, however, along with it would disappear possibly 100 percent of the state's commercial production of directly marketed lettuce hearts, Iranian basil, Japanese yellow carrots and red carrots, Japanese seedless yellow watermelons, Chinese red-fleshed radishes, purple-striped French green beans, and white alpine strawberries. The deed to the farm, dated 1952, describes a vaguely trapezoidal coastal floodplain, bounded by roads on three sides and by the San Dieguito River on the other. Minus the land occupied by buildings and paved areas, and minus a cornfield that the river swallowed during a flood in 1979, there are forty-five arable acres. More than eight million of California's acres are cultivated for agriculture. It is the state's leading resource industry, and this year it will generate revenues of eighteen billion dollars. At least 95 percent of the crops are sold through brokers. The Chinos sell their crops to the public at the Vegetable Shop, and they also sell to a handful of restaurants. Nobody gets a volume discount.

Several years ago, one of my brothers married Alice Waters, whose restaurant, Chez Panisse, in Berkeley, occupies approximately the same place in the new American cooking as does the golden arch in the old American fast food. The most telling measure of the Chinos' esteem for my sister-in-law is that every Wednesday several bushels of their vegetables wind up in the kitchen of Chez Panisse.

"I was absolutely dazzled the first time I saw the Chinos' vegetables," Alice said recently. "It was the most beautiful produce I had ever seen. Now, after years of knowing — or trying to know — this remarkable family, I see that the beauty of those vegetables comes from a commitment to tradition and integrity that is very rare and precious. Their vegetables are endless sources of inspiration, and their standards and approach have changed the way cooks regard vegetables."

A weekly shipment also goes from Del Mar to West Hollywood — to Spago, the flagship of Wolfgang Puck's cooking empire. A Spago dish called the Chino Ranch Chopped Salad — a mélange of corn kernels, diced artichokes, carrots, green beans, red onions, tomatoes, avocados, and radicchio, all dressed with a sherry-wine vinaigrette and presented on a bed of mixed lettuces — is one of the most popular items on the menu. Chino Ranch Chopped Salad also turns up on the menus of a number of California restaurants whose proprietors have never done business with the Chinos, or even necessarily laid eyes on a raw intact Chino vegetable. An analogy would be a bottler of Oregon cabernet sauvignon's slapping a Château Lafite label on his product, in homage.

Alice Waters and Wolfgang Puck have promulgated the notion that if you are going to grow vegetables you might as well grow Chino vegetables or not bother. The Chinos are aware of their important role within the California food culture. They work six and a half days a week, fifty-two weeks a year. They have made of the farm a separate sovereignty, a life and enterprise totally outside the mainstream. The Vegetable Shop is, in effect, a proscenium beyond which they feel no special need to venture.

Manny Farber, the painter/critic/teacher/éminence grise, lives and works in Leucadia, a couple of towns up the coast from Del Mar. "It wouldn't be possible anywhere else," Manny told me over dinner one evening. "The Chinos are selling to rich people who have some aestheticism behind their money." Chino vegetables — bunches of beets and carrots and leeks, fennel bulbs, tomatoes, melons — have turned up as compositional elements in many of Manny's recent sprawling, richly colored and textured oil still lifes. His wife, Patricia Patterson, has painted landscapes of the Chinos' fields.

"In visual terms, the difference between the Chinos' vegetables and all other vegetables is a total difference," Manny said. "They grow vegetables that are charismatically way beyond anyone else's, both in size and in color. They have nothing in common with what you find at Ralph's. Even when they're decaying, they're that way. All those midget vegetables and all the variety — they're growing lorgnette vegetables, ones you'd examine that way. I'm sure the whole process has to do with the most exquisite kind of putting together, and I'm sure they hide that like bloody murder from other farmers."

ONE SUNDAY, I was invited to lunch at the Chino farm. The living quarters have been cobbled together from an assortment of prewar one-story wood-frame-and-clapboard structures. In a hodgepodge manner, the buildings radiate from a brick-paved rectangular courtyard. The courtyard runs north to south. At the south end stands the only traditional Japanese building on the property — a cedar bathhouse, which is reached by a footbridge over a small pond filled with ivory and red-orange koi. At the north end is the only contemporary-looking building — yellow cinder block with sliding glass doors. It contains most of the Chinos' business files, and also a computer system, a photocopier, and a fax machine.

The main house, to the west, where Junzo Chino, the patriarch, lived, with his wife, Hatsuyo, is painted yellow and has a green asphalt-shingle roof. Near the entrance is a large cage that houses half a dozen goldfinches. I removed my sneakers and put them on a bench, beyond the range of Toby and Tommy, a pair of Jack Russell terriers. A low-ceilinged L-shaped space functions as both a kitchen and a family room. Japanese watercolors and calligraphy hang on the walls, along with a poster-size color photograph of Dolly Parton. A meal that Kay had prepared — roast chicken, mesclun salad, steamed broccoli, rice, salt salmon, green tea, banana cake — was set out on a pair of Formica-veneered tables. Frank and Fred drifted in, ate, amiably forgave some breaches of etiquette that I committed in the handling of my chopsticks, and then headed back to work.

Their mother, Hatsuyo, who had been afflicted by a series of strokes, lay on a sofa with her eyes closed. A small television stood on an end table next to her, and across the room were a huge television screen, a videocassette recorder, and a laser videodisc player. An open doorway led to Hatsuyo's bedroom. Tom escorted me there and showed me the butsudan, an ancestral altar, that stood on her dresser. A photograph of Junzo, a gentle-looking, faintly smiling man with black-framed, thick eyeglasses, white hair, and impressively large ears, stood on one shelf of the butsudan, and on another shelf was a painting of the Buddha. Junzo died in November of 1990, at the age of ninety-six, and two months later Tom, Kay, Hatsuyo, and several other family members traveled to Hashiguii, a small fishing village and resort community at the southern tip of Honshu, Japan's main island, to inter a portion of his ashes. Hashiguii was Junzo's birthplace; in the late sixties, he and Hatsuyo had begun making annual visits, and they later built a seaside house there.

Though Tom is the youngest of seven sons, he is now, in some respects, the head of the family. Neither he nor his siblings can articulate how this came about, just as they cannot really explain how their clearly delineated roles in the life of the farm have developed. For instance, only Frank drives the Caterpillar D4E tractor, which he uses for disking, plowing, and leveling. A family friend has described Frank as the Leonardo da Vinci of the big tractor. In effect, Frank is also the marketing manager; only Kay spends more time behind the counter of the Vegetable Shop. The more delicate tractor work — cultivating and furrowing out — is done by Fred. Kay attends to matters in the greenhouses — a quarter of an acre of seedlings, herbs, flowers, cucumbers, and tomatoes — and organizes the main house, cooks meals, keeps the payroll and other employee-related records, pays bills, and balances the checkbook.

Not one of the farm partners looks like a close blood relative of the others. Kay is petite and has a round face and pale skin, a shy, pixyish smile, and short, attractively graying hair. Usually, she dresses all in black. Most days, Fred wears aviator sunglasses, shorts, and a T-shirt that looks ready for the rag bin. Whenever possible, he goes barefoot. He has waist-length straight black hair and a deep tan — he could easily be taken for a Native American — and an ample belly. Frank has inherited his father's lean and graceful physique. His Levi's and button-down Brooks Brothers shirts are always crisply pressed, and he has a fashion-catalog cool and handsomeness. Tom has a compact build, a fleshy face, deep dark crinkly eyes, jug ears, and, despite the fact that he never goes into the field without a baseball cap, a sunbaked complexion. He dresses in a rumpled Eddie Bauer-ish style.

Tom, who got married a few years ago, lives, with his wife and their young son, in Encinitas, a fifteen-minute commute. Neither Kay nor Frank nor Fred has ever married, and all three live on the farm. (Another brother, Junji, also lives there, but he works full-time for San Diego County.) Most of Tom's workday is spent in the fields, overseeing a crew of about a dozen migrants from Oaxaca,

Mexico, and four Japanese trainees; since 1953, groups of agriculture students have been coming to Del Mar from Japan and Brazil as part of an exchange program that Junzo helped organize. Because Tom is also a regular presence in the Vegetable Shop — he monitors the field crews by walkie-talkie — and has tended to speak for the Chinos on those occasions when the Chinos have deigned to speak to the public, most outsiders have the impression that he is the boss. He holds the title of president of Chino Nojo, Inc., the family's corporate entity, but in a practical sense there seems to be no single boss.

When people who have observed the Chinos closely over the years are asked to explain how all this evolved, they tend to fall back on the phrase "very Japanese." Tom, who is an omnivorous reader, owns a large collection of books about Japanese history and culture. At the time of Junzo's death, his siblings deferred to him, because of his deep knowledge of the ordained rituals. Tom's reverence for the elegantly systematic process of mourning ran parallel to his methodology as a farmer. The coalescing of science, art, and ritual is, of course, commonly regarded as "very Japanese." It was natural, therefore, that during the months of Junzo's final illness Tom — the only partner in the farm who has a child — began to assume the role of patriarch.

"The Chinos never tell you anything," Wolfgang Puck has said. "They only ask questions. They ask questions and they read, and that's how, without actually going anywhere, they know what's going on everywhere. They think what they think. You'll be at the stand and a customer will come up and say, 'I just came back from New York. I went to David Bouley's restaurant the other night.' They ask, 'What did you eat?' Item by item, bite by bite, they want to know everything. They ask, 'What did you like the most? What didn't you like? What were the ingredients?' What the Chinos do doesn't involve magic. It comes from tenacity, hard work, some talent, and some love. If there is a magic with the Chinos, I think the magic is that every day they're getting up at five in the morning and working so hard. To see a family like that, doing what they do — I think it's such an amazing thing. Whatever it costs me to buy from them, it doesn't matter. I don't know what anything costs. I just know that they grow it and I want it."

Puck thinks that a combination of lucky accidents, including factors that could have been adverse, have contributed to the Chinos' success, as if the farm itself were a delicate organism that could thrive in no other microclimate. Ten miles farther inland, the daytime temperature runs from eight to ten degrees higher. The morning air humidity at the farm averages around 40 percent — compared with about 85 percent in the prolific farm belt of central Florida, where the produce has a more watery, less concentrated flavor. On the other hand, because nature is reluctant to water the Chinos' crops, they must do it themselves, at daunting expense. This has led to endless irrigation experiments — flood irrigation has gradually given way to drip irrigation, and plastic mulches of various colors and opacities and thicknesses have been tried — that have kept the Chinos vigilant. That they are congenitally vigilant anyway is yet another lucky accident.

"How many people do you know who can look at the sky and pay attention that there's a storm coming?" said Hideo Chino, the seventh-born of the nine children. Hideo is a juvenile-court referee in San Diego, and he also lives there, but he continues to spend a great deal of time at the farm. (For this reason, he is regarded as being more of the farm than the first- and third-born sons, Jun and Shigeru, who are both surgeons living in Orange County, and than the only other daughter, Hazuki, a housewife, who has lived in Los Angeles for more than thirty years.)

"One of the worst things for strawberries near harvest is rain," Hideo continued. "We would always dread rain for the berries. But then, if it looked like rain, my mother would say, 'It'll be OK if it turns windy' — because that would dry the berries. I can remember seeing my father plow up a perfectly good field of cabbage because the price was too low. You're dealing with the facts of life."

FROM A HANDFUL of bamboo leaves Junzo could make a pond-worthy toy boat. From a reed he could make a whistle that looked like a bird. Playing a flutelike instrument called a *shakuhachi*, he could sound like a bird. He understood how to read animal tracks and human tracks. Looking at a footprint in an irrigation furrow, he could tell whether it had been left by a Mexican or a Japanese. On ground that he had made perfectly level he grew perfect celery. He talked to plants and received responses. It is said that he once walked from Peru to California. Words he used sparingly. When he did have something to say, one of his sons recalls, "he spoke in various decibels, in which the specific language was irrelevant."

Junzo was born in Hashiguii in 1894. The Chino family was well established there, and was relatively prosperous; his father had been the village mayor. According to Junzo's immigration card, he arrived in America in 1924, but in fact he came here several years earlier. An older brother had preceded him to California and had then fallen out of touch with the family in Japan; Junzo was dispatched to find him. Immigration restrictions prevented Junzo from entering the country, however, and he wound up in Peru. He spent two years working his way from there toward his original destination, by train in part but mostly on foot. In Oaxaca, Mexico, he learned that his brother was living near Long Beach. When he got hung up at the border outside Tijuana — at the time, he had gone ten days with no food — a Chinese family helped him out. Nearly starving in Baja left an indelible impression on Junzo. Over the years, in Del Mar, whenever illegal aliens showed up on the farm, even if Junzo didn't have work for them he made sure they got fed.

In the family legend, Junzo one day wandered into a supermarket in Los Angeles and by chance, in the produce section, encountered his prodigal brother. Perhaps so. For the next few years, he and his brother migrated from one agricultural oasis to another — Imperial Valley, Coachella Valley, San Joaquin Valley — picking melons, grapes, dates, almonds.

Meanwhile, in 1922, when Hatsuyo Noda was fourteen, her family transplanted itself from Wakayama, a hundred miles north of Hashiguii, to Oxnard, California, and her father began to farm celery there. The Nodas were familiar with the Chinos, and her marriage to Junzo, in 1930, was a semi-arranged matter. Of the two, Hatsuyo had the warmer and more outgoing nature. Friends of the children use adjectives like "supportive," "loving," "intelligent," and "wise" to describe her. She made felt hats and shirts for Junzo, managed the family money, prepared the family meals, filled the house with flowers, and toiled in the greenhouse and the fields. When corn was in season, she waded into the stalks at sunrise and wielded her harvesting knife with terrifying celerity. She had a smile as sweet as early-summer strawberries.

Though Junzo had a gentle spirit, he also had a short fuse. Basically, he remained throughout his life a Meiji man — a product of the Chinese-influenced cultural, political, and technological modernization that flourished in Japan in the late nineteenth century. "Papa wanted everything done fast, and he wanted it done perfectly," Kay has said. "We were told everything one time, and we were supposed to remember it." The farm became a benevolent autocracy, and, in a manner that was typical of Meiji values, the life of the enterprise was coterminous with the life of the family — a self-sustaining universe.

Junzo and Hatsuyo's first child, Jun, was born in the spring of 1930, and by that time they were operating a fruit stand in Los Angeles. Hazuki was born in 1932, Kay in 1933, Junji in 1937, Shigeru in 1938, Frank in 1941, Hideo in 1943, Fred in 1947, and Tom in 1949. The fruit stand lasted until 1934; it was abandoned because, as Hatsuyo later explained, "I didn't like to count pennies." They moved to a thirty-acre leased property near Venice, and for three years they produced vegetables for the wholesale market. Jun remembers running water, but kerosene lamps — no electricity. In 1937, they shifted down the coast to Carlsbad, bought a house and three acres of greenhouses, and raised vegetable seedlings and flowers. More than once, Junzo's asters won prizes at the Philadelphia Flower Show, and that was not at all bad for business. It was less salutary for business when several farmers to whom Junzo had sold seedlings failed to pay their bills. Carlsbad was within commuting distance of Del Mar, and in 1940 Junzo leased land in the San Dieguito Valley and grew peppers there. This property later became Chino Nojo.

For Japanese-Americans living on the West Coast, the Second World War altered every expectation. During the spring of 1942, the Chinos were assigned to an internment camp — Poston No. 3 — near Parker, Arizona. Each member of the family was allowed to bring along a single suitcase. "We had to leave our cats and dogs," Kay has said. "I remember the sound of the door being locked. I just couldn't look." Only the oldest of the children retain vivid memories of the internment camp: an arid square mile, blowing dust, a gun tower, barbed wire, lots of kids, craft groups, outdoor plays, Japanese movies, singing associations, sirens, suicides, Baptist preachers going on about Heaven and Hell. Hatsuyo had a job in the camp kitchen, and Junzo tilled a 50-by-100-foot plot, a vegetable nursery.

Before entering the camp, they had signed over their Carlsbad property to a man named Jim Bailey, who was an employee of a produce shipper, and whom Junzo and Hatsuyo trusted. Putting the title in Bailey's name was intended to be a dummy transaction, a way of protecting assets from possible confiscation by the government. Friends from Carlsbad, a Caucasian couple, made periodic visits to the Poston camp, and on one of their trips they brought the news that Bailey had sold everything — house, greenhouses, clothing, family pictures, dishes, toys, every valued memento. The Chinos were released from internment in the early fall of 1945. Each family member was given twenty-five dollars and a train ticket. Borrowing a friend's 1936 Chrysler, they called on Bailey at his house, in Carlsbad. The children waited in the car while Junzo and Hatsuyo went inside, and when they returned Hatsuyo uttered the phrase *"Shikata-ga-nai"* ("You can't do anything about it"). Not long afterward, Bailey died. Never again was this episode referred to either by Junzo or by Hatsuyo, except on one occasion many years later. "Jim Bailey was a weak man," Junzo explained to Kay — and that ended the discussion permanently.

After a detour to Los Angeles, where they shared rooms in Japantown with relatives of Hatsuyo's, the Chinos arrived in Del Mar for good during the winter of 1947. Junzo could not afford to buy land, so he worked out a sharecropping agreement with a landowner named A. M. Dunn. The property included a farmhouse and four other buildings. The day the Chinos moved in, they discovered that someone had painted racist epithets on the walls and, with a knife, had impaled a photograph of Prime Minister Tojo. They repainted the walls. Because the Second World War had never been Junzo's war — the fanatical Japanese nationalism that triggered it amounted to a repudiation of Meiji Restoration values — he had no desire to prolong it. When a nearby military base announced a sale of surplus supplies, the Chinos bought what they needed to provide accommodations for their work crews: five Quonset huts, and blankets, metal cots, and kitchen utensils.

Dunn, the landlord, was a humorless man who the children thought "looked like a mean Santa Claus." His family then controlled big chunks of the San Dieguito Valley — land that has long since been transformed from monoculture bean fields into golf courses, housing developments, polo clubs, and expensive strip shopping centers anchored by restaurants that specialize in multicolored frozen margaritas. A friendly neighbor, Jennie Collins, who raises fruit and livestock on property a quarter of a mile from the Chinos, settled in the valley in the mid-fifties. "This was always black, black, black country," Mrs. Collins told me. "There were no lights, very few other houses. At night, it was so quiet you could hear the train from Solana Beach, and that's five miles away."

A respectful understanding existed between Dunn and Junzo. Dunn recognized that Junzo was a gifted farmer, and he liked the fact that the rent always got paid on time. He also recognized that Junzo intended someday to own the land. Land very close by was available for three hundred dollars an acre, but Junzo felt that the soil was too sandy. In the summer of 1952, he agreed to pay Dunn a thousand dollars an acre for fifty-one acres, and two months later he paid five thousand dollars for five additional acres. The farm was a crowded place, with fifty-man crews at peak times. Where mechanical cultivation was unsuitable, mules were used. Bing Crosby owned a house about a mile away, and a mule of his named Toby, retired from a career in motion pictures, ended up pulling a plow on the Chino farm. At any given time, four or five issei, or Japanese immigrant, bachelors lived on the premises. Kay and Hazuki were not allowed outdoors after dark.

From the fifties through the late sixties, everything that wasn't grown for home consumption went to the wholesale market in Los Angeles. Junzo also planted unconventional crops like frisée, golden peppers, and Shanghai bok choy, but if the produce buyers for the supermarket chains deemed an item too exotic it could never leave the farm. Diversifying into larger volumes of mainstream products — cauliflower, broccoli, and celery in cool weather, and tomatoes, wax beans, and peppers in warm weather — failed to diminish the Chinos' dependence upon the wholesalers. Every day, they awoke at four-thirty and waited for the phone to ring before going out to pick.

The older children went off to school — Jun and Shigeru to Stanford, Hazuki to study textile design in Los Angeles, Kay to the University of Southern California — and returned in the summer to work in the fields or the packing sheds.

By the mid-sixties, Junzo was past seventy and had begun to

contemplate retirement, whatever that might imply. Some years earlier, Kay, while she was a sophomore at USC, had developed appendicitis and come to Del Mar to recuperate. Then, without explicitly declaring her intentions, she decided to stay. In retrospect, her return seems both fortuitous and foreordained, an expression of the family's collective unconscious. Shigeru and Jun were launched on their medical careers, and Hazuki had settled into motherhood and suburban life.

Over time, however, the others, one by one, came home. Frank, after attending junior college and studying geology at San Jose State, came back in 1965. I once asked him what, specifically, had drawn him home, and he replied, in the epigrammatic way that always makes conversation with him an interesting challenge, "Isn't that what home is for?" Hideo studied microbiology at San Diego State, finished his law degree in 1970, went into private practice for four years, gave up lawyering for a couple of years while he worked on the farm, then resumed his law practice by setting up an office in what is now a bunkhouse a tomato's throw from the Vegetable Shop. Fred attended a nearby junior college, was drafted into the army, and ended up at a missile installation near Fairbanks, Alaska, where one of his tasks was to "tear apart nuclear warheads, put them in cans, and ship them to be rebuilt." He received his discharge in 1968, and having spent eighteen months longing for the climate and the familiar comforts of southern California, headed straight there. The only Chino who actually studied agriculture in college was Junji. At California Polytechnic State University, he majored in crop science and agronomy. But after he, too, came home, a rift developed between him and Junzo. He has spent the past twenty-five years as a mosquito-eradication supervisor for the San Diego County Department of Public Health.

At the University of California at Berkeley, Tom majored in anatomy and physiology and had plans to become a physician. In 1972, he enrolled in the medical school in Guadalajara, but he left after a week and returned to Del Mar, the safest place to be while he contemplated his next move. The Chino Nojo corporate documents at that time listed him as manager, a title that had about it a meaningful vagueness. For several years, he held two jobs: one from dawn to midmorning, at the farm, followed by ten hours of cancer research in a lab at the Scripps Clinic and Research Foundation, in La Jolla. For a year in the late seventies, he moonlighted as a neurobiology researcher at the Salk Institute. At another point, he seriously considered entering a doctoral program in plant pathology. By the time he resolved to embrace the farm full-time, the Vegetable Shop had evolved from a fanciful notion to an institution.

The Vegetable Shop opened for business in the summer of 1969. The first couple of years, it offered quantity and quality but not a great deal of variety — strawberries, corn, melons, tomatoes, peppers, celery, endive, carrots, daikon radishes. Melons and radishes the Chinos had always grown for themselves but never for the wholesale market. Most farmers who set up roadside stands are trying to unload their seconds or leftovers — whatever they haven't sold to the wholesale brokers. Shoppers, of course, are attracted by the prospect of buying fresher-than-supermarket produce at a bargain price. Whenever Frank felt uncertain about prices, he would canvass the produce at a nearby Safeway and mark up everything at the Vegetable Shop 15 percent. If the customers complained that they could pay less at the supermarket, Frank would nod and smile and agree: "Yes, we know that."

Within four years, the revenue from the Vegetable Shop approached that of the farm's wholesale operation. Even Junzo began to see that his children's whimsy was generating far more than pocket change, but his focus remained on the Chino imprimatur. When the impulse struck, Junzo would, like a general surveying his troops, turn up in the Vegetable Shop for a full-dress inspection. Anyone who had been lounging would stand at attention while he scrutinized and rearranged the merchandise. The cucumbers had to be lined up just so; the Brussels sprouts were supposed to be uniform in size and sit in their pint boxes heads up; the tomatoes couldn't look dusty or the beans rusty.

In 1974, Junzo had a heart attack, which he interpreted as a sign that he should relinquish certain prerogatives, such as driving the big Caterpillar. Implicit in each pragmatic decision were all of the deep and complicated feelings that Junzo and Hatsuyo had about the future stewardship of the farm.

"You can't really teach a person to drive a tractor," Frank says. "If you drive a tractor crooked, you have to know in your head that it's going crooked. It's like being a racecar driver: the car is an extension of your body — and how can you teach somebody to feel that?"

Hatsuyo suffered a heart attack in 1978, the year the Chinos sold their last brokered produce, and Kay started to assume Hatsuyo's responsibilities. Tom, meanwhile, had accepted the role of chief agriculturist, and as a result the farm's cropping strategies became increasingly complex. Junzo and Hatsuyo had fertilized with chicken manure, controlled weeds without herbicides, avoided disease-prone plants. Tom stuck to these basic tenets with myriad elaborations. Previously, Junzo might have grown, say, four hundred two-hundred-foot rows of one variety of pepper. Now Tom planted only fifty rows but a hundred varieties. He began ordering seeds from Europe, setting up test plots, studying technical journals, experimenting with various cropping systems. The Chinos had never asked themselves the sorts of questions that concern most growers: How do I grow a tomato that can make it to Chicago? The question Tom and his sister and brothers were now asking was: How can we raise vegetables that will gratify the most subtle palate? They read *Gourmet, Food and Wine, Bon Appétit, Food Arts, Eating Well, Nation's Restaurant News,* and several gastronomic newsletters.

During the winter of 1990, Junzo, who was then ninety-five, developed a bad cold, which was followed by an intractable respiratory infection. When it no longer seemed possible to care for him on the farm, he was hospitalized, and over the next several months he was shuttled between the hospital and a nursing home. One consequence of his illness was that a long-anticipated project — tearing down the prewar buildings and replacing them with more stable ones — had to be postponed. To finance this project, Junzo had planned to use federal-government funds: a twenty-thousand-dollar reparation that was due each member of the family who had been interned during the war — everyone except Fred and Tom. Legislation authorizing the reparations was signed by Ronald Reagan in 1988, eight years after Congress first began holding hearings on "appropriate remedies" for the government's internment of its citizens. The bill that Reagan signed authorized total compensation of $1.2 billion. Junzo's and Hatsuyo's checks arrived in October of 1990, and a month later Junzo died. Hatsuyo had meanwhile developed major health problems — the strokes that severely impaired her speech, her mobility, and her ability to swallow. Junzo's twenty thousand dollars, as well as most of Hatsuyo's share, went to pay medical bills, and Junzo's capital-improvement master plan has yet to be put into action.

LATE ONE SPRING AFTERNOON, Tom gave me a tour of some of the farm's hidden and semi-obscured charms. We started off in a red clapboard barn that sits next to Calzada del Bosque, the paved road that leads to the Vegetable Shop. Much of the barn's interior has been taken over by Maurice McColley, an eighty-four-year-old semiretired carpenter who has been a presence for about fifteen years. Previously, the barn was a storage place and machine shop for irrigation pumps. In addition to Mr. McColley's carpentry tools and supplies, it houses perhaps a hundred worn-out automobile tires, a mile of flexible irrigation pipe, dozens of louvered wooden window shutters, a tractor-driven planting tool that was used only one season, and a khaki-green 1965 Ford Mustang — the second-oldest edition of that model. When Tom showed me the Mustang, he said, "We don't get rid of cars that easily" — a profound understatement. A few minutes later, we walked from the barn toward a group of smaller equipment sheds, along the way surveying a dark-green Chevrolet truck from the fifties that appeared to be turning itself to compost, a well-preserved twenty-year-old avocado-yellow Karmann Ghia, a dull-gray 1965 Volvo, and four stolid, mature Volkswagen Beetles. "There used to be a VW craze here," Tom said. The Volkswagens signified visionary thinking rather than inertia. The hardest-working and strangest-looking vehicle on the farm was a mobile but asthmatic, bodiless 1959 Beetle. Stripped down to the chassis and retrofitted with a flatbed cargo area, it was used to transport workers and supplies to the fields, vegetables from the fields to the stand, and empty plastic crates from the stand back to the fields.

Between the riverbank and the homestead, we passed an herb garden that had once been the site of a chicken coop, and wound up on a dusty path next to a melon field. Behind the main house were two trucks that seemed to be parked there terminally. The trucks occupied what was, in effect, the front yard of a prefab building that the Japanese trainees used as a kitchen. Through a screen door I could see three of the trainees taking a midafternoon tea break while watching a game show on TV.

Parallel to the riverbank were two greenhouses — Kay's domain. At this season, they were filled with flats of vegetables and melons. Year-round, they are the primary source of the Vegetable Shop's herbs. A grape arbor and a row of raspberry and blackberry bushes lined fifty yards of the riverbank. Where the berries ended, a row of rosemary plants began.

Tom had to get back to work, so I was free to wander. I started along the road past the melon field, which was on my right. Weeds were on my left, and strawberries were on my mind. A pair of rock doves crossed my path, and then a bevy of quail burst from the weeds. The fields are a wildlife refuge, populated by squirrels, rabbits, and gophers, and occasional roadrunners, coyotes, badgers, and bobcats. An ancient tortoise used to live in Junzo's celery field.

When Frank and Fred disk a crop, red-tailed hawks gather overhead and amuse themselves and onlookers by dive-bombing for the field mice scrambling in the daylight.

Because I wasn't a farmer desperate for rain, the weather struck me as perfect: cloudless, with a faint breeze and a temperature in the mid-seventies. One of the trainees was furrow-irrigating a field of fennel, cabbage, and broccoli. He had opened several valves and was running along a turnrow, slamming a metal dam into the main irrigation ditch here, shoveling soil to close a furrow there. The furrows filled with such uniformity that opposing irrigation streams would inch along a crop row and meet almost precisely at midpoint. The earth here was flat: the *Niña* and the *Pinta* and the *Santa María* would have sailed right off the edge of Chino Nojo.

I came upon a field of beets, carrots, radishes, and onions. Next door were strawberries — two robust-looking varieties called oso grande and pajaro. A row of fava-bean plants — a combined windbreak and edible organic flypaper to protect the strawberries from a pest called the two-spotted mite — bordered the field. Earlier in the week, at Chez Panisse, I had eaten a salmon-salad appetizer garnished with Chino fava beans. I could see Tom two fields away, bent over, using a short-handled hoe to cultivate between rows of lettuce. The sun was lowering. The Chinos have an injunction against harvesting strawberries past noon, the idea being that a ripe strawberry picked after the sun has peaked will suffer too rapid a conversion from sugar into starch. Lacking such a sensitive palate, and also lacking a habit of self-denial, I decided I didn't care. The fava-bean plants were tall enough for camouflage. I had heard talk of a plan to install a video camera in the cornfield to monitor rustlers, but there were no signs of surveillance equipment hidden among the fava beans. I breached the border and felt safely out of view as I knelt above an oso-grande plant. I plucked three plum-size berries and checked my watch: 4:00 P.M. Forbidden fruit. The hawks and the quail were my only witnesses.

Each strawberry tasted like a perfect slice of fresh-baked pie: firm, plump, juicy, sugary, and agreeably warm.

I wanted the Chinos to explain how I could have been eating and enjoying strawberries for forty years, while all along I hadn't a clue how a strawberry was supposed to taste. I knew, however, that no one on the farm would tell me. Kay can be quite talkative, and is especially gracious to visitors who introduce themselves as friends of friends, but when a dialogue crosses certain invisible lines her responses become elliptic and her memory becomes selective. Tom has mastered the allied arts of conveying a great deal by saying little and of saying a lot to avoid saying anything at all. Frank seems most comfortable saying very little, period. The most garrulous Chino is Fred, so I once asked him point-blank what it was that made Chino vegetables and fruits taste special.

"We know that if it doesn't rain for twenty days we have to water our crops," he said. "You can't be stupid and be a farmer anymore. If you went to school and studied agriculture and then went out in the field to farm, you'd lose your shirt. You know why? Because all you have to do is make one mistake."

Conversations with Fred have a free-associational pitch and yaw. For about a week during one of my visits, a tomato bearing the label "Vine Ripened Extra Large Tomato Packed Exclusively for Big Bear Markets" sat on top of a jar of homemade peach marmalade on the kitchen table. It was like a piece of conceptual art that was daring someone to eat it. One day, I asked Fred what it was doing there, and this launched him into an object lesson on the differences between hothouse and outdoor tomatoes. From there he digressed to why honey is not good for you, the tendency of upper-class Japanese people to wear camellia oil in their hair, the fragrance of butyric acid and the impossibility of ridding oneself of the odor by any process other than metabolism, gene mapping and the possible fallacy of Darwinism, the size of the hole in the ozone layer, microwave technology, dead satellites, life expectancy, and the vagaries of the screen career of the actor Martin Landau. We were eating lunch at the time, and Hatsuyo lay on the sofa, mutely watching a videotape of *Double Suicide,* an adaptation of a Japanese Bunraku play. Fred has no difficulty simultaneously following a movie and discussing whatever pops into his mind. There was a time when he rented a dozen movies a week. Recently, he has averaged about one a day.

After lunch, I followed him from the house to a large, high-ceilinged garage that during the wholesale-market era was the packing shed. It now contains a walk-in cooler and a slightly smaller cooler, a beige Ford van that Frank uses to make deliveries to the airport and to Spago, a silver Mercedes-Benz that was originally owned by Shigeru, an antique white Porsche that Jun gave to Frank, and a Corvette-like kit car that Fred ordered from a catalog more than ten years ago and has never finished assembling. I asked Fred whether he thought the family had enough vehicles. "We're missing a truck that we could drive on the road," he said. Fred uses the Mercedes on his infrequent departures from the farm, mainly to chauffeur Kay, who has never learned to drive. He figures he puts only a few thousand miles a year on the odometer.

"I know what a hassle travel is," he said. "It seems sort of superfluous. What do you really gain from it? Wherever you go, you don't really know anyone. Going to Japan doesn't interest me. You're talking to someone who doesn't believe in experts. You live a life, and no matter what you do you have a limited perspective. The more you know, you realize how much less you know. If I travel, I'm not really going to learn that much more. I'm more interested in people and the mechanisms of people than in places."

In another area of the garage, Frank was installing a motor in a Volkswagen that would replace the one being retired from the field. As he adjusted a metal clamp on a transaxle boot, I asked him whether Junzo had understood the mechanics of automobiles. "No," Frank said. "A farmer does have to learn how to clean a carburetor, do a tune-up. But he just drove." The decapitated blue shell of the VW was parked outside.

"Originally, we were going to do it a little differently, but we just kept cutting it off," he said. "I had this idea in my head of what this car was supposed to look like, because I had this idea of what it was supposed to do."

"How did you learn about cars?" I asked.

"What do you mean?"

"Who taught you to do what you're doing right now?"

"Nobody. You just do it."

"How do you know how to just do it?"

"Well, these cars, you realize, were designed so that any moron could work on them."

Fred, in a welder's visor and a leather apron, was using a welding torch to frame a tall, heavy-duty storage rack — a steel structure that would be fitted with plywood shelves. Sparks flew several feet in every direction.

I asked Frank, "When a Chino learns welding, does he study it or does he just go buy welding equipment and start to do it?"

"No. Actually, it would have been a good idea for Fred to take some classes." Pause. "But he's pretty hardheaded."

Frank stood up to inspect his handiwork and to wipe his grease-covered hands with a terry-cloth towel. He had on smudge-free Levi's and a blue Oxford shirt with the cuffs rolled up in precise, even folds. If he had been wearing a white linen suit, he would have achieved the same fastidious result. After walking around the car, he picked up a socket wrench and went back to work.

"I'm sure a person like Wolf asks himself, 'Am I going to do this forever?'" he said of Wolfgang Puck.

"Do you ask yourself that question?"

"I don't ask myself that, no. Because farming is a lifetime thing. My impression is that my parents never thought any of the kids would do farming. I had a sense of that before the stand started.

Once the stand started, it was something for us to do. The stand was the best thing that ever happened in our lives and theirs. If we just took care of restaurants, we wouldn't be where we are. We don't have to do this. If somebody down the street could do this better than we do, we'd stop doing it."

"What would you do if you weren't doing this?"

"I'd have to start thinking about what I was going to eat." For thirty seconds, he was silent. Then he said, "Maybe I'd be a gardener."

ONE SUMMER DAY in 1978, Jean-Pierre Gorin showed up at the Vegetable Shop "in quest of the perfect green bean," as he later said in a eulogy at Junzo's funeral. Gorin, who is a French-born filmmaker and a longtime friend of Alice Waters, discovered not only the perfect green bean but also "purple-and-white eggplants, yellow, green, and red tomatoes, lettuces encompassing all shades of green — a perfect still life."

While Tom was carrying sacks of vegetables to Gorin's car, he noticed a University of California at San Diego parking permit on the bumper. Was he a faculty member? Yes, Gorin said, he taught film in the visual-arts department. His body of work at that point consisted of two idiosyncratic documentaries, *Poto and Cabengo* and *Routine Pleasures.* Tom dropped Jean-Luc Godard's name into the conversation. As it happened, Gorin and Godard had collaborated on several projects and were in the habit of referring to themselves as "the only two members of a Maoist film collective."

Gorin made a transition from steady customer to occasional employee. Once, Sophia Loren stopped by the Vegetable Shop. Frank, who is unapologetically celebrity-struck, did a double take, allowed for an interval of insouciant silence, then gestured toward Gorin, who was bagging corn, and said, "By the way, he's also involved in film." The more time Gorin spent with the Chinos, the more he felt that they and Waters should get acquainted. A year passed before Gorin arranged a meeting, but soon Greyhound coaches were ferrying shipments from Del Mar to the Chez Panisse kitchen, in Berkeley. The thought of his family's vegetables languishing several hours in a bus cargo bay made Frank uneasy — it took only a few hours for a cavaillon melon to go from sublime to sub-Chino-standard — so a switch was made to airfreight. A couple of years later, Puck opened Spago, in West Hollywood. The day Waters came to the restaurant, whipped a lavender-and-white-striped eggplant out of her handbag, and said, "Look what I've got!" was the day Puck decided that he, too, wanted to meet the Chinos.

The van that Frank drives to Spago every weekend is something of a shrine. Its interior walls are covered with autographs: Puck, Barbara Lazaroff (Puck's wife), several chefs who cook for Puck at Spago or his other restaurants, Waters and others from Chez Panisse (Paul Bertolli, Mary Jo Thoresen, Peggy Smith), Julia Child, Jacques Pépin, Richard Olney, Larry Forgione, Maida Heatter, Anne Rosenzweig, Bradley Ogden, and Mark Miller. There is also a wooden pizza spatula signed by Puck, Lazaroff, and the three-time Tour de France winner Greg LeMond.

One Sunday, I joined Frank for his run to Spago. The trip along the San Diego Freeway takes about two hours and bypasses Carlsbad, where he was born, where his parents once grew vegetable seedlings and hothouse flowers, and where most of the farms have long since become easy-commute housing developments. When we arrived at Spago, three hours ahead of the early dinner crowd, one of the head chefs was standing in the parking lot. Puck had recently leased a cherry-red Mustang for him. While the chef enumerated its surplus of desirable features, Frank nodded sagely. Several kitchen helpers were also hanging around, and soon Frank opened the cargo doors of the van. They lifted the lids of the cardboard cartons as if peeking at Christmas gifts — perhaps two dozen different fruits and vegetables. "Spago doesn't order anything specific," Frank told me. "I basically decide what they need — which is everything we've got. Has anybody ever criticized anything we sent them? No. Because we never send them anything bad. If it's bad, we won't send it."

There is a state prison in the town of Chino, California. Occasionally, a diner who notices the phrase "Chino Ranch vegetables" on the menu congratulates Puck for giving the convicts something worthwhile to do. Frank's time at Spago seems to be evenly divided between pizza making and cultural-anthropology fieldwork. The restaurant has two kitchens: one of them is fully exposed to the clientele, and Frank stations himself there, in front of the pizza oven. He wears a white linen Spago apron and a cream and pink Spago baseball cap, makes vegetable-laden pizzas, schmoozes with the help, and watches the stars and the periodontists and herbalists to the stars pay dearly to amuse themselves. The agent Swifty Lazar invites a hundred and fifty friends to an annual Academy Awards–night party at Spago, and Frank is always on hand. Everyone back at the farm gets a full accounting.

Puck and his wife take short vacations to Rancho Santa Fe or Del Mar to be near the Chinos, though doing so exposes them to the family's relentless generosity. The Chinos bestow gifts — often lavish, famous-label objects — on birthdays, wedding anniversaries, and New Year's Day, and they give them at less predictable moments, with a frequency that leads many of their friends to arm themselves with reciprocal gifts before visiting the farm. "The farm doesn't expect anything other than courtesy," Hideo told me.

"Our parents taught us 'Be generous with what you have in abundance,'" Shigeru said. Obeying this dictum, Kay seems to be endlessly divesting herself of an abundance of Hermès scarves, Chanel handbags, Japanese wooden combs, and Baccarat tchotchkes. Once, I made the mistake of admiring aloud a collection of stout elliptic baskets woven from dyed Torrey-pine needles. They were the work of a local artist, and about a dozen of them, from goldfish-bowl to washtub dimensions, were stored in the office. As I was leaving, a couple of hours later, Kay handed me a small carton; it contained one of the baskets. In a conversation the next morning with Dwight Worden, the family's attorney, I asked what, short of returning it, he thought I should do. "Understand that the Chinos are very selective about who their friends are, but if you're their friend that's the way it is," he said. "You don't get into gift-giving contests with the Chinos. You can't win." A few days later, I mentioned to Tom that I still felt uncomfortable about the basket. Tom's response was to give me another gift — a book entitled *Japanese Etiquette: An Introduction.*

Andy Goldsmith, one of the Chinos' seed suppliers, has described the Chinos as "a basic element of my life-support system." He added, "People bring or send them seeds from all over the world. Tom receives domestic-seed catalogs from Japan, publications from France and Holland and Israel. It's very easy to feel inadequate talking to him unless I really stay on top of my stuff. He's told me that what I do is very important in terms of having new products for him. He makes me feel that I'm integral to the success of his operation. As I visit vegetable research stations, I come away with the idea that Tom should do this or that. The Chinos grow what they grow by some subjective method of natural selection. They try everything and decide what they like. I sell a million and a half dollars' worth of seeds a year, and for the amount of business I do with the Chinos I should be dropping in on them three or four times a year. But I see them every week. When I think of the amount of vegetables they give me in return for the amount of seed that I sell them, I would gladly give them all their seeds free. The Chinos feel that what they do is every bit as important and that they're every bit as professional as my doctor or lawyer. They have a clear sense of their own self-worth. The Chinos are not snobs. They're very warm, giving people."

When it comes to some of the Chinos' friends, their munificence backfires. Manny Farber says, "The reason I don't go out there more often is that they don't let you pay." Henry Knorr, a machinist who has been in business a mile from the farm since before the family owned it, gets a call a couple of times a year from Kay. She says, "We've got some corn for you. Come and get it." Otherwise, he gets his vegetables at Big Bear, where his money is good. Some people have attempted subterfuge, hiding money under a tray of vegetables, only to discover after their next visit that an envelope containing the same money has been slipped into their sack of squash. Tibor Safar, who has a doctorate in experimental psychology — which means that Tom can no longer accurately refer to him as "the most eternal grad student in the history of UCSD" — used to help out behind the counter at the Vegetable Shop. He still comes around regularly, and never departs empty-handed. "It is a problem," he acknowledged. "I know that some people won't come here anymore because of that. But I've come to terms with this. I just told myself that staying away because the vegetables were free was too great a price to have to pay."

ONE MORNING late in June, the plywood unloading platform behind the Vegetable Shop was knee-deep in melons and dew-speckled corn. Tom shucked an ear of corn and handed it to me. It was the first time I had eaten raw sweet corn. I took a bite, then sat down to contemplate the paradox that corn could taste as complexly sugary as a Chino strawberry and somehow stop short of cloying. Though I didn't think Tom would have felt slighted if I had taken only a few bites, I polished off the whole ear. While he went to work on the melons with a cleaver and a knife — there were four varieties of Israeli muskmelon, six varieties of green-fleshed Japanese net melon, fourteen varieties of French cavaillon melon, eight varieties of Eastern market melon, half a dozen kinds of foreign and domestic watermelon — I shucked and ate a second ear, and then a third.

The cavaillon melons had gray-green skins and pink-orange flesh, the Israeli melons fine-netted blond skins and pale-yellow-green flesh. As I switched from corn to the melons, I wouldn't have minded a juicy lime, but it would have clouded my research. The melons all revealed perfumes and other subtleties that I had never encountered. Along the way, I kept losing track of which varieties I was tasting. Tom patiently repeated the same facts several times. I asked him what he told customers when they asked the names of melons. "We call this a French honeydew," he said, holding one at eye level. "It's actually an Israeli galia melon. We've always been paranoid about telling people the varieties of melons, because we don't want them buying the seeds themselves. Also, if you tell someone the name and they like the melon, they'll remember the name and never try anything else."

A couple of days later, I stood with Tom in a melon field at 6:30 A.M. He had already been awake for two and a half hours: he had commuted to the farm from his home in Encinitas, read the *New York Times,* and eaten a pancake breakfast prepared by Kay. Shortly before six, the Japanese trainees and the Mexican workers had assembled behind the Vegetable Shop. Tom gave them instructions for the morning, and they headed out to the fields in a convoy that consisted of the bodiless Volkswagen, two golf carts (one with a trailer full of stacks of empty plastic crates and flats), a hoodless Toyota pickup (also full of crates), and a four-wheeled motorcycle. Harvesting usually goes on until ten o'clock, unless there are strawberries, which can be picked until noon. At the moment, Tom, with the help of Rene Herrera, a small-boned, fine-featured man in his late twenties, who for four years has been migrating to Del Mar from Oaxaca, was looking for ripe melons. Tom had an opaque, skeptical expression, like a customs inspector. Rene carried a pair of long wooden sticks, which he was using to probe the foliage. The mature cavaillons were not much bigger than softballs. Tom judged their ripeness by the presence of a hairline crack at the junction of the stem and the fruit. He moved through the row at a steady, efficient pace, picking ripe melons and putting them in the furrows. When he got to the watermelons, he said, "A ripe watermelon should have a waxy coat and make a low-resonant response when you tap it. Also, the end that touches the ground turns yellow. When you tap an unripe one, it will make a more high-pitched, pinging noise." He held up a seedless red Japanese watermelon and said, "This has a high-pitched ping, but the color tells me it's ready. One determinant does not a watermelon make."

"Does a day make a big difference in flavor?" I asked.

"Eight hours makes a difference."

At 7:00 A.M., it was time to cut corn, and Tom and Rene rode in a golf cart toward the north end of the property. It was a ten-minute walk, but I knew they would be there awhile, so I took my time. I paused to watch Frank, who had put on a red apron and latex gloves to cut lettuce, then strolled past fields where radicchio, green beans, broccoli florets, Brussels sprouts, white cauliflower, green cauliflower, Romanesque cauliflower, turnips, carrots, and fennel were being harvested. In a freshly disked plot next to a row of sugar-snap peas, I saw a pile of more than a hundred melons, mainly cavaillons, a day overripe. Four months earlier, I had seen these melons in their embryonic phase. Tom and two trainees had sat with tweezers at a kitchen table, counting seeds from a large Mason jar. They were assembling sixty-three-seed lots and wrapping and tying them in cheesecloth bundles. After the seeds had soaked in water for two hours, they would be put in an incubator for a day, then planted in flats in the greenhouse. It struck me as excessively painstaking labor, and I was curious about the economics.

"Well, uh, these seeds are rather expensive," Tom said.

How expensive?

"Well, uh, about a dollar a seed."

"How many seeds to a pound?"

"About five thousand."

This was $4,870 more than a California commercial melon farmer would typically pay for a pound of high-end cantaloupe seeds, I later learned. Staring now at the pile of dumped melons, I reminded myself: Tom Chino has a supple mind, and he knows what he is doing. I saw the golf cart parked in a turnrow, and I

could hear the *whack* and *thwack* of knives dismembering corn-
stalks, but when I called out to Tom there was no response.

Tom and Rene were in there somewhere. I waded blindly
through the orderly jungle for a couple of minutes and found
them. Tom was working with frightening speed. Though a single
stalk might produce three ears, the average marketable yield is one
and a quarter ears per stalk. After severing the most mature ear,
Tom would palpate the next largest, testing for worms. Every tenth
ear, he cut off the top leaves to appraise the ear's maturity. The
harvested ears were deposited in every third furrow. Corn pollen
rained on his head, nestled in his ears. Though the pollen didn't
bother him, he was allergic to the corn juice, and chances were that
by the end of the day his eyes would be an itchy, bloodshot mess.
His tool was a fourteen-inch chef's knife, which he sharpened
daily. With it, he estimated, he had in the past ten years cut a million ears. Twice a season, it cut him.

When Tom returned from Berkeley, in the early seventies, corn
had already become a major cash crop, along with strawberries.
Hatsuyo oversaw the planting and cultivating and harvesting, and,
though the public seemed to feel that the end result was sublime,
her system contained imperfections. The basic problem was that
demand often exceeded supply. Frank didn't mind when this happened, and he still doesn't — he thinks running out of things pre-
vents anyone from taking the Vegetable Shop for granted — but it
bothered Tom.

Tom carries a Rapidograph drafting pen and a leather-bound
notebook in his shirt pocket. In a tiny scrawl, legible only to him,
he records cropping and cultivating and harvest schedules, yields,
and sales figures. Beginning last year, some of these jottings were
transcribed to a computer database. In the hierarchy of variables
that Tom must juggle when he's determining his annual planting
strategy, corn ranks first. From one year to the next, all the other
crops are rotated through all the other fields. Corn, however — the

volume of acreage and the specific fields devoted to it — remains constant. The planting schedule is rigid, based on a growth cycle that, depending on the weather, ranges from 70 to 110 days. At any given time, about twenty-five acres are planted with corn. With double cropping in some fields, 60 percent of the land is devoted to corn in the course of a year. The benefits of computerization notwithstanding, one variable has remained unquantifiable. "Studies always look at yield ratios," Tom said. "But what do the studies tell you about flavor?"

From corn, our conversation divagated to Japanese textiles, plant pathology, natural predators, Donald Trump's haircut, and New York City politics. His knife kept swinging and the corn kept coming. At one point, he asked Rene how many ears he had cut.

"All this time you've been talking to me, you've been *counting* to yourself?" I said.

"Somebody has to count them," he said, laughing. *"Jesus."*

At nine-forty, while Tom was still in the field, picking peppers and eggplants, a dozen people were politely lined up in the shade of the Chinese umbrella tree next to the Vegetable Shop. Two women had brought folding chairs, two other women were reading Danielle Steel novels, someone else was busy with a word-puzzle book. One customer had traveled from Rancho Bernardo, a forty-mile round trip. A pretty, dark-haired woman from Rancho Santa Fe told me she had been coming to the stand several times a week for twenty years, and said the only family member she knew by name was Kay. I asked her how high prices would have to get to discourage her, and she replied, "I have no idea what anything costs."

The plywood shutters were raised at ten o'clock, and by eleven-thirty, when Tom was ready for lunch, the corn supply had dwindled severely, and the basil was all gone.

"It seems that there was some confusion about the basil harvest," Tom said.

"What was the confusion?" I asked.

"Well, they didn't pick enough."

"Is that the only thing you're out of?"

"That and patience."

Tom headed for the house, undecided whether to pick more corn. If he cut thirty or fifty dozen ears more, it would all sell. On the other hand, he was too hungry to go cut it himself, and the workers were entitled by law to a lunch break at noon. Strawberries were another possibility. Unless a worker could pick a twelve-quart flat in well under an hour, however, that option was uneconomical. By the time he had finished lunch, his mind was made up: no more strawberries today, and only fifteen dozen more ears of corn. As he got up to leave, Kay came in carrying a seedless red watermelon. Hatsuyo was seated on the sofa, awake but with her eyes closed. She wore a headset attached to a Sony portable tape player.

For more than thirty years, Junzo conducted a weekly ritual. Each Friday night, the trainees would gather at the kitchen table and listen attentively while Junzo delivered extemporaneous lectures on agriculture, ethics, philosophy, history, the foibles of contemporary Japanese society — whatever crossed his oracular mind. These sessions would last anywhere from an hour to four hours, depending upon the pedagogue's mood. If the trainees asked questions that he considered unworthy, he would refuse to answer. Two years earlier, a trainee named Aono Masaru had surreptitiously preserved these monologues by hiding a tiny tape recorder and microphone in his shirt pocket. I listened to some of the tapes, in which Junzo's voice had to compete with Masaru's heartbeat and breathing, the scuffling and barking of dogs, and the jangling of Kay's jade bracelets. It was one of these tapes that Hatsuyo was listening to now, and, looking at the tranquil expression on her face, I could see that none of the static interfered. Rather, the sound and cadence of her dead husband's voice seemed to affect her like a soothing mantra, a means of transport into both the past and the beyond.

As I was leaving the house, Kay began to slice the melon. I stood outside the screen door, tying my shoes and trying to defend myself against an excited Jack Russell terrier.

"Mama, I have a sweet watermelon," I heard her say. "Want a taste, Mama? Hey, wake up!"

HATSUYO CHINO died ten weeks later, on September 17. As the children had done when their father died, they arranged a funeral service for Hatsuyo at a Buddhist temple in Vista, twenty-five miles from Del Mar. A priest from Los Angeles delivered a eulogy, which he began with a quotation from Kobo Daishi, the ninth-century founder of the Shingon sect of Japanese Buddhism: "So as a saint one leaves their hometown, so as a saint one returns."

On the forty-ninth day after her death — as it happened, one day after the year's corn harvest was completed — a *nokotsu* ceremony was held, signifying that she had made the transition from *shiryo* (newly dead soul) to *nii-botoke,* or new Buddha. An urn containing half of Hatsuyo's cremated remains was interred in a *haka,* or family tomb, in San Diego. A week later — just a few days shy of the first anniversary of Junzo's passing — I was invited to go to Tokyo with Kay; Tom and his wife, Nina MacConnel, and their two-year-old son, Makoto; and Hideo and his fiancée, Sheridan Reed. When I met Kay in the airport departure lounge, she was carrying an amorphous package that was small enough to balance in the palm of one hand and was wrapped in a knotted Hermès yellow-white-and-black silk scarf. "Here's Mama," she said.

Several times during the next few days, I heard Kay address her mother's ashes as if she were speaking to a living, breathing being. In Tokyo, she perused a brochure that described the attractions of a lavish hotel where we would be staying in Osaka, and said, "Oh, the hotel has nightspots. Did you hear that, Mama? Nightspots." In Hashiguii, when someone showed up with a box of *imo-manju,* delicate yam-shaped pastries, she said, "Oh, let's give one to Mama.

She loves *manju*." Only in the most limited sense, the corporeal, had Hatsuyo departed.

Hazuki Chino Ho, with her husband, Clarence, and their son, Steven, met us in Tokyo. We flew in darkness to Osaka, and spent the night. The next morning, we caught a train bound for Hashiguii by way of Wakayama, Hatsuyo's birthplace, where the family made ritual visits to the *haka* of several relatives. The ride from Osaka to Wakayama had revealed an anomalous landscape — pollution-spewing factories and ubiquitous vegetable plots. This contrast repeated itself along the route from Wakayama to Hashiguii until eventually the urban industrial sprawl thinned, giving way to greenhouses, harvested rice fields punctuated with conical heaps of straw, grape arbors, persimmon groves, pine and cedar and bamboo forests, glimpses of ocean. Dusk was approaching when we arrived.

From Hashiguii harbor, you can see the nearby island of Oshima, and a group of huge rocks that rose from the ocean floor. Kobo Daishi, legend says, built a bridge from Hashiguii to Oshima, using the rocks as foundation stones. The site is now a national park. Junzo and Hatsuyo's house, which had an off-white masonry exterior and an obliquely sloped green copper roof, was perched on a cliff above the park and was protected by a tsunami-proof thirty-foot seawall. A red Shinto gateway, like a stately piece of freestanding sculpture, had been erected on an outcropping below. From aeries on the rocks, cormorants studied the ocean — Hashiguii and its neighboring town, Kushimoto, enjoy a reputation for extraordinarily clean waters — and abruptly launched themselves and dived for fish. Seafood venders worked in tidal pools, washing squid, which they would later hang from drying racks in front of their shops.

I stayed in Hashiguii three days, during most of which Hatsuyo's sister-in-law and two of her nieces occupied the kitchen, orchestrating what seemed like a nonstop meal. A low table in the house's main room had been made into a butsudan, and a black-and-white photograph of Junzo and a color photograph of Hatsuyo, smiling, were propped there. Huge floral sprays and large plastic-wrapped baskets of fruit flanked the altar. Whenever a visitor entered the house, he would proceed directly to the butsudan, kneel, light incense, ring a brass bell with a wooden mallet, pray briefly, and bow. Several times a day, unprompted, the family members would do the same.

The funeral took place on an afternoon, at two o'clock. Shortly after seven that morning, when I wandered over to the house from a rented room where I was staying, I found that everyone had been awake for at least a couple of hours, as if it were a workday on the farm. Kay and Hazuki had been busy wrapping packages. "Well, the things that Mama wanted done today, I've done," Kay said. "She wanted to be in this room today, and she wanted these things wrapped." Months earlier, Hatsuyo had given Kay money and instructions to buy certain people gifts that they would use and never give away — Mont Blanc pens, Chanel handbags, crystal Baccarat monkeys, photographs of Junzo and Hatsuyo, *manju* and tea. In midmorning, Shigeru and Junji arrived. So did several former trainees — including some who had worked on the farm in 1953, the first year of the exchange program.

An hour before the service, I drove to the Buddhist temple with Tom. We left the village on a paved road but in less than a mile we were in a rural setting that seemed ages removed from the center of Hashiguii. The road ascended a ridgeline and then wound down into a sparsely populated valley of rice fields and small gardens. Though the area was formally named Kujira Kawa (Whale River), after the nearest ocean inlet, it was commonly called the Chino Valley. Chino ancestors had controlled most of the land and, eight hundred years earlier, had built the temple we were heading for.

The sanctuary was no larger than a spacious living room. The altar was in the center. Dozens of *ihai* — thin blond wooden memorial tablets — were set on the altar. Photographs of local soldiers who died during the Second World War hung from teak beams. Glassed-in shelves containing dozens of brass and gold-leaf Buddhas and saints filled one wall. We set the photographs of Junzo and Hatsuyo on the altar, placed the flowers from the butsudan on bamboo tables, and rested the fruit baskets in front of the flowers. Cushions directly in front of the altar were reserved for the immediate family, and friends and other relatives were directed to positions left and right. Because Jun was absent, Junji was given the cushion designated for the eldest son.

A priest appeared — a slender hollow-cheeked man in his seventies, who, ten months earlier, had conducted the rites for Junzo. He was joined by another priest, who, it turned out, was his son. Kneeling and facing the altar, they began a chant accompanied by a percussive progression: alternately, they used a goatskin-covered drumstick to strike first a large bronze bowl, then a wooden drum, then a smaller bronze bowl. The chanting, which Tom later explained was "a rendition of a sutra and also the recitation of a person's life," lasted about fifteen minutes. Then the older priest took a pair of three-foot-high memorial slats called *sotoba* — oversize *ihai* — and held them horizontally to bathe them in smoke that rose from a block of incense on a brass tray. The tray also contained granular incense. Each member of the immediate family approached the altar, pinched a bit of incense three times, touched it to the forehead, and put it on top of the burning block. After the other mourners repeated this ritual, the older priest again sanctified the *sotoba* with incense smoke. An elderly cousin named Torao Chino, a career bureaucrat in the Japanese Diet, fulfilled the duty of chief mourner. At the conclusion of the service, he delivered a brief speech expressing the family's gratitude — remarks that he would later embellish, during a longer speech at a hotel in Hashiguii, where an uncountable-course meal would be served, along with crippling quantities of sake and beer. The mourners gathered briefly in front of the temple, where many photographs were taken, and then walked down a stone path in bright sunshine. Two farm women wearing bonnets were working with hoes in a nearby field.

At the cemetery, each mourner bowed before the *haka*, lighted incense, dipped a myrtle branch in water three times and sprinkled the *haka*, then bowed again. The *haka* comprised seven pieces of granite, including an obelisk, one side of which was engraved with Japanese lettering painted white, another with lettering painted red. Hatsuyo's side of the obelisk had the red lettering. It had been in place since Junzo's death, and now that she was joining him the red would be scraped off and replaced with white lettering.

It was a springlike day in November. The cemetery was nestled in a narrow, steep-sided valley a quarter mile from the main drag of Hashiguii. A pair of eagles glided above the ridgeline. On a real spring day earlier that year, I had entered the courtyard of the farm in midafternoon, looking for Kay, and had seen only Hatsuyo, seated in her wheelchair beneath the bougainvillea — the first time I had ever seen her outside the house. She wore a windbreaker, an Hermès scarf, and a Spago baseball cap, and she was reading *Hokubei Mainichi*, a North American daily Japanese newspaper. The world's most businesslike Jack Russell terriers watched over her, a cool breeze was blowing, and the finches were chirping. She seemed the image of serenity, secure in the lap of a self-sufficient world to which she had given her life.

Early on the morning of the funeral, I had walked with Tom to the cemetery. After praying at the *haka*, he decided that he wanted to look inside. This required lifting three granite markers and a two-slab plinth. He removed the urn containing his father's ashes, studied it briefly, then replaced the plinth and the other stones.

I had been looking at the trees on the surrounding hills, and I asked Tom if he knew what kind they were.

"No, I'm sorry," he said. "I don't really know plants that well."

He lighted another bundle of incense, bowed, and stood quietly.

Then he said, "It's my feeling that you can never pray too much. There are some sects of Buddhism that believe that the more you pray the better chance you have of acquiring Buddhahood. But that's not really why I'm praying. It's more a matter of paying respect. I'm paying respect for what my parents did. What they did made me who I am."

— 1992

Keepers of the Flame

*Tom Mix played a good man who rode into a new town and
innocently got into trouble. Then he had to solve the troubles.
He only managed to solve the troubles after a series of crises
that demanded the most dangerous stunts imagined.*

— Explanatory text, Tom Mix Museum, Dewey, Oklahoma

B EFORE I MET Richard Seiverling, my grasp of the facts and
the significance of Tom Mix's existence amounted to not much.
This was true despite two coincidences: first, I grew up in north-
east Oklahoma, within easy driving distance of the Tom Mix Museum, and second, as I negotiate the routine chores of everyday life
I am guided by an interior dramatic vision of self, a psychic simul-
cast, almost identical to the heroic persona and exploits of the legendary cowboy movie star. Richard Seiverling — who has earned a
couple of graduate degrees and likes to be referred to as Dr. —
is the founder and chairman of the National Tom Mix Festival.
When I phoned him a while back, a few weeks before the eleventh
annual festival, to get driving directions to his home, in Hershey,
Pennsylvania, he asked, as he evidently does whenever he deals
with a member of the fourth estate, "Do you need me to be dressed
in Western regalia?" My plan was to tour the second floor of Dr.
Seiverling's house, where he has installed a private museum — a
collection of artifacts documenting his life and its intertwining
with the life of Tom Mix. Because I didn't intend to take photo-

graphs, I suggested that he wear whatever made him comfortable. A spotty, cool rain was falling when I arrived in Hershey, headquarters of the candy company, and each moist air molecule seemed to have bonded with a fresh warm cocoa molecule, bathing the landscape in a sweetly fragrant pale-chocolate fog. Dr. Seiverling, who has blue eyes, gray hair brushed straight back, and a softly pleasant, uncowboylike face, greeted me dressed in a manner that implied local chauvinism — chocolate-brown slacks, belt, and necktie, a cream-colored dress shirt, and a cream-colored sports jacket.

The downstairs portion of the house, where Dr. Seiverling and his wife, Gladys, have lived since 1963, was rigorously tidy, with nothing that hinted at the rich, variegated lode upstairs. Before I could get a close look at that, however, Dr. Seiverling proposed that we sample the noon buffet in the Circular Dining Room at the Hotel Hershey, and as we drove there and then ate our lunch he began to fill me in on the National Tom Mix Festival.

"This is a labor of love," he said. "Planning the festival that's coming up has become almost a full-time job for me. It's been causing me a lot of stress. But it's still a labor of love."

The eleventh festival — the first to be held outside Pennsylvania — was to take place in Las Vegas. Dr. Seiverling's background and loyalties are all-Pennsylvania. He was born in Lancaster County, and is an alumnus of the Hershey Industrial School and Hershey Junior College. He earned his bachelor's degree from Lebanon Valley College, in nearby Annville, a master's degree in education from the University of Pennsylvania, and a doctorate in education from Penn State, and he spent almost his entire professional career with the Pennsylvania State Department of Education. He is now seventy years old. When he was in his late fifties, Gladys Seiverling advised him that with his retirement years approaching he needed an avocation.

"My wife said, 'You'd better get yourself a hobby,' and the first thing I thought of was Tom Mix," he told me. "He was my boyhood hero. I had saved a lot of Tom Mix memorabilia, which I'd collected as a result of going to see Tom's movies or listening to his radio program. When I was nineteen and a cub reporter for a weekly newspaper called the *Ephrata Ensign,* I got to interview him, and I had my picture taken with him. That was in June 1940, three and a half months before he was killed, in an automobile accident. I'd looked at the memorabilia in the intervening years, but I hadn't thought about them a lot."

In 1979, when Dr. Seiverling began to think seriously again about his hero, the centennial of Mix's birth and the fortieth anniversary of his death were only a year away. Not surprisingly, the merchants in DuBois, the town in western Pennsylvania to which the Mix family moved, from the backwoods hamlet of Mix Run, when their son was eight, did not require excessive prodding to go along with Dr. Seiverling's idea of an annual Tom Mix festival. Among the special guests at the first festival was Kurt Klotzbach, a journalist from Dortmund, Germany, whose book *Tom Mix — König der Cowboys* Dr. Seiverling esteems as an indispensable contribution to the ever-expanding corpus of Mix hagiography. Attracting a Mixophile as exotic as Kurt Klotzbach conformed to Dr. Seiverling's sense of what the festival might become — an internationally recognized annual ritual devoted not to nostalgia but to a celebration of stalwart, manly courage. Thanks to a thoughtful donation from the Hershey Corporation, Dr. Seiverling was able to arrange a nice photo opportunity: Kurt Klotzbach receiving a five-pound chocolate bar.

"We did it as planned," he said. "We brought in a photographer and I gave him the big chocolate bar. But guess what! Kurt's a diabetic. He couldn't enjoy it."

The festival had a ten-year run in DuBois. Attendance was steady. Thousands of out-of-towners, who were not necessarily deep-dyed Mix lovers, would show up for the centerpiece parade. Much smaller crowds would drop in on film screenings and swap meets that Dr. Seiverling orchestrated. Across the years, however, a series of small and large disagreements accumulated. Before Mix impersonated a cowboy, he had been a bona fide range-riding cowboy. In almost all his film appearances, he did his own stunt work. As a circus performer, he drew worshipful crowds all over America and Europe. "We have had our differences," Dr. Seiverling told me, his polite way of saying that what the DuBois organizers thought of as appropriate National Tom Mix Festival–related activities — tobacco-spitting and bed-racing contests — were not what he had in mind when he contemplated ways to glorify the memory of the most accomplished and charismatic cowboy who has ever lived. "Let's put it this way," he said. "I was never smiling when I went to the bank." When he learned last year that the Imperial Palace Hotel and Casino, in Las Vegas, had added to its collection of antique automobiles the 1937 Cord 812 Phaeton Coupe that Mix was driving at the time of his fatal accident, he decided to get in touch with the new owner.

"Promoting this festival is just a big PR job," he said. "I had to convince people at the Imperial Palace that this was worth their while. They didn't come after me, in other words. I had to write three different proposals. I can tell you that the logistical challenges for this festival far exceeded my expectations. For instance, I'm planning to take gifts of chocolate to all the Imperial Palace PR people — but what if it melts?"

"WHAT YOU'RE LOOKING AT is Cowboy Corner," Dr. Seiverling said when he guided me to the second floor of his house and I got my first glimpse of his museum. Roughly half the upstairs floor space was occupied by the museum, which was L-shaped; the other half was a bedroom that the Seiverlings' grown daughters or grandchildren or such guests as Kurt Klotzbach use when they come for a visit. (The Seiverlings' own bedroom was downstairs.) Cowboy Corner was a telephone-booth-size niche filled with photographs. One double frame featured, on the right, Tony II — a white Arabian that was the successor to Tony, Jr. (the Miracle

Horse), himself the successor to Tony the Wonder Horse, the equine prodigy memorialized in a hundred and fifty or so early Mix movies and in Dr. Seiverling's 1980 treatise *Tom Mix and Tony: A Partnership Remembered* — and, on the left, the picture of Mix and the nineteen-year-old Richard Seiverling taken at the time of the 1940 *Ephrata Ensign* interview. Nearby were two autographed photographs of Mix and a wide-angle shot of the entire company of the 1935 Tom Mix Circus and Wild West Show. There was also a montage that included many of Mix's contemporaries from the oaters — among them Buck Jones, Ken Maynard, Hoot Gibson, William Desmond, Bob Steele, Fred Thomson, William S. Hart, Pee Wee Holmes, and Leo Maloney — lined up beneath a portrait of Dr. Seiverling at the age of forty-five astride Dolly, the first horse he ever owned. On a shelf in Cowboy Corner was a collection of souvenir pins from the first eight National Tom Mix Festivals, and also a souvenir oversize coffee cup, slightly smaller than a chamber pot — one of a limited edition of four from the 1982 festival. Dr. Seiverling said, "I got one of these, one went to the Tom Mix Festival Committee, one went to the DuBois Chamber of Commerce, and who do you think got the other one? A fellow by the name of Willard Scott. I think you've probably heard of him."

As it happened, 1982 was the first year that the Ralston Purina Company, which had sponsored the radio program *Tom Mix Ralston Straight Shooters* during the thirties and forties, sent a representative to the festival. Subsequently, the company hired Dr. Seiverling as a consultant and reintroduced Mix-related gift premiums to consumers of its hot-cereal products. These promotional items, which Dr. Seiverling and his like-minded pals recognized as instant collectibles, included a comic book titled *Tom Mix and the Taking of Grizzly Grebb;* an 8-by-10 photograph of Mix and Tony, Jr.; a sew-on cloth patch with the Tom Mix brand; two LPs of old radio broadcasts; a cereal bowl; and a wristwatch with Mix's image on the face. Dr. Seiverling showed me a specimen of each. In 1983, the wristwatch sold for a box top plus $19.33. "I'll be taking this with me to Las Vegas," he said. "I know of one dealer who hoarded these, and last year was selling them for two hundred dollars apiece. I don't plan to let mine go for less than two-fifty."

When we ventured out of Cowboy Corner and into the main part of the museum — an area about ten by twelve — Dr. Seiverling took from a shelf an antique wooden Straight Shooters pistol. "In 1933, one box top and ten cents would get you one of these," he said. "I had no problem with the box top, but I did with the ten cents. Well, I wanted that gun badly, so I waited. I waited and waited. I waited fifty years. I got this gun in 1983, and I paid a hundred and twenty-five dollars for it. If I'd had a hundred and twenty-five dollars in 1933, I could have bought the Ralston Purina Company."

Dr. Seiverling's pedigree as a Straight Shooter dates from 1927, the year his mother recorded on an index card the recipe for a concoction that she took the liberty of calling Tom Mix Chocolate Cake. He showed me that. He showed me thirty-six Danish Tom Mix comic books from the thirties. He showed me a Tom Mix hobbyhorse; a 1934 photograph of Tom and Tony, Jr.; a 1934 catalog of Straight Shooters premiums; a still from *The Great K and A Train Robbery*, which he rated "among the best William Fox films that Tom Mix made"; a Ralston Purina photomontage of stars from the radio show (among them the very young George Gobel); photographs of four of the five Mrs. Tom Mixes; and five spent cartridges from a Tom Mix shooting exhibition (sent to him by a woman in Ohio and impossible to authenticate). He showed me his collection of Big Little Books: novels (or, in some instances, novelizations of Mix's films for Universal Pictures), also from the thirties, whose immediate aesthetic virtues — vividly colorful covers and pocket-size convenience — were matched by the bristling vitality of their prose. I picked up *Tom Mix in the Range War* and read on the first page, "A vicious WHIR-R-R-R at the side of the trail brought lightning action. Tom Mix twisted in his saddle, his right hand streaking to the big forty-five Colts at his hip. Tony, his trail-wise horse, danced lightly aside on quick, sure hoofs, snorting his anger at the writhing, evil-eyed little reptile which was gliding through the sage-brush stems."

Regularly, Dr. Seiverling receives overtures from people who mistakenly assume that his passion for Tom Mix has rendered him feeble-minded. "For instance, I got a call a while back from a dealer in Little Rock, Arkansas," he told me. "She said she had a saddle blanket worn by Tony. She was willing to sell it for, as I recall, six hundred dollars. Naturally, I asked her, 'How can I authenticate that it was really worn by Tony?' And she said, 'I thought you were a Tom Mix fan.' And I said, 'I am, madam. But I'm not a nut.' And she hung up."

We pored over the contents of two leather-bound volumes of sepia, brown, and purple penny-arcade cards, the cream of Dr. Seiverling's collection of five thousand. "In 1927, I got my first Tom Mix arcade card in Rocky Springs Park, in Lancaster, and I've been collecting them ever since," he said. "I will trade any arcade card of any cowboy for any Tom Mix that I don't already own. I swap these all the time. The only tricky part of swapping by mail is: Who sends it first?" Several cards depicted the Mix mansion, in Beverly Hills. "You see the front door in these pictures, right? That's the one I have the front-door assembly to." From Cowboy Corner he retrieved an oblong cardboard box, opened it, and removed a peephole, a door knocker, and a door latch of unpolished gray metal, about eight pounds' worth. These objects came into his possession, he explained, in 1987, when he went to Los Angeles to pay homage to the mansion and other Mix-related shrines and was unable to repress an urge to introduce himself to the present occupants of the house.

"The owner, who wishes to remain anonymous, had replaced the door assembly but had saved this. She sent her butler to the basement and he retrieved it," he said. "When she handed it to me, she said, 'I've been waiting all these years to give this to the right person.' That's a nice story, isn't it? Sounds dramatic, doesn't it?"

We made excursions to the other sections of the museum: to Education Corner (framed diplomas), to Family Corner (mainly pictures of the Seiverling daughters, and not to be confused with His and Her Corner), to Military Corner (photographs documenting Dr. Seiverling's service during the Second World War, and in Korea, and twenty-seven years with the Army National Guard; his Bronze Star and Purple Heart; and also the remnants of his collection of Second World War — mainly Nazi — artifacts, most of which was deaccessioned a decade ago to pay off debts incurred by the first National Tom Mix Festival). But we always returned to Tom Mix.

After about three hours, knowing I had a two-hundred-mile drive ahead of me, I suggested to Dr. Seiverling that he was probably ready to send me on my way. This he interpreted as a cue to open an album of photographs of Tony the Wonder Horse and of Mix's other horses. "Now, here's another aspect that I haven't shared with you," he said — a favorite phrase of his. The horses reminded him that we had not yet discussed *Tom Mix: Portrait of a Superstar — A Pictorial and Documentary Anthology,* a book he had been writing for the past ten years. "Obviously, these are pictures I'm getting ready for my chapter titled 'Mix's Magnificent Mounts,'" he said. "As you'll see, I'm a great one for these alliterations."

Several drawers of a sideboard in Military Corner were full of book material, most of which had already been set in type and made camera-ready. It was clear to me that Dr. Seiverling had no wish to diminish the accomplishments of Kurt Klotzbach or of M. G. (Bud) Norris, the author of *The Tom Mix Book* (1989), or of Paul E. Mix, the author of *The Life and Legend of Tom Mix* (1972) and of the recent monograph *Tom Mix: The Formative Years.* Earlier, describing Bud and Paul to me, he had said, "Now, these are both avid Tom Mix fans, and they are both excellent resource people." Nevertheless, as he recited the table of contents of his book his natural modesty began to elude him. "My book represents a whole different approach," he said. "It will be over three hundred pages long, with over five hundred pictures. And I'll have a picture of Tom Mix and me together, which none of the other books have. I have a printing bid of ten thousand dollars. My plan is to price it at twenty-nine ninety-five, plus three dollars' shipping. I think I'll have no problem unloading five hundred copies. I'd hoped to have it ready for the festival, but this festival has required more of my time and energy than the first ten festivals combined."

THE MORNING the festival opened, two weeks later, I tracked Dr. Seiverling down as he was finishing his breakfast in the Emperor's Buffet, one of eight restaurants in the Imperial Palace. What recommended the Emperor's Buffet was not its cuisine but its proximity — a distance of less than ten yards, with only a keno parlor and a bank of slot machines to divert traffic — to Royal Hall A, a six-thousand-square-foot exhibition space that had been rechristened the Tom Mix Festival Memorabilia Room. Dr. Seiverling was seated with Serge Darrigrand and his wife, Brenda, both members of the festival staff, and with Hal Verb, who had come to Las Vegas from San Francisco at his own expense to display his amateur skills as a comic impersonator. All three men wore Western regalia. Dr. Seiverling's and Hal's costumes were understated and generic. Serge, on the other hand, who was the official Tom Mix look-alike — a man of indeterminate age equipped with the requisite chiseled jaw and cheekbones, prominent nose, oversupply of teeth, and brilliantined dark hair — had paid conspicuous attention to detail. He had on a dark-brown bib-front shirt with cream piping and with an authentic-looking TM monogram on the left sleeve, cream-colored slacks with dark-brown piping, a trademark wide-brimmed ten-gallon hat (black), a white neckerchief, and shiny brown boots. This getup made it not immediately obvious that for the past twenty-six years he had worked in a General Motors hydromatic plant in Ypsilanti, Michigan.

With the opening of the festival only an hour away, Dr. Seiver-

ling excused himself to finish setting up his exhibit in the Memorabilia Room. Serge, who had stashed his spurs behind one of Dr.
Seiverling's display tables, was headed there, too. Going along with
him and his wife, I asked about his career as a look-alike.

"I've been involved with horses all my life," he said. "You know
the saying — once a cowboy always a cowboy."

"And Serge has always dressed Western," his wife said.

"I used to dress more like Buck Jones than like Tom Mix," Serge
continued. "I did sharpshooting at the Stage Coach Stop. It's also
called Michigan's Village of the 1800s. It's in the Irish Hills, near
Clinton, Michigan."

"That's why he's known as the Michigan Cowboy," Brenda said.

"I've been doing sharpshooting since I was fourteen years old.
The first time I saw a Tom Mix movie was in 1957, at the Henry
Ford Museum, in Dearborn. It was *Riders of the Purple Sage*. People
had always been telling me I looked like Tom. I wasn't at the first
Tom Mix Festival, but after I heard about it I got in touch with
Dick Seiverling. I sent him some pictures."

"Pictures don't tell the whole story, but after Dick saw Serge, and
then Hickman Hill, Tom's grandson, saw Serge in person, they
were convinced," Brenda said. "And Serge decided that if he was
going to do it he'd do it absolutely authentic."

All of Serge's cowboy shirts are made by Brenda and patterned
after an actual Mix shirt that is in their possession. "An elderly
man who'd retired up to the Dakotas sent it to us," Brenda said.
"His mother had worked on the movie sets, in the costume department, and she had this shirt. He was old, he had no children, so he
gave it to Serge. It's made of some kind of orange cotton, I would
say. It has the regular T-bar-M — Tom's brand — on the sleeve."

That Serge looked a lot like Tom Mix was plain to see, and I
gathered that the similarity would have seemed even more striking
if I could have viewed Serge in profile, perched on his horse Dynamite and cantering across a television screen. I asked whether he
often got accosted by admirers.

"Even if he's just in the supermarket wearing jeans and a black cowboy hat, people recognize him," Brenda said. "They stop us and say they saw him in a parade, or whatever. Serge has ridden in the Tournament of Roses parade for six years now. I have to admit that teenagers don't remember Tom Mix. But they know that Serge looks like someone. With them, the name that comes up a lot is Johnny Cash."

As Serge knelt to strap on his spurs — silver, with jinglebobs and double-spoked rowels — I asked how tall he was.

"Five-eight in my stocking feet, almost five-ten in my boots," he said. "According to the Tom Mix Museum, he was about five-eight. According to the movie-studio publicity departments, though, he was six feet. I wrote to the Blucher Boot Company, in Fairfax, Oklahoma, and found out that not only were we the same height but we've got the same-size foot. When he died, they had an order ready for him, a size eight D with two-and-three-quarter-inch heels."

I caught up with the Darrigrands again later that morning, in the Tom Mix Theater, a partitioned-off section of Royal Hall B that had been equipped with chairs, a couple of film projectors, and a portable movie screen on a tripod. We had just watched the 1932 classic *Destry Rides Again* (not to be confused with the 1939 classic of the same name, starring Marlene Dietrich and James Stewart) and were waiting while the projectionist rewound it and prepared to thread another 1932 classic, *Hidden Gold,* into one of the projectors. To keep the audience stimulated, Brenda commandeered a hand-held microphone. She could have gotten by without amplification — there were only about a dozen of us in the audience — but the microphone lent a show-biz tingle to the proceedings.

First, Brenda introduced Hal Verb. He led off with an impression of Ed Sullivan and then presented Ed's special guests Gabby Hayes, Gary Cooper, James Stewart, Rodney Dangerfield, Al Jolson, Ronald Reagan, and Richard Nixon. After Hal was done, Brenda said, "Now, ladies and gentlemen, I'm going to introduce you to a man you've already met if you've been to the Memorabilia Room," and Serge, who had left when the lights went up, came on for a sharpshooting demonstration. The Tom Mix Theater was only about ten yards wide and Serge was using live ammo, but the bullets were made of wax, and that reduced the chance of serious ricochet injuries. From eight paces, he aimed a Colt revolver at some small balloons that had been attached to an upright plywood table six feet in diameter. He connected squarely with the first two balloons, then, with his back to the target and a mirror in one hand, missed a couple of times, then, turning around, popped a couple more. His final trick involved suspending a kitchen knife between two balloons so that its blade could split a wax bullet — a two-in-one shot. When he squeezed the trigger and nothing happened, Brenda said, "I'd like to tell you that Serge has done this many times. He doesn't usually forget to reload." There was a patch of dead air as Serge reloaded, and Brenda filled it by describing how, during his routine visits to nursing homes and in his talks with Boy Scouts, Serge stresses patriotism, obedience to parents, and gun safety. Then Serge gave it another try, and it worked.

After *Hidden Gold,* a transportation hybrid that featured horseback chases and car chases ("It's the cops!" "Come on, step on it!") and some canyon-size plot holes, I wandered back into the Memorabilia Room. There I met Gene Gammel and Melbourne Robison — respectively, a sergeant on the Reno police force and a salesman and commercial photographer who works for an outfit that sells novelty T-shirts. They told me they had just endured a hair-raising transportation adventure of their own. "We're in a real pickle," Gene said. "We just pulled in on a bus from Tonopah, about two hundred miles from here. Our car broke down on the way from Reno last night. That car has a hundred and thirteen thousand miles on it, but it's never given me that kind of trouble before." Breakfast at the Emperor's Buffet — especially the cold scrambled eggs — had not dulled the memory of their bus ride.

B-Western fans cross-pollinate in endless permutations. Melbourne, who specializes in Buck Jones — he owns two of Buck Jones's "personal pistols," including the one he was carrying the night he died, in the famous Cocoanut Grove fire, in 1942 — happens to own one of Mix's hats. He also has a sideline in Daisy BB-gun memorabilia. Six years ago, Gene began collecting Roy Rogers and Hopalong Cassidy artifacts, or what he calls "Roy and Hoppy stuff," and he takes pride in his accumulation of Lone Ranger and Cisco Kid souvenirs.

"There's a guy back East who's documented over twenty-three hundred Hoppy items," he said. "I've got over four hundred myself, and that's not counting comic books. In the fifties, there were a million members of the Hopalong Cassidy Troopers. It rivaled the Boy Scouts."

It was Gene who exploded for me the myth of the cereal-box-premium decoder ring. "There were a lot of rings offered as premiums, and there were several types of decoders, but nobody made a decoder ring," he said, contempt creeping into his voice. "Nevertheless, I'm always hearing guys talk about how rich they'd be if their mamas hadn't thrown away their Tom Mix decoder rings or their Captain Midnight decoder rings. Right."

A couple of weekends a month, Gene and Melbourne hit the road and look for Roy and Hoppy and Buck stuff. They like to visit flea markets and street fairs in places like Folsom and Old Sacramento. One of their techniques is to arrive before sunrise, while the traders are still setting up. At that hour, Gene and Melbourne have to compete with other collectors, who try to gain an edge by wearing miners' helmets.

"He didn't really know about collecting until he met me," Gene said of Melbourne.

"That's true," Melbourne acknowledged. "I didn't really understand how to access stuff."

What made the trouble with Gene's car so inconvenient was the demand of another of Melbourne's passions — camel racing. He was a past vice-president of the International Order of Camel

Jockeys, and he was due that weekend in Virginia City, four hundred miles north, to compete in a camel race. Also, his nine-year-old daughter, Rachel, was supposed to join him there. A dentist friend from Texas who usually raced ostriches but dabbled in camels was coming out to Virginia City to get married on camelback, and Rachel was to be a flower girl of sorts. Before Melbourne left Las Vegas, however, he wanted to get his hands on six Buck Jones arcade cards in Dr. Seiverling's collection.

As the founder and chairman of the Tom Mix Festival, Dr. Seiverling had had a direct hand in the layout of the Memorabilia Room, the perimeter of which was lined with exhibitors' tables. Practicality had forced him to leave certain items behind in Hershey — his hobbyhorse, his fragile Danish comic books, the door knocker to the Beverly Hills mansion — but he had brought plenty of treasures, both priceless and negotiable, including his albums of arcade cards; a lock of hair from the mane of Tony the Wonder Horse (circa 1929); his Straight Shooters wooden pistol; nouveau Ralston premiums (Ralston Straight Shooters Club membership card, sew-on insignia, Tom Mix watch, and catalog); posters from previous Tom Mix Festivals; a couple of hundred copies of *Tom Mix and Tony: A Partnership Remembered,* priced at five dollars apiece; a couple of dozen 2-by-3-inch engraved Tom-and-Tony mirrors; Tom Mix Chewing Gum booklets; thousands of Tom-and-Tony stamps, which he had printed himself; a 1935 letter from Joe Bowers, of Beverly Hills, to Miss Vandella Moyer, of Lebanon, Pennsylvania, written on Tom Mix Circus and Wild West Show stationery; two copies of *Tony and His Pals,* a 1934 collaboration by F. M. and H. M. Christeson, priced at fifty dollars each; and several Big Little Books, priced from twenty to twenty-five dollars, among them *Tom Mix Plays a Lone Hand, Tom Mix in the Fighting Cowboy, Tom Mix in the Range War, Terror Trail, The Rider of Death Valley, Texas Bad Man,* and *Tom Mix and the Hoard of Montezuma.*

Dr. Seiverling said, "Incidentally, I should point out that Bud Norris's collection of Tom Mix Big Little Books is probably the most inclusive and comprehensive in existence, and it's in the best condition of any I've seen. I'm negotiating with him right now for a copy of *Flaming Guns* — it's the hardest one to find, and he has an extra. So far, we haven't been able to agree on the terms."

Dr. Seiverling's exhibit covered several tables and extended along much of one wall, turned a corner, and blended into Bud Norris's exhibit — with only a bouquet of red carnations, the gift of Dominick Marafioti, of Rochester, New York, who was the national chief of the Buck Jones Rangers of America Club, separating them. Flanking Bud on the other side was Paul E. Mix, whose grandfather was Tom's first cousin. "I was born in 1934," Paul said. "The only time I saw Tom was when I was five years old. My uncle Leroy took me and held me up on his shoulders. This was at the Clearfield County fairground, in Clearfield, Pennsylvania. He said, 'Over there, wave at Cousin Tom.' I don't know if I remember it because I remember it or because I was told about it so many times." Paul worked on *The Life and Legend of Tom Mix* from 1964 to 1970. When he wasn't busy researching or writing, he was an electrical engineer for Du Pont. I'm told that the book is quite good, but I haven't actually read it, because Paul had only one copy for sale in Las Vegas and he wanted a hundred dollars for it. A while back, the book's printer mistakenly destroyed the photographic plates of the pages.

I discovered, to my gratification, that Dr. Seiverling and Bud Norris, Western civilization's two most fervid non-blood-kin authorities on the life of Mix, do not allow themselves to indulge in petty rivalry but, rather, are magnanimous mutual boosters. Bud is grateful for the energy that Dr. Seiverling has devoted to the festival planning across the years, and Dr. Seiverling, for his part, has only praise for Bud's methodology as a scholar and collector. "Bud's accumulation of factual information is really kind of encyclopedic, especially regarding filmography," Dr. Seiverling said, referring to *The Tom Mix Book*. "His book is probably the most thorough of its kind. Now, I'll let other readers and historians decide where to place my book when it comes out. I feel that my book, whenever it's published, will make its contribution and take its place."

At the time of the festival, Bud was six weeks away from retirement, having spent thirty-five years as an employee of the United States Postal Service in Columbus, Ohio. *The Tom Mix Book* was the culmination of a fifteen-year effort that is part of an almost seamless fifty-year continuum. Lionizing Tom Mix, Bud told me, "is a lifelong disease for which there is no cure." His collection, which is particularly strong in Ralston Straight Shooters radio premiums, reflects a forthright approach to connoisseurship: almost everything is in mint or near-mint condition. It is displayed in the Tom Mix Memorial Theater and Archives, in the basement of his house, in Columbus — like Dr. Seiverling's museum, a by-appointment-only operation. Less than 10 percent of the collection was on view at the Imperial Palace. "I tried to get some variety, and then packed in as much as the van would hold," he said. His portable display cases contained Straight Shooters items that no one else seemed to have — a telescope, a signal arrowhead, spurs, a bandanna, a sun watch, a pocketknife, a rocket parachute. He also had an ample inventory of *The Tom Mix Book*, at $24.95. The book was dedicated to his mother, who not only "bought the cereal so I would have the box tops to send away for Tom Mix toys," he wrote, but also had the foresight to preserve the toys for posterity. The other woman in his life, his wife, Peggy, was helping to collect tickets at the Memorabilia Room door and projecting a consistently cheerful attitude, which I found noteworthy in the light of a fact about the Norris marriage that Bud shared with me. "I've told Peggy if our house catches fire I'm gonna grab my Tom Mix stuff first and then grab her," he said. "And she knows I'm not kidding."

From Dr. Seiverling I learned that Bud, if he was asked to identify virtually any production still from a Mix movie, could recite its provenance and the accompanying dialogue with alarming accuracy. Bud himself, however, says that Peter Schauer, a freelance cinema archivist from Vienna, and Janus Barfoed, a film historian from Copenhagen, possess skills in this regard superior to his own. In the introduction to *The Tom Mix Book* he thanks Schauer at length for his help in compiling the book's filmography, and on the acknowledgments page he cites Barfoed. At the Imperial Palace, Schauer manned a table directly across the room from Bud, and, as far as I could tell, had made the trip all the way from Vienna not to sell anything but just to hang out with pals. He was an amiable man with a mustache and what appeared to be a serious appetite for *Topfenstrudel,* and he spent most of the weekend seated in a folding chair, welcoming conversation with anyone who cared to discuss Mix or ancillary topics. When I inquired about the source of his admiration for Mix, he said, "I think this man was the best ambassador America has ever had." Barfoed, who was attending his second festival, had brought along several dozen movie-lobby posters and other carefully preserved items of B-Western promotional material, all for sale, and also prints of two rare silent films, *Den Glade Tom* and *Hest Contra Bil.* Their screening had been scheduled by Dr. Seiverling for the "matinee extravaganza," on the final day. Though both films were released in the United States during the First World War, the whereabouts of any English-language versions (*The Conversion of Smiling Tom* and *Taking a Chance*) were unknown. Not only would the prints from Copenhagen bolster Mix's reputation for physical courage and masculine charm but their intertitles would demonstrate his fluency in Danish.

In all, the festival attracted fewer than a dozen official exhibitors, some more Mix-specific than others. They included Colonel William O. Mueller, of Livermore, California, whose array of one-of-a-kind items included a pair of elaborately engraved silver six-shooters that he said had awesome sentimental value, because Mix had given them to him, but that could be pried from his possession for $125,000; Oliver Drake, an eighty-seven-year-old former producer, director, and screenwriter of Westerns, who was hawking his memoirs at eighteen bucks a pop; Leo Reed, a veteran of the Tom Mix Circus and Wild West Show, who credited his youthful experiences as a roustabout, ticket taker, and cotton-candy salesman with enabling him to overcome his natural shyness; Michael Lyonais, of Maple Valley, Washington, a dealer in and collector of Native American and Old West artifacts; and Russ Campbell, a hatmaker from Seattle.

An average of three hundred paying customers a day would have pleased Dr. Seiverling. It became evident early, however, that this figure was quite optimistic and that problems with crowd control were unlikely to arise. Daily tickets sold for five dollars. The first thing a ticket buyer noticed, smack in the center of the room, was the canary-yellow supercharged Cord Phaeton Coupe that Mix had died in. The car had been carefully restored after the accident, subsequently changed hands a few times, and was obviously regarded as an important fixture of the Imperial Palace's collection, right up there with Hitler's Mercedes and the Alfa Romeo that Mussolini gave his mistress. For $9.95, Dr. Seiverling was selling four-inch replicas of the Cord. He had also persuaded the Franklin Mint to donate a 1/24-scale model, and he planned to give it away as a raffle prize.

It is an article of faith that all Mix devotees undertake certain pilgrimages, and high on the list of obligatory sites is Mix Wash, the spot on the road near Florence, Arizona, where Tom Mix lost control of the Cord (as it careered into a dry creek bed, he received a mortal blow to the neck from a metal suitcase), and where there is a memorial marker, a stone cairn crowned with a riderless bronze horse — unless, as can and does happen, vandals with blowtorches have recently paid a visit and reduced it to a horseless cairn. True disciples also flock to the birthplace, in Mix Run, Pennsylvania; to the boyhood home, in DuBois; to the site of the 101 Ranch, near Marland, Oklahoma, where he put in four years cowboying; to the Tom Mix Museum, in nearby Dewey ("Mecca for Mixomaniacs, the museum houses the largest collection of personal belongings of our hero," Bud Norris has written); to the pavement outside Mann's Chinese Theater, in Los Angeles, where Tom and Tony left impressions of their hands, feet, and hooves; to the mansion in Beverly Hills; and to Forest Lawn Memorial Park, in Glendale, California, which was Tom's next, and final, stop after Mix Wash (and where Bud, when he visited it recently, left a red rose; Dr. Seiverling, who accompanied him, left a yellow rose).

Other than the death car, Las Vegas has no historical connection to the life of Mix. Even before the festival set up shop at the Imperial Palace, a consensus existed among Dr. Seiverling and the other members of the festival staff that there was a need for a new, permanent home for the festival, with low overhead and rich historical significance. DuBois had, of course, ceased being an option. When you got right down to it, the big crowds in DuBois were nothing but tourists, fly-by-nighters who didn't know a Ralston Straight Shooters' Manual from an L. L. Bean catalog. Their genuine interest in Mix ran about as deep as their genuine interest in Amish folkways. They were no more likely to go out of their way to lay a yellow rose on Mix's grave than they were on Mr. Ed's.

So one item of business that Dr. Seiverling had to address in Las Vegas was the future. Bud had mapped out a post–Las Vegas itinerary that called for him to travel an indirect route back to Ohio, with a stop at Forest Lawn and another in Florence. And as long as he was in Arizona it made sense for him to check in with some people in Tucson who had expressed interest in creating a home for the festival there. Old Tucson had a lot of charm and was within easy driving distance of some of the locations for the Selig silent one-reelers from the early years of the Mix oeuvre. Another possibility was Guthrie, Oklahoma, a preservation-conscious town that was the home of the Blue Belle Saloon, where Mix tended bar eighty-six years ago. If Guthrie had an inside track — as I gathered it did — it was because the executive director of the Guthrie Chamber of Commerce and the landlord of the Blue Belle Saloon had troubled themselves to come to Las Vegas to talk numbers.

"The Blue Belle is where Tom Mix first made his mark," I over-heard Dr. Seiverling tell the Guthrie boosters at one point, as if re-citing a script that they might have written. "He was a bartender, and also a drum major in 1904 for the Oklahoma Cavalry band. Two of his wives were from Oklahoma. He did his first cowboying for the old Miller Brothers 101 Ranch. I visited that a couple of years back. Obviously, Guthrie has the advantage of having the lo-cale that is historically significant in the life of Tom Mix."

"It's hard not to like it," the Chamber of Commerce man agreed. "There are a lot of things going on there. You know, the world's largest Masonic temple is there. Also, the world's largest privately owned indoor rodeo arena."

The Blue Belle landlord said, "I know the governor, and I'm sure he would designate an official Tom Mix Day" — a prospect that Dr. Seiverling seemed to find tantalizing.

ABOUT THIRTY PEOPLE showed up in the afternoon at the Tom Mix Theater for a silent film called *Trailin'* and a talkie called *The Fourth Horseman.* Again Serge performed at intermission, and again Brenda provided a play-by-play that was both scripted and improvised. In three attempts, Serge failed to split a bullet on the knife blade. Holding a pair of six-shooters and crossing his wrists, however, he connected with one mounted balloon and with one that Brenda was holding in her hand — an act of bravery that she announced entitled her to a Caribbean cruise. Serge was followed by Ted and Ruth Reinhart, who operate a country inn in Alexan-dria, Pennsylvania, and bill themselves as the Singing Sweethearts. The Reinharts are exponents of so-called pure Western music, which they croon while wearing matching regalia with maximum froufrou. Ted had a plummy voice and a manner that suggested a Jonathan Winters version of an aggressively friendly cowboy. He said, "Thanks again, Serge Darrigrand, our very fine, competent Tom Mix look-alike." Then he sang "I'm a Cowpoke Pokin' Along," one of his favorites. Ruth was pretty and had prematurely graying hair and a high-wattage smile that went great with bright-red lipstick. When she sang "Home on the Range," she recruited three unsuspecting men from the audience to back her up with coyote howls — a move that I took as a warning to head back to the Memorabilia Room. There I noticed that Colonel Mueller was idle. First, I reminded myself of something Hal Verb had told me — that to place the colonel's reminiscences in proper perspective it was "often necessary to separate fiction from fiction" — and then I introduced myself and asked which branch of the armed forces had commissioned him.

"I'm a colonel because I spent nineteen years in the army," he said. "Doing what? Government service, that's what. From the age of sixteen until I went into the army, I used to spend my summers with Tom Mix. I have never capitalized on Tom, because he was too close to me. Let these goddamn yoyos who had their pictures taken with him one time and think they knew him — let them capitalize."

The colonel had a close-cropped gray beard, a voluble, raspy, nicotinized voice, and an arthritic condition in both hips that forced him to depend on a cane. He was dressed in black and wore dark-tinted wire-rimmed eyeglasses. For two dollars he was selling autographed copies of *The Life and Times of the Fabulous Tom Mix*, a typescript memoir that began with the moment in 1920 when the future colonel was six years old and living in Cincinnati and, through the intervention of his father, had a face-to-face meeting with his hero. "I guess he took a liking to me," the colonel wrote, and his narrative continued:

> I'd go out in the summer time and see Tom whenever he was geographically within 100 miles of me. When he'd go over to New York and go overseas to make his tours, I would go to New York and bid him a bon voyage. When he would get into Washington to do a command performance for the President, I would go there and visit

with him and Tom always put $100 bill in my hand and told me to always be a straight shooter and make something of myself.

The typescript was bound inside another reminiscence, which Colonel Mueller printed up a few years ago, and in which he recalled being sixteen years old and receiving a Colt six-shooter from Mix — "the first gun he bought when he came out of the Army." Colonel Mueller listed some other gifts: a 101 Ranch badge, an Oklahoma deputy badge, a Texas Ranger badge, spurs, a Stetson, and lots of pictures. In nearly four hundred films, Colonel Mueller wrote, "Tom Mix never drank, smoked, chewed or swore — or kissed an actress," feats of self-restraint that the colonel was not claiming to have accomplished personally. Nor, as it happens, would Mix have been able to make such a claim truthfully; in *The Tom Mix Book* Bud Norris has cataloged cinematic episodes of smoking, drinking, gambling, kissing leading ladies, and uttering oaths like "dammit to hell." I sensed, however, that Colonel Mueller would not be receptive to this information.

A plastic binder on a table in front of the colonel contained dozens of photographs of Mix and an assortment of other provocative material, including publicity stills of an actress who Colonel Mueller said was one of his ex-wives. "That's my number five," he said when I got to that page. "She was in all the Sean Connery movies. She got the house in the Isle of Man. A million bucks. They each got a million bucks."

"What year were you two married?"

"Shit, now you're pinning me down," he said. Lowering his voice, he added, "Listen, the reason I hesitate is, I'm not even sure we ever got divorced, to tell you the goddamn truth."

Once it had become clear to Colonel Mueller that I wasn't going to buy the engraved silver six-shooters, he showed me a Tiffany silver hip flask with a TM monogram. "Sid Jordan gave him that flask," he said, referring to the sharpshooter and longtime sidekick who appeared in scores of Mix movies. Twenty-five hundred dollars, give or take, would buy the flask.

Splaying the bejeweled fingers of his right hand, the colonel said, "Tom gave me that ring when I was twenty-one years old. That's a seven-and-a-half-carat emerald and three and a half carats of diamonds. And that ring he gave me when I was thirty. It's a three-and-a-third-carat diamond."

I tried running some numbers through my brain — when Colonel Mueller turned thirty, hadn't Mix been dead four years? — but got distracted by a pocket watch engraved "Thomas Edwin Mix," a keepsake from a Masonic-rites initiation ceremony. I remarked that Dr. Seiverling had told me — and Bud had pointed out in his book — that Mix's given middle name was Hezekiah, which he later changed to Edwin. The colonel said, "Listen, he had to give his fucking right name to become a Mason. What does that watch say? 'Thomas Edwin Mix.' There's more assholes that'll tell you more shit."

Hidden between stills of Mix and Ken Maynard was a photograph inscribed "To Col. William Mueller, With Best Wishes, Ronald Reagan."

"Oh, no, I covered up Ronald?" he said. "That asshole. What did Reagan do wrong? I'll tell you what. He made legitimate businessmen of the savings-and-loans thieves, and look at all the poor people he hurt. And I'm not telling you anything I wouldn't say to his face, and, in fact, already have."

The colonel showed me a photograph of a handsome, slender young cowboy, lariat in hand, posed against a split-rail fence. I asked who it was.

"That's me, when I was twenty-one years old. I was an extra on *The Miracle Rider*. I did two Wild West shows at the 101 Ranch, in 1931 and '32. Those were the days. Well, the days weren't bad, but the nights . . ."

A man called Ewing (Lucky) Brown stopped by. It seemed he had made a career as a bit player in Westerns and had known Mix's daughter Thomasina. He remembered some guns she had once shown him. "If you're into his guns, maybe you could answer a question for me," Lucky Brown said.

"I'm not into his guns. The man gave me those guns," Colonel Mueller said. "He gave me nine guns — six Colt single-actions and three Winchesters."

After that, the conversation never quite achieved a tone of cordiality.

"Another expert," Colonel Mueller said before Lucky Brown was out of earshot.

One other impressive item that Colonel Mueller had on display was an enlarged copy of a black-and-white diagram that had appeared regularly in editions of the Ralston Straight Shooters' Manual. This was the official Tom Mix injury chart, which purported to identify only the most serious of his actual wounds — traumas that were consequences of his having been "blown up once, shot 12 times and injured 47 times in movie stunting." According to an explanatory note, he had been "shot by cattle rustlers in Texas . . . shot twice in left arm by Oklahoma outlaws . . . shot below elbow by outlaw . . . shot through abdomen by killer he arrested . . . shot by bad man while Oklahoma sheriff . . . shot in leg when 14 years old . . . shot through leg by bank robbers . . . shot through elbow in real stage coach hold-up . . ." For graphic simplicity, the diagram omitted the "scars from twenty-two knife wounds" and "the hole four inches square and many inches deep that was blown in Tom's back by a dynamite explosion."

"Tom Mix lived nine lives before he ever made a picture," Colonel Mueller told me.

I told him this was the first copy of the diagram I'd ever seen.

"Yeah, I'm surprised, with all these supposed Tom Mix collectors in this room, I've got the only one here," he said.

I thanked the colonel for his time and was headed toward the casino for a breather when I ran into Gene Gammel and Melbourne Robison.

"We saw you talking to Colonel Mueller," Gene said. "Get an earful?"

I said I had.

"Did he show you the picture of himself when he was twenty-one?" Gene asked.

I said he had.

"You know, he showed me that picture one time at a show in Reno," Melbourne said. "I thought it looked familiar, and when I got home I checked in a reference book and, sure enough, there it was."

"Only, it wasn't the colonel," Gene said.

An expression of shocked dismay must have registered on my face, because Gene rested a comforting hand on my shoulder.

"It was an actor named Allan (Rocky) Lane," Melbourne said. "Actually, it was a pretty well-known picture. Otherwise I don't guess I would've remembered it. Yep — Allan (Rocky) Lane."

DESPITE THE LIGHT TURNOUT the first day — fewer than a hundred tickets were sold — Dr. Seiverling was in a sanguine mood when I found him that evening at his station in the Memorabilia Room. I had just sat through *Riders of the Purple Sage* in the Tom Mix Theater, and had decided to skip *The Man from Texas*. Leo Reed, the veteran of the Tom Mix Circus and Wild West Show, had joined Dr. Seiverling, and so had William E. Thrush, a Mixophile from Las Vegas. Bill Thrush was recounting his dealings with an impostor, a woman who years earlier had claimed to be an illegitimate daughter of Mix and also to be an actress who was a stand-in for Clara Bow. "Do you realize she got five thousand people to give her a standing ovation at a benefit in Beverly Hills in 1981?" he said. "I had to go after her with all the powers at my disposal. Of all the common women I have seen in my life — and I have seen a *lot* — there was nobody that could come close to her."

Somehow, Dr. Seiverling managed to guide the conversation to his magnum opus, *Tom Mix: Portrait of a Superstar*. He had the page proofs handy. "What do you think of that, Leo?" he said, riffling the chapter on Mix's circus career. "All right, Leo, here we are with the Sells-Floto Circus in 1929. And here's a souvenir program from 1930. Still Sells-Floto. Always in this pose on Tony the Wonder Horse. The circus was headquartered in Peru, Indiana. Now, here's a montage of posters. He spent 1934 with the Sam B. Dill Circus, but when Dill died that's when he bought it out and the next year it became the Tom Mix Circus and Wild West Show. They wintered in Compton, California. Here's a group picture from, I think, 1935. Here's a 1936 photo. Here we have a chart of dates played from 1934 to '37. Now, Leo, you were with the circus the entire 1935 season. I can get those route books for 1935 and show you the itinerary, day by day. Wherever you were, I can go right to the route book and give you every performance. Now, here I've reproduced the pages from the 1937 route book. Here's Ruth Mix, in 1938. Shortly after this photo was taken, he went on his European tour. And by then, you can see, of course, its name has been changed, and it's just the Tom Mix Circus. In 1938, it seems there was no route book — that's when the circus folded up. OK. Here's the quintet touring Europe that spring, while in the U.S. the circus was falling apart. Did you ever see a better picture than that one of Tom clowning around? Now, over here you've got Tom with the lord mayor of London. Here's a lot of baloney that he told the newspapers in England. If you think Tom told some whoppers, wait till you read the story of how the redskins captured him. And then here on the left is the picture on top of the Savoy. Here he is riding in London. Here he is standing with Tex McLeod. Here he is in Hyde Park. Maybe you can tell me who the girl is — she's in a lot of these pictures. Now, Leo, these are pictures that have never before been seen in this country. Then he goes to Germany — here's Billy Jenkins, the German Buffalo Bill. I just want to show you the finale. He goes now to Denmark. Here he is in Denmark while the circus is failing in the U.S. Those are very rare pictures. I'll bet you never saw these — Tom Mix in his military ribbons. He never wore these in the United States. And here's Mabel in 1944, performing as Mrs. Tom Mix, with, I think, Tony III."

Dr. Seiverling also had a proof of the book's jacket illustration — an electric-hued image of Tom and Tony the Wonder Horse, which he had discovered on a mid-thirties cigar box. "We all know what four-color separation can cost, but this is the way Tom Mix would've done it," he said. "The only hitch is Tom had a little more money than I do."

There was a momentary silence, during which we became aware that the easy-to-eavesdrop-upon Colonel Mueller, across the room, had a captive audience of two — the affable Hal Verb and an equally affable member of the hotel's PR staff. "Now, look," the colonel was saying. "Listen to me. I worked for the FBI and the CIA. There's certain things I can't tell here. But listen carefully. You want to talk about who killed JFK. All right, let's start with who convicted Jimmy Hoffa . . ."

Stacking the page proofs neatly, Dr. Seiverling returned them to a manila envelope, laid the envelope on the table, and slapped it firmly with his palm. "Now, gentlemen," he said. "You talk about research. *That's* research for you. It's no longer a project. It's an *obsession.*" He looked each of us in the eye and solemnly nodded.

The next morning, I watched *The Rider of Death Valley,* a convincing demonstration of Mix's knack for existential drama. "Death Valley fills me with terror," says Lois Wilson (playing a character named Helen). Mix (playing a character named Tom) replies, "I kind of like it myself. It doesn't pretend to be anything it isn't." Then they spend the rest of the movie getting thirstier and thirstier. Afterward, I found Dr. Seiverling where I expected — in the Memorabilia Room, engrossed in conversation. He was talking to Bob Wolter, a collector from Reseda, California, who evidently had access to an important trove of Mix's belongings.

"I won't say who has it, just that it's the people who sold his personal items to the Tom Mix Museum," Wolter was saying. This description was insufficiently elliptical; I knew he was referring to a man in Van Nuys, and Dr. Seiverling, of course, did, too. I was flattered that Wolter, having just met me, had sized me up as a potential predator.

"There's a Big Little Book I've been after for three years," Dr. Seiverling said. "*Flaming Guns.*"

"Bud has it, you know," Bob Wolter said.

"I know, but it's not the only copy in the world and he's asking a lot for his."

In a manner that struck me as less than tactful, Wolter went on to describe a watch that the man in Van Nuys was offering to sell for $250,000. Dr. Seiverling and I let that number sink in.

"And, you know, your friend in the corner there" — Wolter used body language to indicate Colonel Mueller — "just sold the watch that Olive gave to Tom for his twenty-ninth birthday, in 1909. And it's authentic. It's engraved, and everything. He sold it for twenty-five hundred."

Dr. Seiverling shook his head, as if remembering a dead friend.

"Well, Dick, that's a good price."

"Maybe," Dr. Seiverling said, unconvinced. "You know, I love Tom Mix, but I sure won't remortgage my house for him."

"Don't worry about that Big Little Book, Dick. I'm gonna get it for you."

After Wolter departed, I asked Dr. Seiverling whether he had a strategy for separating *Flaming Guns* from Bud. Simply paying the sixty dollars Bud was asking, I understood, was an approach he opposed in principle. And yet he had to have it.

"My objective by the end of the festival is to induce him, and I think I'm going to prevail," he said. "What is the inducement? To get that book, I'm willing to give him a one-of-a-kind item — a wall clock with the same four-color picture of Tom Mix that appears on the cover of his book. There it is, right down there." Not only is Dr. Seiverling a collector and purveyor of Mix memorabilia; he is a promulgator of it. The custom-made clock, its walnut face decorated with the laminated image of Tom and Tony, was displayed next to a cardboard box that contained entries for the mati-nee-extravaganza door-prize drawing.

"How are you going to give him this wall clock if it's being raffled off?" I asked.

The smile on Dr. Seiverling's face said that he was several jumps ahead of me. "This one here is eight by eleven, and the one I'll be offering him is eleven by fourteen."

"But then you'll have your Big Little Book but you won't have a clock."

"I can always have another one made."

"But then you won't be offering him a one-of-a-kind item."

"But he won't know that," Dr. Seiverling said.

Because he is a thoroughly scrupulous person, I knew he didn't really mean that. It was just a symptom of how his desire to acquire *Flaming Guns* on his own terms was confusing his moral logic. I wanted to suggest that Bud's copy seemed to be in mint condition and ask why he didn't just go ahead and pay the sixty bucks, but that would have been out of line.

"I think you realize the only way you can enhance or increase your collection is by swapping," Dr. Seiverling said. "I'll own a copy eventually."

I missed the start of that evening's screening — the double fea-ture *Just Tony* and *Rustler's Roundup* — because I got busy witness-ing a conversation between Janus Barfoed and Peter Hogue, an English professor and film historian from California who was re-searching a critical biography of Ken Maynard. They were scruti-nizing some arcade cards, including one of an actor named Eddie Cobb, who was misidentified in the caption as Fred Gilman.

According to Barfoed, the Exhibit Supply Company, the chief manufacturer of arcade cards, was notorious for making mistakes of this sort. He showed me a production still from *The Fourth Horseman,* and remarked, "This says that the character of Gabby was played by Raymond Hatton. But Raymond Hatton doesn't even appear in the movie. How they came up with that I have no idea."

Barfoed is a slightly built gray-haired man who grew up in Slagelse, fifty miles west of Copenhagen. Even in the cowboy hat that he wore all weekend, he managed to look exactly like a Danish film historian. "It was Tom Mix's visit to Denmark with his circus in 1939 that made me a collector," he said. "My mother's brother was a rancher in Panama. I have an aunt who believes in reincarnation and says that in an earlier life I was a cowboy." His favorite star is Maynard, and then comes Mix. He once met Maynard, and in 1968 he spent several days in Montana with another of his idols, Wally Wales. Western films made after 1954 hold no interest for him. During the German occupation, members of the Danish Resistance bombed the office of a German film-production company — a favor that the Nazis returned by destroying the headquarters of a company that distributed films made by Universal, Paramount, and Republic studios. As a result, the posters and other artifacts that Barfoed owned became much rarer and more valuable. At Det Danske Filmmuseum, where Barfoed is curator of stills and posters, his boss has expressed limited curiosity about his extensive private collection of Western-movie memorabilia. "In Denmark, I am the only professional film historian interested in this material," he told me. "In fact, I believe you could safely say I am the only Grade B–Western nut in all of Scandinavia."

BEFORE THE FESTIVAL, I had been to Las Vegas a few times, but never with enthusiasm. Only once had I stayed longer than twenty-four hours and that was almost thirty years ago, when my parents detained my brothers and sisters and me for three days at the Desert Inn. (That tour of duty was also the occasion of my single sublime Vegas moment: each of the Mills Brothers gave me his autograph.) Anticipating four nights at the Imperial Palace, I had envisioned the usual dreads and frightening temptations — the orange food-warming lamps at the buffets, the ubiquitous TV sets all tuned in to golf tournaments or dog races, the gaming tables and their relentless processions of chinless Fellini extras, the long pantyhosed legs and exploding bodices of the casino hostesses — and they had loomed as a daunting challenge to my emotional stamina. As the final day of the festival dawned, I forced myself to account for the way I had spent my time, and realized, oddly, that I wanted it all to go on much longer. I had ventured out of the hotel only once, briefly, to buy talcum powder and post cards. I had not paid my proper respects to the Imperial Palace's antique-automobile collection, much less to the white marble statue of Joe Louis across the street at Caesars Palace. Forty-eight hours had passed during which I had not even seen the sky. I had gambled only intermittently, and, unsatisfyingly, had broken even. I had visited with Art Evans, a white-haired, string-tied, former parks-department employee from Coquille, Oregon, who in the early hours of the first day of the festival had paid twenty dollars — a steal, by consensus — for a Tom Mix Western Comic Book No. 1 but still was more than twenty shy of a complete collection of sixty-one. (Art Evans was also the only man on the premises with a baseball autographed by Mix, and it had been autographed by Bob Meusel, Chuck Dressen, and Jimmy Foxx as well.) I had conversed with Frank Finn, a John Wayne look-alike who worked as a satellite technician at the NBC studios in Burbank, and who had actually gotten to know, and had received an inscribed glossy photograph from, the real Duke, back in the days when he would obligingly appear on *Laugh-In* in a bunny suit. I had failed, however, to muster the energy to chat with Jim Mecate, who showed up one afternoon in parade-caliber regalia — a Roy Rogers look-alike, someone explained to me.

"But isn't this guy Filipino, or something?" I asked.

"Well, if Roy had been Filipino, that's what he would have looked like," I was told.

On my way out of the Emperor's Buffet the last morning, I saw

Gladys Seiverling perched in front of a quarter slot machine. She had a determined look on her face and a bucket full of quarters in her lap. Trying to win enough to stake her husband to *Flaming Guns,* I thought for a moment, but then I remembered something Dr. Seiverling had said when he was showing me through his collection in Hershey: "Now, mind you, the money for this does not come out of the household budget." In her attempt to beat the stuffing out of the slots, Mrs. Seiverling was trading for her own account.

"Obviously, today will have to be the banner day, because it's the final day" was the first thing Dr. Seiverling said to me that morning. I wasn't about to press him on how ticket sales had been going. His mood, in any event, was typically upbeat. The matinee extravaganza was scheduled for that afternoon, and two of Mix's grandchildren, Vickie and Dan Matthews, would be on hand. The grandchildren had dropped by the previous day, but I hadn't met them. I had gotten the news from Colonel Mueller.

"Hey, kid, Tom Mix's granddaughter was here," he told me. "I said to her, 'Do you have anything personal of your grandfather's?' She said, 'Not a thing,' so I told her, 'Well, you do now.' Remember that little horseshoe charm I had here?" He pointed to a spot on his black leather vest. "It was a pair of dice studded with seven diamonds. I gave it to her. Then I said, 'Now, do you want to feel your grandfather? Pick up that gun.' And she held that Colt in her hand, and it broke me up. Seeing her holding that gun just broke me up. I had tears running out of my fucking eyes."

The Matthewses were the youngest children of Thomasina — the daughter of Tom and his fourth wife, Victoria Forde.

"I'm named after my grandmother," Vickie said when I was introduced to her, just before the matinee. "Our two older brothers are Tom and Tony."

"If my brother Tony was named after the horse, then we figure our grandfather must have owned a dog named Dan and that's who I'm named after," Dan said.

Vickie, who runs a Montessori school in Ojai, California, was wearing boots, a suede skirt and vest, a silk blouse, a souvenir straw hat from one of the festivals in DuBois, a silver necklace with a TM-monogram drop, and the diamond-studded horseshoe-and-dice charm that Colonel Mueller had given her. Dan, a computer consultant in Lakewood, California, had not previously owned any Western regalia. He wore blue jeans, a pair of boots borrowed from his nephew, a bolo tie borrowed from a friend of Vickie's, and a felt cowboy hat and a leather vest that he'd bought on the Strip the day before.

Originally, the matinee extravaganza was to have been held in the Imperial Theater, which is the site of *The Legends in Concert,* a nightly stage show featuring impersonators of no-longer-breathing show-biz giants. The Imperial Theater has a capacity of more than eight hundred. When it became apparent that the matinee extravaganza was not likely to draw a crowd of more than sixty, the venue was shifted to the Tom Mix Theater. The ever-cheerful Ted Reinhart introduced Dr. Seiverling, who wore a light-blue Western-cut suit and a solid-navy necktie embroidered in white script with "Tom Mix and Tony."

"Thank you, Ted, and, once again, welcome, Straight Shooters," Dr. Seiverling told the gathering. "I hope you all have your Tom Mix Ralston Straight Shooters wristwatches on. It's Ralston time. We're very glad that we've been able to bring our Tom Mix Festival from the mountains of Pennsylvania to the glittering lights of Las Vegas, here to the Imperial Palace Hotel. We don't know exactly what's in store for the Tom Mix Festival. It appears that since we've traded the mountains of Pennsylvania for the glittering lights of Las Vegas we have other options available to us. So we don't know which of those options we'll exercise, but we hope that wherever we wind up, you'll be there with us." Before presenting the Mix grandchildren, he said, "Unfortunately, I could not persuade their mother, Thomasina, to come over here from Auckland, New Zealand. So let me introduce Victoria Matthews, granddaughter of our hero, Tom Mix, and her brother Dan."

Vickie read a poem about Mix that had been written by a neighbor, Lydia Marcus. Dan limited his remarks to "Thank you for keeping alive the memory of our grandfather."

It was lucky-drawing time. In addition to the miniature Cord 812 Phaeton Coupe, Dr. Seiverling was giving away a 1933 Duesenberg Twenty Grand and a 1935 Auburn 851 Speedster. He acknowledged the presence of Neil Haworth, who had owned the full-scale Cord 812 before it entered the collection of the Imperial Palace, and recalled that three years earlier he himself had "had the honor of seeing and sitting in the car." This reminded me of something I had heard Colonel Mueller say the day before as I passed by his table: "I wish right now — I could use ten dollars for every time I drove that goddamn car there. But most of the time I used the Cadillac or the Packard." The miniature Cord was won by Jim and Loretta Murray, who had stopped in Las Vegas on their way from Maryland to California, where they planned to pay homage to Tom and Tony's footprints, in Los Angeles, and to the gravesite, in Glendale. Jim was a retired customs officer and had been the recipient, in 1937, of a firm handshake from Mix and a signed photograph of him astride Tony. "That was the biggest thrill in my life," he told me, in a manner that left no room for doubt. Peter Hogue, the Ken Maynard scholar, won the one-of-a-kind wall clock.

After a final display of precision sharpshooting from Serge, *Den Glade Tom* and *Hest Contra Bil,* the two films that Janus Barfoed had brought with him, were screened. I had no trouble recognizing Mix — more than ever, he resembled Serge — but I couldn't easily track the plots. I would have had less difficulty, I suspect, if I hadn't bogged down trying to transcribe the dialogue in the intertitles: *"Og den gang lykkes det ham"* and *"En gaestfri engel"* and *"Jeg har manden!"*

Dr. Seiverling, I learned after the matinee, had made a glorious appearance in the *Legends in Concert* spotlight when I wasn't looking. The previous evening, he had accepted a complimentary ticket to the midnight show, and the Marilyn Monroe impersonator had picked him out of the audience and had some fun with him. Photographic proof of this memorable event was available, and he was more than happy to share it with me: a color 8-by-10 that showed him seated in a chair with Marilyn on his lap. One of his trouser legs was rolled up, his hair was mussed, lipstick was smeared all over his face, and he was minus his eyeglasses, which had disappeared down the front of her dress. The photograph was inscribed "Darling Dick, My Heart Belongs to Daddy, Marilyn."

"She pulled my pants leg up, ripped open my shirt," he said. "You know, that's pretty hard to take. I had so much lipstick on my face I walked in here afterward and Janus thought I was bleeding to death."

Bud, who had already seen the photograph a few times but didn't mind another look, said, "I just noticed something about this picture, Dick — where your thumbs are."

"One of her pressure points," Dr. Seiverling said. "But I didn't squeeze. My glasses were in there. When I got them back, they were all steamed up."

"What did Gladys say?"

"I woke her up in the middle of the night. I told her, 'Honey, I just had a dream. And it wasn't about you.'"

Across the room I saw Colonel Mueller packing up. He had on the same all-black outfit — trousers, shirt with rose-and-white-brocade stitching, boots, leather vest, neckerchief (with United States Marshal–badge neckerchief holder) — and the same tinted shades he had worn throughout the festival.

"Are you all done, Colonel?" I asked him.

"Done?" he growled. "I got here at three o'clock Wednesday and I was done at four. I have never spent four more boring days in my life. You know how women go through a change of life? Well, I experienced a change of life just sitting here. Boy, I'm tired. This just wore me out, doing nothing. Doing this solitary nothing."

I excused myself for a final chat with Bud, who I was certain had had a more diverting experience. Had he and Dr. Seiverling come to terms on *Flaming Guns*?

"I sold it ten minutes ago," he said. "To that fellow over there."

The buyer, for the sixty-dollar asking price, was Gary Brown, the deputy city manager of Visalia, California, and a former police chief of San Clemente. I accompanied Bud while he broke the news to Dr. Seiverling.

"I hate to tell you this, Dick," he said. "*Flaming Guns* is gone."

"Who bought it?"

"Gary Brown."

Dr. Seiverling reacted graciously and philosophically. "I told you if you could sell it, sell it," he said. "And it's in good hands, because he's a younger collector. And that's the kind of guy who's got to keep this going when we're gone. His father was an old Tom Mix fan. If anybody should have gotten that book, Bud, Gary's the one." Then, barely missing a beat, Dr. Seiverling announced that he wanted all the members of the festival staff to pose for a group picture with the Cord. He and Bud and Bill Uhler, his projectionist, and their wives, the Reinharts, and Brenda Darrigrand all lined up next to the car. Serge, who was wearing an orange shirt with black piping and black buttons on the bib, navy slacks with orange piping, a black scarf, and a beige sombrero, sat behind the wheel. When Dr. Seiverling said, "Serge is going to drive us to Florence, Arizona!" everyone else said, in chorus, "Oh, no!"

Several hours of packing lay ahead for Dr. Seiverling, whose plane wasn't scheduled to leave until the next afternoon. He was tired, of course, and as soon as he got home he had to start thinking about an African photography safari that he and Gladys would be embarking on within a week, but he seemed satisfied. "The high point for me was seeing 'Welcome National Tom Mix Festival' on the marquee of the Imperial Palace," he said. "And, as far as actual fans are concerned, we had our best turnout ever. You understand, I'm not talking about commuters and parade lovers. I'm talking about real Tom Mix fans."

He held up a beige promotional poster, one of several that had been on display in the hotel — a smiling headshot of Tom Mix, with an appliquéd border of lariat rope. "Isn't this something?" he said.

I agreed that it was really something.

"I'm going to make sure every member of my staff gets one of these," he said. "Someday this is going to be a real collectible."

— 1991

Mom Overboard!

WHAT THEY HAD IN MIND was not complicated. Falling in love had been a snap, an act of faith in gravity. Other basic laws of nature, surely, would apply along the way. Details would resolve themselves. They would live in the city or a suburb, wherever they pleased. They would make room for two children, maybe three — unblemished surfaces upon which they would imprint their best selves. Somebody, a "nurturing" woman with no threatening presumptions, would look after the kids each day while Mom and Dad worked at their important jobs. Nights and weekends, Mom and Dad would divide the labor fifty-fifty. Dad would be a New Man, and Mom would be a Fulfilled Woman.

What they hadn't specifically foreseen: that the baby would start calling the sitter Mama; that the pipe would burst, the roof would leak, the train would stall; that the dry cleaner could never get out the spit-up stains; that indelible bags would materialize under the eyes; that the stay-at-home moms would invoke the No Nannies rule for play dates; that the Entenmann's cake sent to school for the bake sale would become an object of brutal gossip; that the forty-five-minute session locked inside the conference room with the breast pump would end with everything spilled all over the final draft of the Armbruster agreement; that Dad's secret motto would become "Thank God it's Monday."

Above all, they hadn't precisely anticipated that maternal instinct was a dull double-edged knife, and that Mom would tire of having it lodged between her ribs. One evening, while talking on the portable phone with that weasel Peterson in Denver, she put the boys in the tub. The synchronicity — explaining to Peterson that his proposal implied multiple felonious breaches of securities law and hearing Nathaniel announce, not actually in time, that he needed to go potty — seemed, in retrospect, a gift from the cosmos. As she angled for the floater with her free hand and fantasized about FedExing it to Peterson, the fog magically lifted. She could quit. She would quit. She would be free at last. She would downsize, lateralize — call it anything you liked. She didn't care. Finally, she would call all the shots, run her own outfit, answer to no one she didn't feel like answering to.

WHEN SERA QUIT, in 1990, at the age of thirty-three, she already had in place a highly evolved child-development-oversight system. Her training as an architect had given her the discipline to do "visual mapping inside my head." She could see a path to her children's future and engrave it in her brain. After her first baby, also named Sera, was born, in the spring of 1984, her maternity leave lasted three weeks. Sera and her husband, Tom, a publishing executive, then lived — and still do — a half hour from the city (in a town where I also happen to live). Each morning, she was on a train by seven-thirty, and on a good day she caught the 5:39 or the 6:01 coming home. While she was gone, the live-in Haitian nanny's job was to remember to follow instructions and fill in the blanks. A new day meant a fresh 8½-by-11 sheet, with an hour-by-hour timeline on the vertical axis and, across the horizontal, five categories: "Intake," "Sleep," "Alert," "B. Movmt.," "Special Note."

Little Sera was fifteen months old when her brother William arrived. Sera redesigned the gridwork so the nanny could track both babies on a single page. Several minutes a day, as ordered, the nanny directed each child's attention to the prints of Matisse paper cutouts that hung on the walls outside their bedrooms. "I wanted them to study the hard edges of the cutouts so they would focus their eyes," Sera told me. Unless the children were sleeping, she wanted classical music wafting through the house. The regimen would change as the children grew older, when she would devise more elaborate charts and daily-activity requirements. For a toddler, the nanny followed a printed menu of activities that Sera had prescribed to stimulate visual, motor, and auditory progress: finger painting, crayoning, stencils, Colorforms, Legos, Bristle Blocks, puzzles, tools, Mr. Potato Head, alphabet tapes, farm toys that made animal sounds. Television was out of the question. ("TV is just like sex. The more you have it, the more you want it. And you don't need it. There are better things to do.")

To monitor the children's diets, Sera itemized suitable foods from five groups. In her absence, the nanny was expected to record what they ate, using a customized shorthand. Spaghetti with meat sauce was "V-4, P-1, C-4" (tomatoes, vegetable group; ground beef, protein group; noodles, carbohydrate group). A yummy helping of spinach, kosher steer liver, and rice was "V-4, P-5, C-2," and so on. Dessert was maybe a little F-4 (watermelon, fruit group) but not too much D-4 (dairy group, asterisked note: "Ice cream no more than once a week").

Again, after William was born, Sera's maternity leave lasted less than a month. Her boss congratulated her: "Now you've got two kids. You've got a daughter, you've got a son. You're all done. Great. Welcome back to work." This was during a boom cycle in commercial construction. The architectural firm that employed her had been around for almost ninety years, and she was the first woman ever to be designated a project manager: to oversee from A to Z, from schematic designs to final drawings, the planning of a major piece of work — in this case, a twenty-two-story office building on Fifth Avenue. ("Mom, didn't you build a building in New York City?" "Yeah, I built more than one." "Wow, that's incredibly cool.")

In the late summer of 1988, she delivered what is called a bid set.

("The instructions for how to build the building, complete documents, every single nail, screw, you name it.") To finish this project on schedule, she worked several consecutive weekends, bringing little Sera, who was four, with her. Little Sera drew tiny pictures on Post-it notes and distributed them throughout the office, or she sat under a drafting table and played with her Barbies. Big Sera's recollection of this passage in her life included a vivid memory of feeling sick. She was pregnant again. The choice to have a third child, she later grasped, was a subconscious acknowledgment that "something had to give" — and, indeed, her entire body conveyed this message emphatically; she was confined to bed during much of the pregnancy. A second daughter, Meta, was born in the spring of 1989, at which point Sera's extended pregnancy leave became a permanent maternity leave. Late in 1990, she gave birth to her fourth, and final, child, a boy named Thaddeus.

CATHY: *When she got a call asking her to organize the Girl Scout cookie sale, she said yes, both because of and despite certain aesthetic objections. Handling this administrative task was preferable to, say, camping in the woods with a bunch of little girls. The cookies, however, were inedible. Her daughter once left a couple of undelivered boxes of cookies in the pantry, where they might have remained forever if the dog hadn't gotten to them.*

Oven-fresh homemade cookies, on the other hand, had intrinsic value. She enjoyed baking with her children during Christmas vacations and delivering plates of cookies to the neighbors. This friendly gesture demonstrated that she was no mere erstwhile luminary of the banking-law department but also a mom who had what it took to mobilize an army of gingerbread soldiers.

In time, she began to bake with a vengeance — cakes for birthdays, but mainly cookies. The cookie jar was always full, and her children were perpetually grateful. The approach of Christmas each year meant raising the ante. She started weeks ahead of time with rum balls, which improved with age, and shortbreads and nut-butter balls that would last. She made decorated cutouts and shaped other cookies into wreaths and candy canes. She made maple-pecan cookies and spiraled chocolate-and-vanilla freezer cookies, peanut-butter cookies and cranberry-orange cookies — five dozen per batch, fifty dozen by the time she was done.

Her triumph was the annual cookie exchange, the holiday party to which a hundred or so women brought generous samples of their wares, drank wine, complimented each other on their craftsmanship, and then took home a box of whatever looked appealing. Unfortunately, the cookie exchange developed a competitive undercurrent, and some women panicked. What they brought to the party was conspicuously bakery-bought; the tip-off was a cookie that looked too perfect. Her cookies looked real — because they were — and everybody loved them. To be polite, she gathered an assortment of other people's cookies and brought them home. When she set them on the kitchen counter, her children said, "Why didn't you just bring home the ones you took with you?" There was no chance they would deign to feast on these. Which was where, once again, the dog came in handy.

THE NEBULOUS CONCEPT of "free time" presented itself to Sera. Years earlier, before children, she had belonged to the Junior League, but she had allowed her membership to lapse after discovering that "you don't know some people until you get on a committee and they start ordering you around." Now she decided to join the executive board of the local arts center, where she had once curated an exhibit on suburban-community development. A campaign to relocate and expand the town library was under way, and she was eager to donate her expertise. "I pass by that corner three times every day of my life," she said, referring to the new site. "I'd hate to have to look at an ugly piece of architecture."

Her child-care arrangements fluctuated (the Haitian nanny had gone off to have a baby of her own), but Sera didn't mind. She felt like making up for lost time. She continued to draw up lists because keeping pace with her instincts and impulses required plotting and budgeting. "I'm a designer," she said. "You have to design your children's future to a certain point. You have to create the environment for them to flourish. Sometimes I wake up at night and have an anxiety attack — that I've forgotten about this or that part of my child's brain."

There was a daily list of rudiments ("Sera & William: 7:00–7:15 A.M. — Wake up, Shower — body lotion & powder — check finger & toe nails, Brush Teeth, Dressed . . . 7:45–8:30 A.M. — Breakfast (vitamins), Pack snack & lunch . . . Meta & Thad: 4:00–4:30 P.M. — Bath, Bath oil/lotion, Medicine for Thad, Check nails, Pajamas . . . 7:30–8:30 P.M. — Bed time, Reading, Prayers") and there were also individualized charts that combined daily, biweekly, and weekly routines. When William was in second grade, for instance, his checklist consisted of thirteen items. Every day, he was expected to do his homework, practice the piano, practice the drums, make his bed, read aloud for thirty minutes, and tidy his room. Twice a week, he would work on a book report, read to his younger siblings, set the table, empty the dishwasher, play educational games. At least one day a week, he was either supposed to hone his computer skills or study Korean. The final item on his checklist was: "13. Observe stars."

CAROL: *Even after you quit work, she knew, you carried your demons with you. When she no longer practiced law, what she missed — even more than knowing that her time was being billed at around $250 an hour — was the gamesmanship, the rituals of Type A personalities meticulously sharpening their knives. She had a habit of reading the preliminary school budget or the proposal for the new school-governance mandate the same way she used to vet a securities prospectus. Her self-anointed role, as she defined it, was that of fiduciary for every child in the school district. She would attend public hearings and, with insistent politeness, raise points and ask questions until she wore out her welcome.*

There was a tenured second-grade teacher at her children's school who, it seemed, had to go. The teacher intimidated children, belittled them, convinced them that they would never learn. Quietly, she helped organize a petition drive, soliciting the signatures of parents of first graders who didn't want their children assigned to this teacher's classroom. One day, after learning about a fresh insult that the teacher had inflicted upon her daughter, she lost it. She called the superintendent directly, and after that she called the principal and told him what she had done. Twenty minutes later, she got a phone call from the teacher, whose attempt at contrition did not get far. "Listen, I'm from the South," she told the teacher. "My people have a long-standing tradition of horsewhipping people like you to run them out of town. Or else they'd shoot you. You should be grateful you're living in this century."

Six weeks later, the teacher was gone from the classroom.

SERA REFLECTED upon her own childhood experiences: born in Korea; emigrated at twelve, after her mother married an American; adopted by her stepfather; schools in New Jersey and Virginia. She was an only child and a conspicuous achiever. She had become skeptical of the child-rearing philosophy her mother subscribed to, which stressed performance — recite this, show that, demonstrate your knowledge — too often at the expense of self-esteem. Her own children, she decided, would develop a wide range of skills (art, music, nature study, team sports), but the emphasis would be upon enhancing social development rather than proving individual superiority. With four children spread over six years, she needed a master plan with an overriding theme and focus. This she defined as "raising each child as an only child and a middle child."

The summer when little Sera was four and William was almost three, they started taking swimming lessons and tennis lessons. For the next several years, they competed on the country-club swimming and tennis teams and brought home trophies. (The progress of William's golf game was a casualty of a decision that Sera's husband made a year ago: to deactivate their country-club membership. Sera regretted this, because "golf is something you can't start too early.") Little Sera enrolled in dancing school at three and began to specialize in jazz and tap at four. Around the same time, she started taking a eurhythmics class, which integrated music and full body movement, and William started a year later. From nursery school through first grade she attended gymnastics classes, and so did William. Both children were enrolled in drawing and ceramics classes at the arts center, but, because of scheduling conflicts, they dropped out when little Sera started second grade. To compensate, big Sera made private arrangements with an instructor from the arts center, who agreed to come to the house every couple of months to do projects with the children in an "art room" that had been carved out of the basement play area. Little Sera was five and William was four when they learned to play chess — an enthusiasm that seemed to flag after a couple of years. When William resumed playing, in second grade, Sera hired a private chess tutor, and he started winning tournaments.

After two seasons of Little League T-ball and baseball, little Sera retired. This coming Little League season might or might not be William's swan song as well. Little Sera also gave up basketball after fifth grade, which in hindsight could have caused her parents to question the wisdom of their investment in her sleep-away basketball camp. The two summers she spent at sailing camp, on the other hand, were a can't-lose proposition. "You know how you can eat a banana and it gives you so much of what you need?" big Sera said. "That's also true with sailing. It's multidisciplinary — math, physical exercise, nature." The sport that little Sera has stuck with longest is soccer; she has played on a girls' traveling team for four years, and for three summers she attended one-week sessions at soccer camp. This coming summer, she'll be attending soccer camp after she returns from a month in Europe at an international children's camp. After that, she'll head to Virginia for a week with her mother's parents; big Sera wants her to use that time working on her Korean and learning to sew. At one point, big Sera was looking for a charm school for little Sera. Instead, she persuaded a friend who was a former model to come around for a few private sessions — one on clothes, one on poise, one on skin care. The former model also gave little Sera a copy of *Tiffany's Table Manners for Teenagers.*

As a child, big Sera was given daily private piano and violin lessons. One of her goals is to play trios with little Sera and William. Piano lessons for little Sera began in first grade. Until recently, the piano was in the kitchen, which enabled big Sera simultaneously to cook and observe little Sera as she practiced or worked with her teacher. "You have to be there with them to show your interest," she told me. "You have to make it pleasant." Little Sera took up the recorder, clarinet, and flute in the third grade, and by sixth grade she and the other members of her flute club had performed during a party at the White House. William, by third grade, had stopped playing the piano and the drums. When Sera persuaded him to concentrate next on the clarinet, her husband warned, "William's not going to be in the marching band. He's going to be on the playing field, in the game."

The skating lessons that William began when he was three led to hockey at six. He now plays in a traveling hockey league that specializes in ice time at exotic hours in inconvenient locales — say, Sunday morning, six o'clock, at West Point. Every Tuesday, William takes supplemental power-skating lessons. Next summer, he will attend two weeks of hockey camp in New Hampshire, a week of puck-handling camp on Long Island, and a couple of weeks of defensemen's camp in Connecticut. Sera hopes that William, like little Sera, will stick with the traveling soccer team he's played on for the past two years. He has been one of the leading scorers, a fact that is possibly attributable to the one-on-one private soccer coaching Sera arranged for him. One of my sons plays on the same team. Often, I find, the pleasure and natural excitement of the game are enhanced by the suspense of wondering when the referee is going to warn our coach that if that mother on the sideline doesn't stop hollering he's going to award the opposition a penalty kick.

CAROL: *Fundamentally, she was happy. She was conditioned to believe she could accomplish whatever she wanted or adopt any persona she pleased, and after she stopped practicing law no one could pin an easy label on her. Once, a friend said, "If you'd told me ten years ago that I would become a housewife, I never would have believed you," and she replied, "Who says you're a housewife? I'm not!" She wasn't a floor scrubber, a pillow puffer, or any version of Martha Stewart wannabe. She was proud that her daughters had witnessed the hollowness of her husband's threat that, if the house wasn't cleaned up, this year there wouldn't be a Christmas tree. "Guess what," she would remind the girls. "We got a tree anyway, didn't we?"*

Her own mother, who also disdained domesticity, used to pick her up after school every day and they would do stuff— cruise the countryside, pick corn, go fishing, visit a divertingly ditsy alcoholic aunt. Mainly, they drove. She enjoyed doing the same thing with her daughters, though with a bit more focus. Her favorite weekday afternoon was Wednesday, when she would climb behind the wheel of her Taurus wagon and emulate Cha Cha Muldowney.

The girls should learn to ride horses, she decided, so she arranged back-to-back half-hour lessons— with a particular teacher whose only available time slot was Wednesday from four o'clock to five. That her older daughter had a one-hour swim-team practice every Wednesday at four-thirty— as well as a Brownies meeting every other Wednesday at five-thirty— she regarded less as an inconvenience than as an amusing challenge. That Carol herself was also the Brownie troop leader provided a bonus hurdle.

The older girl wore her bathing suit under her riding clothes, and as soon as she got off the horse her mother bombed off to swim team — less than ten minutes in manageable traffic. She would double back in time to pick up the younger girl at the stables, then retrace her route in plenty of time for the end of swim practice. Every other week, she arranged for the older girl to catch a ride from swimming, because the drive home from the riding lesson usually left about forty-five seconds to spare before the Brownie troop members began to arrive. "Pay attention, I might be micromanaging your lives now and turning you into little ax murderers," she told her daughters. "But trust me, you'll be happy ax murderers."

SERA AND TOM live in the same house Tom grew up in and their children attend the same public schools he did. Last fall, little Sera started middle school. At the end of the first marking period, when she brought home a report card with all A's, big Sera decided it was probably safe to take a break from her weekly hour and a half of private tutoring in math and English. The identity of the tutor, who has been on retainer since little Sera was in second grade, is proprietary information. "I don't want to say who it is," Sera told me. "But I have a very good source." The tutor continues to meet every week with William — working on math, English, and study skills — and Sera is thinking of finding someone else to teach him Spanish.

Meta is now in first grade and soon, Sera thinks, she wants her to start working with the math-and-English tutor. Because Thad is still in nursery school, he's not quite ready. Sera knew Thad would be a good skater when, soon after he learned to walk, he started motoring around the house in William's Rollerblades, so she bought him a pair of his own. Both Meta and Thad participated in the same hockey clinic this winter. This spring will be Meta's second season of T-ball. A few months ago, she started piano lessons, and Sera says that Spanish and Korean are "in the wings." Thad will probably begin recorder lessons this summer. William has been teaching him and Meta chess.

All four children attend catechism classes one morning a week. "And they read the Bible," Sera told me. "You know, for each age there's a different edition of the Bible they can read. But I'm not sure how much I like it, because it's very violent." The afterlife that Sera envisions for herself runs counter to Catholic dogma. What she looks forward to is really more a form of reincarnation. "In my next life, I'd like to be born a man," she told me. "I wouldn't have any emotional attachment to anybody. I'd just have fun making money. And have a wife who takes care of everything."

CATHY: *Always, she played by the rules. In school, she never once turned in an assignment late, and in business she operated the same way. Her firstborn, a daughter, was five months old and not yet weaned when she returned to work because an important deal suddenly had to close. It didn't help that the closing was scheduled for immediately after Father's Day weekend and that her husband also had to work. She had no choice but to bring the baby with her. She ended up in a room with ten men who spent their Father's Day taking turns holding her daughter while she redrafted and shuffled the closing papers. Every couple of hours, she excused herself to nurse. It was a revelation: this was not how she intended to spend her time with her children.*

After more than a year on the mommy track — which at her firm meant being at her desk every morning by seven o'clock to earn the right to leave at five-thirty, for three-quarters pay — she threw in the towel. But her sleeping habits never changed. By 5:30 A.M., she was alert, except in summer, when the sunrise woke her up even earlier. She did the laundry, emptied the dishwasher, made lunches and snacks, straightened the house, got the kids dressed and fed and off, and as soon as they were out the door she had a block of time that she was willing to give away.

To anyone who asked, it soon became evident that she could coordinate any local project and deliver on schedule. She joined the arts-center board, became a library trustee and recruited other library volunteers, served on the committee to screen school-board candidates, agreed to be president of both the Junior League and the PTA, typed the whole school directory and the whole annual literary magazine, and didn't object when her husband volunteered them as co-commissioners of the soccer league, even though she correctly suspected it would become the family albatross. Beginning in spring, it fell upon her to process six hundred registration forms, deposit every check, account for every expenditure, assemble teams, draft coaches and assistants and team mothers and publicity managers, plot the availability of playing fields. In late summer, it actually got worse — fifty-hour weeks sorting T-shirts, printing and mailing rosters and schedules, packing balls and whistles and cones and goalie vests and goalie gloves and first-aid kits in equipment bags. She had the kids gathered around the dining-room table stuffing envelopes as they whined, "We want to go to the pool!" She accused herself of child neglect. She tried denying what the situation reminded her of, but, of course, she knew too well: this was exactly how she felt right before she realized that she would have to quit her job.

FRIENDS OF SERA'S gave a New Year's Eve party and invited a tarot-card reader, a palm reader, and an astrologer. The palm reader told Sera that she had a tendency to get into traps, and she didn't enjoy hearing that, because it implied that motherhood was a trap. The good news came when she gave the astrologer the dates and hours of her children's births and was informed that many of the signs were auspicious. "Thad has, like, eight planets that are cardinal signs in the tenth house, which means he can't help being famous," she said. "When he's twenty — it will be just the tip of the iceberg — he's going to be incredible. And Meta's child is going to be famous. So it'll be my child and my grandchild. It's on the map."

As if she didn't know what to make of her own fatalism, she went on, "The secret of this whole thing is there is no secret. Whether a mother works or doesn't work probably makes no difference. I believe in supernatural power — inherent things that you have no control over. What I find hard in my life right now is being in a vacuum. I'm no longer in school, where I got a report card, or at work, where I would get a salary review. We don't get grades, we don't get paid, we don't know until we die — actually, we don't know until *they* die. There are no guarantees. This is the way I approach any project. I have children and I have to make sure that I do the best that I possibly can. How do I define 'best'? When you go to bed totally exhausted and saying, 'I couldn't have done one more thing for them today.'"

One morning when it was snowing and sleeting and Sera's kids were home — along with the plumbers, who were there because the main sewer line had backed up — I went over to her house to hang out. When I arrived, I found her in the living room, where there was a checkerboard-top table, a Calder lithograph above the family photographs on the mantel, a large fluorescent geometric painting brightening an adjacent wall, and, near a row of windows, two glass vases of dried flowers standing on a large round table that was draped with a floral-print cloth. Southeastern light streamed in, and, despite the weather, everything inside felt clear and cozy. A stereo piped a Handel flute sonata from the next room. Sera was curled up on an off-white sectional sofa with Meta, who first read aloud from a storybook and then recited sight words ("meadows," "famous," "cough," "terrible," "hungrier," "cellar," "calendar") from index cards that Sera was holding. It was a deceptively serene moment.

Though the phrase "snow day" strikes terror in a lot of parents, Sera regarded this as an opportunity. She had a long list of tasks to accomplish: all kids finish writing Christmas thank-you notes; have William assemble table grandfather sent for Christmas; bake birthday cake for Tom; shop for Tom's gift; work on summer-camp applications; organize den; go to bank; get rid of Christmas candy; return Christmas gifts; buy William personal organizer; buy colored index cards for Meta's sight words; make about twenty phone calls (including clarinet teacher, insurance company, masonry contractor, soccer telephone tree).

When the sight-word exercise was done, Sera announced,

"Meta, it's time to write your letters." She set a box of purple floral stationery on the checkerboard table, handed Meta a pen, and said, "OK, Meta, now let's make a list. Who do you have to write to? Grandpa — Dad's father — gave you what? A hundred dollars. And Grandma — Dad's mom — gave you the black pants and the Gap clothes that you like. And Grandma and Grandpa, my parents, gave you the handmade wooden chest. All right, Uncle Thaddeus and Michael gave you a bracelet and that tape and book — how do you say that — *Jumanji*? You can just write it out the way it sounds. Who else? Patty? Patty gave you wonderful things. The candy and the colors and the book. And the Conroys gave you — OK, the chocolate. And Uncle George gave you a Gap check — money you can spend. Now, who did we forget? What about Mommy and Daddy?"

"Daddy gave me the T-shirt and Mommy gave me . . ." Meta paused, momentarily stumped.

"*Meta,*" Sera told her. "Mommy gave you everything."

— 1996

The Book Eater

WHILE AMUSING HIMSELF at an antiques fair in Rhinebeck, New York, one day a few years ago, Michael Zinman, a sixty-three-year-old polymath who has acquired an international reputation for his prolific and idiosyncratic habits as a book collector, came across a large plywood heavy-jowled caricature of Richard Nixon. For Zinman — whose day job is buying and selling, in a market understood by himself and very few other people, enormous natural-gas turbines — seeing the ex-president's oversize red-and-white-painted mug was, he says, "like an epiphany." Epiphany du jour seems more like it. The next morning, having invested a hundred dollars in this curio, he nailed it to the front of a weathered-cedar two-story office building he owns on one of the main avenues of Ardsley, a suburb about forty minutes north of New York City. The political establishment there is mainstream Republican, and two days later a village official dropped by to inform him that he was in violation of the local sign code. "It ain't a sign," Zinman replied — the previous owner had in fact used it as a basketball backboard. "An omen, maybe, but not a sign." Nevertheless, he was told, proper procedures hadn't been followed, and it would have to come down. "You want me to take it down?" Zinman baited his visitor. "Go ahead and issue me a summons. And you'll be reading about this in the *Times* by the end of the week." The official departed, and not long thereafter a cohort of his came around and suggested that the presence of the Nixon head could complicate a zoning proposal Zinman was preparing to submit to the village planning board. Zinman blithely made an allusion to the potential pleasures of litigation. Since then, the Nixon head has stayed put, and its owner has occupied himself with other self-gratifying endeavors. This vignette offers a concise illustration of the Zinman rules of engagement: obey your whims, inflict no physical harm but get in the other guy's face as much as circumstances dictate, and be poised for the next skirmish.

Zinman has a nimble verbal manner, a cheerful seen-it-all-but-show-me-some-more bluntness, infused with a nasal Yonkers inflection, and a look that would have engaged Daumier — elfin, slightly paunchy, bemused. His red hair has mostly gone white and there's not much left on top, and he has a pink complexion, a neatly trimmed beard, hazel eyes, and a consistent air of benign, sage alertness. When I first visited his office, more than a dozen years ago, at the outset of our friendly acquaintanceship, a sublime oil painting of a grizzly bear by J. J. Audubon greeted me — one of nine Audubon quadruped originals that Zinman has at one time or another owned, and all of which he has since parted with. The grizzly loomed over a large maple partners' desk from which Zinman carried out his duties as chief executive of Earthworm Tractor Company, a firm that traded heavy earthmoving equipment. After conducting some quick business over the phone — arranging for a Caterpillar dealer in the Pacific Northwest to acquire a winch that Zinman happened to know was situated on the lot of a Caterpillar dealer in New York, a conversation that netted him about a thousand dollars a minute — he ushered me next door to show me a collection in progress of books that appealed to him for their titles alone: *Frog Raising for Pleasure and Profit, Pamphlets by an Ass, How to Be Happy Though Married, The Cult of the Goldfish, Colon Cleanse the Easy Way!, Hell: What Is It? Who Are They? Can They Get Out?, The Truth About Baking Powder.* Not far from the bizarre-titles collection was a bookcase containing several hundred thousand dollars' worth of fragments, plus many intact volumes, of Early American Bibles. Such odd juxtapositions, along with a decorating motif that inclined toward high-low eclecticism and clutter — a not quite life-size carved wooden pig posed next to an uninviting brown cotton upholstered sofa, above which hung a brass plaque engraved "When You've Got Them by the Balls Their Hearts and Minds Will Follow" — struck me as a fitting analogue to Zinman's peripatetic intelligence.

When I began dropping by again recently, the ambience was unchanged. Shelves and storage rooms throughout the building were burdened with tons of books. In the place of the Audubon bear, Zinman had mounted four framed business documents, mementos of financial calamities he's been a party to — each being a complex long-term investment and thus a deviation from his proven talent for, as he puts it, "trading on my own instincts."

"Every time I think I'm smart," he told me, "those four relics are my lesson in humility. The point being that virtually every undertaking that is not transactional in nature — anything that doesn't primarily involve buying and selling or brokering — I've been singularly unsuccessful at." These vicissitudes notwithstanding, Zinman's trading instincts have over time kept him liquid and, remarkably, have supported his insatiable fervor as a collector. And, within the past year, one transaction in particular has affirmed his dominance of a certain niche of the rare-book market. In the process, the improbable wisdom of his unorthodox methods has been permanently vindicated.

IN 1958, at the age of twenty-one, Zinman made what he considers his first serious book purchase, spending two hundred dollars for a three-volume octavo edition of Audubon's *Quadrupeds of North America*. The rest of the world's preference for Audubon birds was precisely what attracted him to the quadrupeds — "because no one liked the furry little creatures." He paid for the books at the rate of ten dollars a week, and the day he made the last payment he bought another Audubon work, again on the installment plan.

At that point in his life, he'd already matriculated at Cornell and at New York University, in both cases departing without a diploma. Given the chance, he would have graduated from Cornell, but he became persona non grata after he and a confederate, on the eve of an alumni reunion weekend, orchestrated the theft of all the toilet seats from six dormitories. He dropped out of NYU because his father asked him to join his merchant trading company. This enterprise was the precursor of Earthworm, which enjoyed twenty generally prosperous years, culminating in Zinman's decision, in the mid-eighties, to sell shares to the public. As founder, he retained about 20 percent of the stock, which in time became worthless. First came the dubious decision to import excavators from Russia. ("They just didn't work. We had a lot of press, and the biggest contractor in D.C. bought one of our machines and the thing kept breaking down. Why didn't we see that coming? We were stupid.") Next, he imported tractors from China, with similar results. ("Why? We didn't learn our lesson after Russia.") I once asked Zinman whether his book collecting had gotten in the way of managing Earthworm, and he said, "No, it was the other way around."

Over two decades, he progressed from Audubon to natural history in general, then to American natural history, then to voyages to and travels in the New World (with special reference to natural history). During this odyssey, his enthusiasm endeared him to a network of bookdealers who tended to cluster in New England, New York, Philadelphia, and London. Impassioned book collectors are driven by, among other things, the conviction that bookdealers usually don't realize the extent of the treasures squirreled away in their own inventories. As the focus of Zinman's collecting evolved, he often sold books in one corner of a shop and then spent hours scouring the premises, walking out with a lot more baggage than he'd just deaccessioned. At certain London shops, Zinman was welcomed as a one-man swarm of locusts — relentless, contrarian, gluttonous. He'd work his way through the basement stocks — the so-called hospitals, where "crippled," or incomplete, books were consigned — of several dealers: Bernard Quaritch, Francis Edwards, Pickering and Chatto, Maggs Brothers. The consensus at Quaritch, which has been around since 1847, is that in terms of numbers of imperfect volumes bought Zinman is the most active customer in the company's history. (He was surely among the least self-restrained. In London, Zinman made a habit of staying at the Savoy Hotel and of not overexerting himself fretting about the house protocols. Once, when a staff member reminded him that gentlemen were required to wear jackets and ties in the Savoy parlor, Zinman apologized for his faux pas, retreated to his room, and returned wearing a jacket and tie but not a shirt.)

Zinman's omnivorousness made it inevitable that he would come across examples of Early American printing — a category comprising what was produced from 1639, the year the first mechanical press showed up on the Atlantic shores, through 1800. This is the same span of time surveyed by the ur-text *American Bibliography,* a reference work whose primary author, Charles Evans, labored more than thirty years, completing twelve volumes before his death, in 1935. Evans identified forty thousand individual items — books, pamphlets, chapbooks, broadsides, magazines, newspapers — of which 10 percent were "ghosts," known to have once existed but evidently no longer extant. Updatings of Evans subsequently added fourteen thousand or so items. The largest holding of such material, at the American Antiquarian Society, in Worcester, Massachusetts, consists of twenty-two thousand items. When Zinman first started acquiring Evans items, conventional wisdom held that there simply weren't enough of them loose in the market for him to build a substantial, much less a definitive, collection. So, naturally, whenever an opportunity arose he bought. And the more he bought the more he wanted to buy. Over the past twenty years, Zinman has sought and, with infrequent exceptions, bought anything — *anything* — printed in colonial America.

ONE SUNNY DAY late last winter, as a blue Plymouth Voyager van inched its way up a ramp of the Cross Bronx Expressway and onto the George Washington Bridge, the driver, a New Haven book-dealer named William Reese, and his front-seat passenger, Zinman — on their way to Philadelphia, with me riding in the back seat — noticed the same thing at the same moment.

"I assume you want to buy that," Reese said, and Zinman immediately replied, "Of *course* I want to buy it." A minute later, the van had drawn even with a panhandler who was standing on the narrow shoulder of the ramp, holding a rectangular piece of cardboard on which he'd written "Homeless Hungry God-Bless." Reese rolled down his window, and Zinman shouted across a lane of traffic, "I'll buy your sign for twenty dollars!" The panhandler, who had bloodshot eyes, stringy reddish-brown hair, and a beard, studied his handiwork as if maybe something about it had eluded him. Nope, it was just a cardboard sign.

"You got it," he said, approaching the van.

"You have to sign your name on the back of it," Zinman said.

"Are you serious?"

"I'm serious."

"My real name? My name's Wayne."

"Here's twenty bucks."

"I'm not gonna ask what you're gonna do with it."

"I'm giving it to a library."

"You made my day!" Wayne said, then headed down the ramp and hopped over a railing, quite possibly planning to take the afternoon off.

"I'm putting the word out all over the country," Zinman said as the traffic moved forward. "I want signs like this. You'd be surprised. Some people are very sincere in saying these things are important to them and they can't part with them. That's fine. How many do I have so far? I have four — well, now five. I'm just getting started."

"It's a new collection that stores flat," Reese said, and then, gesturing toward the cargo area of the van and a Ryder rental truck that was following us, he added, "Michael's got to get rid of this shit first."

The shit: the supposedly impossibly elusive stuff he'd begun vacuuming up twenty years earlier, now known as the Zinman Collection of Early American Imprints, valued at eight million dollars, which that day was being transported from Ardsley to the home of its new owner, the Library Company of Philadelphia. As we proceeded along the New Jersey Turnpike, Zinman and Reese, who had acted as his agent in negotiations with the Library Company, explored a topic dear to both of them — what they refer to as the "critical-mess theory" of collecting. Reese, an affable and droll fellow in his mid-forties, started out in the book trade in 1975. His own collecting specialties are Melville and American color-plate books, but his main distinction is that through a combination of entrepreneurial ingenuity and scholarly discipline he has established himself as the country's preeminent dealer in Americana. In 1998, the Morgan Library expressed interest in buying the Zinman Collection, and Reese and a pair of assistants spent six weeks preparing an item-by-item appraisal. Most of what Reese scrutinized during that exercise was already familiar to him; he either had sold it to Zinman himself or had bid for him at auction or had heard Zinman expatiate upon it during their almost daily phone conversations. Discussions with the Morgan never got very far, but a byproduct of Reese's appraisal was "100 Exemplars from the Zinman Collection," a prospectus of sorts that would prove handy whenever the next potential buyer came along. In a prefatory note, Reese wrote, "Zinman's primary concern as a collector has been the assembling of the physical evidence of printing in early America, in as broad a range of subjects as possible. The result is a collection almost without equal for the study of the history of the book in America." When Zinman lent me his annotated copy of "100 Exemplars," I wasn't surprised to find that the marginalia read like the bibliomaniacal equivalent of a diary of amorous pursuits, the reminiscences of a protagonist in a state of perpetual satyriasis.

"The most intriguing thing is how a collection like Michael's gets built," Reese said, by way of explaining the practical ramifications of the critical-mess theory. "When you start on something like this, you say, OK, here is a genre, here is a field. And I'm just going to buy it, whatever it is that I'm collecting — signs from homeless people, imprints from before 1801. You don't start off with a theory about what you're trying to do. You don't begin by saying, 'I'm trying to prove x.' You build a big pile. Once you get a big enough pile together — the critical mess — you're able to draw conclusions about it. You see patterns. You might see that this one lithographer in Philadelphia does all the scientific works. You start to see that certain early printers were much better than other printers. You start to see that homeless people in the South put together wordier signs than people in the North because people in the South like to read billboards, so they'll slow down and read the sign. People who have the greatest intuitive feel for physical objects start from a relationship with the objects and then acquire the scholarship, instead of the other way around. The way to become a connoisseur is to work in the entire spectrum of what's available — from utter crap to fabulous stuff. If you're going to spend your time looking only at the best, you're not going to have a critical eye.

"Michael went about this by crawling around book fairs and antique shows and going to see crackpots in the country and bartering and using any number of Zinmanesque devices. Certain institutions collected Early American imprints during the late nineteenth and early twentieth centuries, but then a time came when they no longer had the money to do it. From 1920 on — until Michael got active, in the early eighties — hardly anyone paid attention to this stuff. He started out just picking up all the float, whatever was in the market. After that, stuff started coming out of attics and estate sales. And that's the amazing thing — that at a point when everybody said you can't form a collection on this scale because it's all in institutions already, he went ahead and did it. And now nobody can ever do it again."

"Zinman's determined to a fault," a New England book scout named Matthew Needle told me. "He'll call people day and night. He won't browbeat them necessarily, but he has a way. He starts a conversation: 'What'd you buy yesterday? What have you got for me?' Social niceties were never his strong suit."

Steve Weissman, formerly a bookdealer in New York, now living in England: "Michael has persistence, but he doesn't have patience. Voracity is a kind of impatient quality. He's incapable of waiting even for a nice copy. But he knows it when he sees it."

Near Trenton, Zinman was reminded of an emblematic transaction, an encounter with a dealer from New Jersey who had brought to a book fair "a very nice seventeenth-century Mather item" — specifically, a 1684 sermon by Nathanael Mather on the obligation of Christian believers "to live in the constant exercise of grace." Bracing himself for disappointment, the dealer told Zinman he assumed that he already had a copy. "So I look at it," Zinman recalled. "And I say, 'Actually, I've got two copies.' He says, 'I guess you don't want it.' I say, 'Of course I want it. Then I'll have three.'" His collection included three complete copies, four substantially complete copies, and about a dozen fragmentary copies of Increase Mather's *Kometographia* (1683), one of the first scientific works published in America. Also: five copies of William Hubbard's *Narrative of the Troubles with the Indians in New England* (1677); seven copies of *Wisdom in Miniature; or, The Young Gentleman and Lady's Pleasing Instructor* (1796); five copies of Nathaniel Morton's *New England's Memoriall*, the first history book printed in the colonies (1669); eight copies of Timothy Dwight's *Conquest of Canäan: A Poem, in Eleven Books* (1785). On one of the few occasions when he sold a book "because I needed cash, a book I would not have parted with otherwise," it was John Smith's *Generall Historie of Virginia, New England, and the Summer Isles*. Distressing though it was to separate himself from the book, Zinman drew consolation from the fact that he still owned thirty-three copies.

SO HOW WAS IT he'd agreed to relinquish, en masse, his Early American imprints? Nicholas Poole-Wilson, the managing director of Quaritch, told me he figured that Zinman, having entered "the late afternoon of his life," wanted to make arrangements for his worldly possessions. If he'd been describing a sixty-three-year-old other than Zinman — whose mother, at ninety-seven, is alive and kicking, though not quite as high as she did when she was a Ziegfeld chorus girl — I might have found this plausible. The chief reason was quite mundane. He and his wife, Barbara Weingarten, had decided they wanted to move from the suburbs to Manhattan, and he was having trouble finding a co-op apartment in a building where his joist-threatening library would be welcome. In other words, he wasn't selling because he was strapped for funds. Though eight million dollars was a fair market appraisal, the Library Company was paying only five million; the three-million-dollar difference was a gift from Zinman. And even as he was surrendering the collection he was adding to it.

"He bought a book from me last week," Reese interjected.

"Yeah, for ten grand. And I'll give it to them. I've been giving stuff to the Library Company for the last fifteen or twenty years, and I have absolutely no intention of stopping. I give books to a lot of people. I really don't have a possessive instinct. I don't have to *own* anything. I do have an acquisitive instinct, but once I've acquired it I'll give it away. I've been asked what kind of trauma am I going through because I'm giving up this collection. I'll tell you something: if I am, it's news to me. Sure, you mess around with the books and they're wonderful. But it's, you know, like revisiting old girlfriends."

The Library Company's pedigree — Benjamin Franklin and friends founded it in 1731, originally as a subscription lending library — destined it to become the august American-history research facility it is today. Its archives of printed materials and manuscripts focus mainly on the colonial period through the late nineteenth century, with particular strengths in the revolutionary, federal, Jacksonian, and Civil War periods. The fact that its Early American imprints were skewed toward the Middle Atlantic region, while Zinman himself had gathered an inordinate amount of New England material, meant that the combined holdings would dovetail neatly. Thanks in large part to Zinman's obsessiveness, in both quantity and quality, the Library Company is now second only to the American Antiquarian Society as a repository of early imprints.

When we arrived — the Library Company owns a pair of red-brick buildings on Locust Street in downtown Philadelphia — a delegation of board members and employees was on hand not only to hail Zinman but to unburden him. Carefully and efficiently, the contents of Reese's van and the rental truck were unloaded and stacked in the trustees' room, on the ground floor — 231 banker boxes filled with books, pamphlets, broadsides, medical and scientific texts, sermons, almanacs, psalters, Bibles, atlases, magazines, poetry, fiction, commercial catalogs, state constitutions, city directories, sheet music, children's literature. The items were in eight languages, including the Massachusetts dialect of the Algonquin nation, and among them were the earliest work of fiction by an American (1715); the first modern novel published in America (1767); the first American sporting book, a sermon on the pleasures of fishing (1743); the first arithmetic book published in America (1719); Cotton Mather's account of the Salem witch trials (1692); a 1729 printing of *The Bay Psalm Book,* the original edition of which, in 1640, was *the* first book printed in colonial America; the only colonial-era book identified as having belonged to a slave (1741, inscribed "Lucinda her Book given by her Mistress"); ten editions of Thomas Paine's *Common Sense* (1776); multiple editions of the *Journals* of the Continental Congress; the first American edition of *Paradise Lost* (1777); a perfect 1783 copy of *The New England Primer,* the most famous colonial schoolbook; the most complete known copy of Jacob Taylor's *Tenebrae,* the earliest illustrated scientific book (1698); a 1794 memoir of Marie Antoinette, printed in New York, that made her out to be a low-rent floozy; Charles Perrault's *Fairy Tales* (1794), among the rarest of American children's books, complete except for the title page; *The Indian's Pedigree* (1794), a racist broadside printed in Boston; the first American edition of a Shakespeare play (*Hamlet,* 1794); *Aristotle's Masterpiece,* the first American sex manual (1766); and a frayed but unique copy of a 1770 broadside poem by Phillis Wheatley, a slave woman who became a celebrated literary figure. The Wheatley broadside was sold by Reese to Zinman for fifteen thousand dollars at a book fair in New York on a day when the object in question changed hands two times before Zinman arrived. That it wound up with him surprised no one.

When the delivery was completed, Zinman and Reese broke for lunch, along with some members of the Library Company board and James Green, who is the associate librarian and someone Zinman has consulted several times a week for the past fifteen years on the topic of Early American imprints. En route to the felicitously named Bookbinder's, a seafood restaurant, Zinman stooped three times to pick up objects he spied on the pavement. A couple of hours later, during the drive home, he reported, "It wasn't a bad day at all. I found two pennies and a marble." Then, when we were about fourth in line at a tollbooth, he announced, "You usually find money here," and jumped out of the car.

"We ought to leave him," Reese muttered.

"There's a lot out there," Zinman said when he returned, having increased his net worth by more than a dollar. "To quote Franklin, 'Waste not, want not.'"

"No, Michael," Reese corrected him. "What Franklin actually said was 'A dime found near a tollbooth is a dime earned.'"

"These toll collectors start getting mad, so I leave some for the next guys. You know, this is easy, not like when you're walking in New York on a hot day and you've got to use a knife to pry pennies out of the tar and then you've got to go find a newspaper in the garbage to wrap them up so the tar doesn't stick to your pocket — now, that's a problem."

Assuming that he'd developed a system for cataloging what he scavenged, I asked, "What do you do, write down where and when you found it and then file it away in a specimen box?"

"Are you kidding? I spend it!"

WHEN THE SPIRIT moves him, Zinman is willing to squander financial opportunities. While he was confident, for instance, that the John Carter Brown Library, of Providence, would ultimately have offered more for his Americana collection, he nevertheless went ahead and sold it to the Library Company. This attitude — it's only money, isn't it? — was evident in his dealings with Donald Oresman, a New York lawyer who sits on the Library Company's board. After he and Reese had agreed on the price, Oresman told me, he called Zinman for the name of his lawyer so they could draft a contract. "You write the contract," Zinman proposed. When Oresman inquired how and when he wanted the five million dollars delivered, Zinman said how about a million a year for five years. What rate of interest, Oresman asked, should the Library Company pay on the balance due? Zinman: "Forget the interest."

This was consonant with Zinman's track record as a capricious philanthropist. During the seventies, feeling oppressed by the non-existence of live classical music on the radio, he arranged to sponsor one-hour broadcasts five nights a week, beginning at midnight, on WQXR, the FM station owned by the *Times*. In the course of this, he created a charitable entity, the Haydn Foundation, to function as the formal underwriter. (The various ways in which Zinman has deployed the Haydn Foundation in the intervening years have prompted Clarence Wolf, a Philadelphia bookdealer and a close friend, to refer to it on occasion as the Hiding Foundation.) Occasionally, Zinman took the role of on-air host. At one point, he got a phone call from a fledgling enterprise called National Public Radio. Zinman: "They said, 'Hey, Zinman, we're setting up this nationwide radio network and we think you've got the greatest thing since chopped liver! No one else is producing any live music in the country. You're putting on two hundred and fifty concerts a year. We want you on NPR.' To which I rejoined, 'Are you kidding? I'm already on QXR! Who the hell are you?'"

A different sort of missed opportunity occurred several years ago when New York University Medical Center solicited a major donation. Zinman offered to endow urinals, at a thousand dollars apiece, provided each was equipped with a plaque that read, "The pleasure you are now experiencing has been made possible through the generosity of Michael Zinman." The hospital fundraisers vacillated before declining, and Zinman said fine, but if you change your minds the offer stands. "They came back to me later and said, 'Here's the problem: What about women?' I said, 'You want to put urinals in the ladies' rooms, too? No problem.'"

The apparent relish with which Zinman dispenses his largess — the joy of giving, compounded by the joy of tax deductibility — is at odds with a tendency that for a long time characterized his affairs both in and out of the book trade. "I love Michael," Clarence Wolf has said. "He's the least petty person I know. But he can be as exasperating as anyone I've ever dealt with." This was an oblique reference to the fact that for years Zinman was notorious not as a flat-out deadbeat but as someone who paid his bills *very slowly.*

Steve Weissman: "He'd buy from little dealers, from big dealers, and he tended to pay the ones who needed the money and make the ones who didn't wait a long time. I don't think he ever took advantage of anybody who really needed the money. In the end, it always came out all right."

Zinman's unbusinesslike predilections were never more evident than when he operated a conventional business. During the Earthworm era, he had frequent dealings with a Caterpillar franchisee in Cincinnati named Albert Norman. A basic ingredient in their relationship was a shared disdain for the guys in suits at the Caterpillar Tractor Company's main office, in Peoria, Illinois. Zinman and Norman traded used earthmoving equipment in ways that, though entirely legitimate, albeit too convoluted to go into here, proved too imaginative to be tolerated by Peoria. Eventually, his dealings with Zinman cost Norman his Caterpillar franchise. Along the way, Zinman somehow managed to get — and for long periods of time to stay — deeply in debt to Norman without alienating him.

"He's able to get credit when almost no one else possibly could," Norman told me recently from Florida, where he's happily and prosperously retired. "He's either the smartest or the luckiest guy in the world. I once sent my finance manager to New York to collect some money. Michael put his arm around him and took him home and showed him his book collection. My finance manager came back to Cincinnati and said, 'You ought to see the books he's got there.' I said, 'I hope you at least got a half million from him,' and he said, 'I didn't get anything.' Michael showed him some books and convinced him he was good for the money."

In gratitude, Zinman dedicated to Norman a book he wrote and self-published in 1986, *The History of the Decline and Fall of the Raterpillar Tractor Company*. The book, which consists of photo reproductions of correspondence and legal documents, accompanied by an explanatory narrative, recounts a quite expensive practical joke that Zinman perpetrated to get on the nerves of the then chairman of Caterpillar, to whom the book is also, rather more ironically, dedicated. This saga began in the late seventies, when Caterpillar sued Earthworm, alleging unfair competition. The litigation, along with a Zinman countersuit, took about six years to settle. Deciding that he hadn't had quite enough fun, Zinman subsequently incorporated the Raterpillar Tractor Company, a shell whose main asset was a letterhead bearing the disclaimer "Raterpillar Tractor Co. is in no way connected with Caterpillar Tractor Co. Caterpillar Tractor Co. sells 'Cats' — Raterpillar Tractor Co. sells rats." As he had hoped, this provoked a new, though far less protracted, bout of legal jousting. The net result, for Zinman, was a bill from his attorneys in the middle five figures and the file of documents that provided the fodder for *Decline and Fall*. He printed thirty-five hundred copies, gave away hundreds, and sold the rest, including hundreds at a kiosk in the Peoria airport. *Decline and Fall* is now, by any measure, a rare book, and Zinman himself is down to only three copies.

DURING THE LATE EIGHTIES, Zinman bought a library that had been bequeathed to a synagogue in Yonkers by Irving Levitas, a rabbi, Talmudist, and American historian. To emphasize the esteem in which he held Levitas as a scholar and collector, Zinman told me, "I have a short list of heroes, and Irving was one of them." Another was A. J. Liebling, the *New Yorker* writer. As an homage, Zinman formed a corporation, which he has continued to use as a vehicle for some of his book buying, and named it Liebling and Levitas. Among the zillion items in Zinman's desk drawers is a bundle of business cards that Levitas kept handy for opportune moments and that say "Yes, I have read all these books. Thanks for asking. Irving Levitas."

Which, when Zinman showed me the card, raised in my mind the corollary question, How much of what passes through his hands does he actually read? I can vouch that he's thoughtfully digested Liebling (who occupies a spot on my own short list), because he readily sprinkles conversations with illustrative quotations from *The Earl of Louisiana* and *The Honest Rainmaker* and *The Telephone Booth Indian*. But the broader answer seems to be that reading books is subordinate to Zinman's extraordinary need to play with them. What he derives from books is mainly bibliographic knowledge — about books as objects, about the mercantile considerations that went into the production of those objects — rather than a direct absorption of what library professionals refer to as their "intellectual contents." But he clearly has a reverence for learning, for the importance of words, and a ravenous desire to find answers to things, not because he's seeking cosmic truth in books but because he finds pleasure in taking scattered pieces of evidence and constructing a frame and a context. Lacking the discipline and attention span for conventional scholarship, Zinman for several years employed a full-time librarian, Keith Arbour, a highly respected bibliographer and historian, to catalog his Early American imprints. Arbour published several scholarly papers based upon Zinman's holdings.

One day not long ago, Zinman and I were having lunch at a sushi restaurant near his home. ("If this is the only sushi you've ever eaten, you never know how good it is," he said. "You have to try a lot of other stuff to appreciate it fully.") Our agenda that afternoon called for me to witness an active application of the critical-mess theory; I wanted to see him in action. Flying to Los Angeles one day last spring, it happened that Zinman had been reading a pile of booksellers' catalogs and come across one from an English dealer titled "The Atomic Age from Hiroshima and Nagasaki to Star Wars." From the air, he called the dealer and bought the entire collection, eighteen hundred books and pamphlets. A few days later, he rang the dealer back and bought two hundred and fifty duplicate items.

Not much to my surprise, before we could begin to burrow into the "Atomic Age" collection, we got sidetracked. During lunch, I had dislodged a gold crown from one of my molars, which prompted Zinman, back at the office in Ardsley, to remove from a desk drawer a small cylindrical glass specimen jar. Inside was a bunch — I hesitate to call it a collection — of Zinman's erstwhile dental crowns. He set the jar next to a stack of colorful handbills, a few hundred from his collection of a couple of thousand prostitutes' calling cards, a species of ephemera typically found in London telephone booths. While studying these, I noticed, also on the desktop, a pintsize porcelain vase half filled with tar-encrusted pennies.

"Just for the record," I proposed, "how many different collections would you say are in this building at the moment?"

"Let's figure it out," Zinman said, launching a show-and-tell tour. "We can start in this room. Does my caca shelf count?" He was referring to a heap of found objects on a fireplace mantel, an agglomeration that looked like crumbs from the bottom of a vast toy chest — miniature cars and trucks, paper airplanes, automobile hood ornaments, Slinky-eyeball spectacles, Mardi Gras beads. Well, if that counted, I suppose so did the ceramic tub brimming with golf balls that we passed on our way upstairs. ("I found a place where all the golf balls go to die. I could sell them and probably make about a thousand dollars a year, I find so many. But I just give them away.") The second floor was subdivided into Earthworm-vintage office cubicles that are now used to store Zinman's embossed pre-Braille American printing for the blind (a hundred items); nineteenth-century American almanacs (thousands); books-in-parts (two hundred examples of books issued serially, usually by subscription, nineteenth century to the present); American magazines from 1800–30; nineteenth-century lithographed sheet music; Restoration plays (two boxes full); and constitutions (more than seven hundred, from all sorts of organizations, very few governments among them). When we came back downstairs, Zinman noticed that a large shipping carton had been delivered, part of an auction lot of almost two thousand miscellaneous nineteenth- and twentieth-century pamphlets, for which he'd bid five thousand dollars at Swann Galleries, in New York, a couple of weeks earlier.

Skipping the bizarre-titles collection (two hundred and fifty items), which now resided in the basement, we moved to a part of the building that was formerly leased to an aerobics studio. In one big room, just enough space remained to permit navigation among the floor-to-ceiling stacks of boxes — many unopened, such as the dozen or so brown-paper-wrapped parcels containing the "Atomic Age" collection. Then, there were the fifty-four unsold units of Zinman's *American Bible* treatise, a quixotic project he embarked on in 1993: the publication of a four-volume text-and-image portfolio (text by Zinman) of leaves removed from his collection of incomplete Early American Bibles. He printed an edition of a hundred, priced at just under nine thousand dollars apiece, "did everything wrong" in the process, and, to his amazement, still managed to recoup his costs and then some.

The rest of the room was occupied by scores of open cartons of pamphlets, dating from the seventeenth to the twentieth century, which Zinman acquired almost four years ago from an ephemera dealer who had procured them, for the price of scrap, from the New York Public Library. This was material that the library had recorded on microfilm as part of a "preservation" program that deemed the original documents expendable. In 1997 and 1998, Zinman — unable to resist the impulse to rub a great institution's nose in its ill-considered behavior — dispatched to friends, as well as to the library's trustees, poster-size holiday greeting cards devoted to the theme of the library's "trashing" of its own collections.

The following year's holiday missive was again quintessentially Zinmanesque, yet infinitely more somber and stirring. Zinman is the father of four — a son, Peter, and a daughter, Lisa, from a first marriage, and two daughters, Marisa and Alison, whom he raised with Barbara Weingarten. Alison died of cancer in the spring of 1999, at the age of twenty. On a poster that featured full-size photographs of selections from her collection, Zinman included the following text: "Why look to question the motives of collectors? That the collector expends the time and energy to create a collection alone trumpets its importance to the world. This is Alison's trumpet. What a merry tune it plays." And what did Alison Weingarten collect? Airsickness bags.

"The Atomic Age" would have to wait for another day, Zinman announced, because a different critical mess beckoned: "I can't wait to get in there and see what's inside that box from Swann." So we retraced our steps and arrived in a shelf-lined room where he keeps his twenty-five-hundred-volume reference library. He slit open the shipping carton, fished from the plastic-foam peanuts three metal-reinforced gray cardboard portfolio boxes, and set them on a worktable. "I have no idea what this will be," he said brightly, as if preparing to eat an exquisite meal blindfolded. All he knew was that he would find pamphlets that had been consigned for auction by the New Jersey Historical Society. The first box seemed to be mainly First World War vintage, with quite a bit of material on German atrocities, plus a hodgepodge from all over the map: an essay on Robert Burns; an 1883 New York and Brooklyn Bridge guide; a chemical-company promotional pamphlet, *Mulford on Land and Sea; The Commercial Future of Baghdad* (1917); *The Pre-Historic Remains Which Were Found on the Site of the City of Cincinnati, Ohio* (1876); an 1856 *Catalogue of Officers and Students of Beloit College; Vital Problems Affecting the New Rumania* (1919).

According to an arrangement he'd already worked out, he began sorting and making small piles. After gleaning what he wanted, he planned to sell the bulk, for four thousand dollars, to a dealer who'd been the underbidder at Swann's. "I'll send a bunch of pamphlets to friends," he said. "I'll sell a few. I don't want to make any money, but I won't lose any, either." He came across two Evans items from 1800 ("Oh, look, here's something for my collection") — Major General Henry Lee's eulogy for George Washington, and a sermon printed in Hartford, his second and fourth copies, respectively. These would, of course, go to the Library Company. He fingered another pamphlet, chuckled, and handed it to me: *Twenty-ninth Annual Report to the General Assembly of the Presby-*

terian Church in the United States of America, in Relation to the Re-
lief Fund, by the Presbyterian Board of Relief for Disabled Ministers
and the Widows and Orphans of Deceased Ministers, Philadelphia,
1884. Just trying to transcribe the title, I felt my eyes glaze over, my
brain go slack with fatigue. I looked up at Zinman, across the table,
as he opened another portfolio box and gently dumped out its
contents. His eyebrows were arched, he was nodding thoughtfully
and smiling faintly. He seemed no happier than usual, but terrifically happy just the same.

— 2001

The Man Who Forgets Nothing

Now, WHERE WERE WE? Oh, right, Martin Scorsese's stream of consciousness. OK, so one afternoon late last summer, seven weeks shy of the opening date of his most recent film, *Bringing Out the Dead,* we happened to be in a sound-mixing studio in the Brill Building, on Broadway, in the Forties. The floor was raked like a theater's, and Scorsese was situated at a console so that he was literally overseeing a couple of craftsmen — a rerecording mixer and a sound editor — who knew how to operate a control panel with about five hundred knobs and switches. For more than a month, Scorsese and Thelma Schoonmaker, who has edited each of his films since *Raging Bull,* in 1980, had been scrutinizing every millimeter of the film's dialogue, music, and sound effects. A thirty-foot-wide screen spanned one wall, and at the moment it was filled with a medium shot of Nicolas Cage and Tom Sizemore, playing a pair of Emergency Medical Service workers named Frank and Tom. Heard but not seen as their ambulance cruised midtown was Scorsese himself, cast as a sardonic radio dispatcher, delivering dialogue courtesy of Paul Schrader (by way of a novel written by Joe Connelly) in a voice that was unmistakably, quintessentially New York — a quick-tempo wise-guy patois with a don't-tempt-me edge of neurotic potential. He had bad news for Frank and Tom. He was assigning them to pick up a notoriously foul-smelling alcoholic derelict, and to escort him to a hospital: "First of all, I want you to know how sorry I am about this. I've always liked you two. A unit above none. A legend in its own lunchtime. So it hurts me deeply to do this. But I have no choice. You must go to Forty-eighth and Broadway. In front of a liquor store, you'll find a fifty-year-old man unconscious. It says here, 'Man smells real bad.' Do I have to say more?"

It sounded snappy, funny, and fine to me. However, according to a batch of typewritten notes that had been prepared after a work-in-progress screening the previous week at a small theater on the East Side, Scorsese's voice was perhaps "too piercing."

"'Too piercing'?" Scorsese now said. "It's one of my best performances. I can hardly hear myself."

As Tom Fleischman, the rerecording mixer, paused the film and got busy modulating the pitch of this speech, Scorsese's thoughts sprinted off in a different direction. He was reminded of the old Harry Belafonte calypso tune "The Banana Boat Song" — or, rather, a parody of same by Stan Freberg, which included a reference to "piercing," and that reminded him of another Freberg routine, a parody of the television series *Dragnet*, which in turn reminded him of *Pete Kelly's Blues*, a feature film directed by Jack Webb, the star of *Dragnet*. The production designer of *Pete Kelly's Blues*, in which Webb played a bandleader during the twenties, was a Disney veteran who brought to it a remarkably vivid palette, a reality-heightening Technicolor glow reminiscent of the live-action Disney children's films of the forties — stuff like *So Dear to My Heart* and *Song of the South*. And, Scorsese further recalled, *Pete Kelly's Blues* had a screenplay by Richard L. Breen, whose name, curiously, Webb had heralded before the title. When the picture was released, in 1955, the year Scorsese turned thirteen, he followed it from theater to theater, as was his habit. He did most of his growing up on the Lower East Side, on Elizabeth Street — a self-contained Sicilian urban village where it was understood that you needed a good reason to venture far from the neighborhood.

Going way uptown to see a Jack Webb picture in a first-run theater wasn't a good enough reason, even for an adolescent movie addict. You waited until it came downtown to one of the second-run chain theaters — the Loew's Commodore, at Sixth Street and Second Avenue, or the Academy of Music, on Fourteenth Street — and the ticket price dropped from a dollar-fifty to seventy-five cents. For second and third viewings, you went to the independently owned Stuyvesant or St. Mark's or Orpheum, all on Second Avenue, where the price was about a quarter. One particular Saturday-afternoon double feature at the Orpheum came to mind: *Bomba the Jungle Boy* and *Great White Hunter*. He'd gone hoping to see "something totally mindless," and *Bomba the Jungle Boy* certainly qualified. But *Great White Hunter* turned out to be a rerelease of *The Macomber Affair* (based upon the Hemingway story "The Short Happy Life of Francis Macomber"), a whoa-what's-happening-here sexual psychodrama directed by Zoltán Korda and starring Gregory Peck, Joan Bennett, and Robert Preston as the unlucky Macomber. On a Sunday afternoon when the Loew's Commodore was completely packed, Scorsese and his father, Charles, saw Hitchcock's *Rear Window*. Afterward, still tingling, they got caught in an intermission crowd on the Second Avenue sidewalk outside the Anderson Theater, a Yiddish house where Molly Picon's name was on the marquee (not to be confused with the lower-echelon Yiddish theaters on the Bowery, where Charles Scorsese, as an adolescent, used to sneak in and spend the night when he'd gotten into trouble at home).

I'd brought along a laptop computer, and, though I type very quickly, I was laboring to keep up. Hoping to slow Scorsese's stride, I interjected that while I was growing up in Oklahoma my impressions of New York derived from the TV series *Naked City* and, most memorably, from the movie version of *West Side Story*. No doubt the Leonard Bernstein overture helped, but mainly I'd been hooked by the opening image — an abstract graphic representation of the Manhattan skyline that dissolved into the real thing.

Yes, absolutely, Scorsese agreed, those graphics were the extraordinary handiwork of Saul Bass, who later designed the titles of *GoodFellas, Casino, The Age of Innocence,* and the four-hour documentary *A Personal Journey with Martin Scorsese Through American Movies.* And the production designer of *West Side Story* was Boris Leven, who worked on Scorsese's *New York, New York, The Last Waltz, The King of Comedy,* and *The Color of Money.* Not that Leven was necessarily to blame, but he also designed a 1954 stinker called *The Silver Chalice,* in which Paul Newman made his screen debut, for which Newman later apologized with an advertisement in the *Los Angeles Times.* The performance that really stood out in *The Silver Chalice* was that of Jack Palance as Simon the Magician, "who gave Jesus a run for his money. . . . He was one of the holy men that the quote pagans unquote rallied around as an answer to the Jesus cult. He was said to have raised the dead — twice! — and he disappeared completely while being interrogated by the emperor." That digression led naturally to Apollonius of Tyana, Hannibal, the Punic Wars, the fact that when you go to Tunisia it's mainly Roman rather than Carthaginian ruins that you see, and how that landscape invariably evokes Federico Fellini's *Nights of Cabiria.* Scorsese was barely warming up, I gathered, but Fleischman had by then solved the "too piercing" problem, and it was time to move on.

ACROSS MANY MONTHS, I had many conversations with Scorsese, encounters that tended to engender a mixture of awe and sympathy. Along the way, I would speculate about this agreeably garrulous fellow: What's the weather like inside his brain? Evidently, every movie he'd ever watched — and he'd probably seen more than any other living director, more than most movie critics — was stored there, along with five-plus decades of personal history, sensory memory, family mythology, music heard, books read, all of it seemingly instantly retrievable. Was it painful, I wondered, to remember so much? Scorsese's powers of recall weren't limited to summoning plot turns or notable scenes or acting performances; his gray matter bulged with camera angles, lighting strategies, scores, sound effects, ambient noises, editing rhythms, production credits, data about lenses and film stocks and exposure speeds and aspect ratios. Instinctively, he'd engraved facts and images and feelings that he'd been able to draw upon throughout his creative life. But what about all the sludge? An inability to forget the forgettable — wasn't that a burden, or was it just part of the price one paid to make great art?

Since 1973, the year *Mean Streets* appeared — long before the label "America's greatest living film director" became routinely appended to his name — moviegoers throughout the world have known what a Scorsese movie looks and sounds like, even if only from seeing the work of other auteurs, disciples, and wannabes who've gone to school on his camera moves, narrative innovations, and editing tropes. Scorsese once mentioned to me that the best new movie he'd seen during the previous year was *Rushmore,* an unpredictable and winsome comedy directed by Wes Anderson — who, he learned after sending Anderson a fan letter, was an ardent admirer of Scorsese's exemplar, Michael Powell, the British director of such masterpieces as *The Red Shoes, The Life and Death of Colonel Blimp,* and *A Matter of Life and Death.* When I asked Anderson how he'd reacted to hearing from Scorsese, he replied, "I wrote back to him probably twenty-five seconds after receiving his letter." Of course, Anderson also proved to be a careful student of Scorsese.

"So many Scorsese ideas have been used so much that they're no longer Scorsese ideas," he told me. "They're just part of the grammar. The most obvious things are the ways he moves the camera and the cuts. And the way he uses music. Also, using documentary-style information in a fiction movie. . . . Take the counting of the money in *Casino.* The movie just sort of stops for a few minutes, nothing is happening with the characters, because he's telling you how the money works. He does it differently in *Mean Streets,* when he shows you how that world works. He's not the first director to do these things, but the way he does it combines realism and this dreamy and surreal expressionism."

"Marty hates plots," Thelma Schoonmaker often says, echoing remarks that Scorsese has uttered along those same lines. He is, of course, a masterly storyteller, one who refuses to settle for conventional three-act linear dramas with tidy resolutions, because since when does life work that way? What drives a Scorsese tale is his talent for weaving variegated optical and aural and emotional textures, for devising solutions to the paradox that truth and beauty and depravity must share the same frame. Underlying these dazzling gifts is Scorsese's compulsion to provoke discomfort in himself and his audience. For instance, there's the slaughter at the Norbulinga Palace in *Kundun,* or the torment and torture of Jesus in *The Last Temptation of Christ,* or the tattooed torso of the jailed Max Cady (Robert De Niro) in *Cape Fear.* Or there's that sidewalk confrontation between Travis (De Niro) and Sport (Harvey Keitel, playing Jodie Foster's pimp) in *Taxi Driver,* during which De Niro expresses his revulsion — and our revulsion — by stiffening his spine and looking away, into the uncertain distance. Our sympathy lies squarely with Travis at that moment, as opposed to the chill we feel in the famous "You talkin' to me?" sequence. (For my money, and this is, I concede, a minority viewpoint, the most unnerving scene in the Scorsese canon is the passage in *The King of Comedy* where Rupert Pupkin, in a successful effort by De Niro to establish a gold standard for putzlike behavior, shows up uninvited, luggage in hand, along with a girl he's trying to impress — Diahnne Abbott — at the weekend home of Jerry Langford, a Carson-like talk-show host played by Jerry Lewis. Pure skin-crawling terror, and nobody ever comes close to getting hurt.)

Barbara Hershey, who played Mary Magdalene in *Last Temptation,* spoke to Mary Pat Kelly, one of Scorsese's many biographers, about the disturbing scene in which she copulates with a series of strangers while Jesus watches silently: "There was one shot, just a simple shot, where an Indian man is watching me make love. Christ is sitting out of focus in the background. . . . The camera slowly starts to move in, and you think it's going to move onto Christ, but it swoops slightly and moves into the close-up of the eye of the Indian man, and then it locks focus and Christ is in focus as well, in the background. When I saw it I said to Marty, 'How did you think of that?' and he said, 'I thought of that four years ago. I woke up in the middle of the night with that one.' I realized that he had been preparing for this film his whole life. . . . Who knows what talent is? . . . I don't think talent is as rare as the need to express it or the strength to handle the rejection. I don't think Marty can help it; there's nothing else he can do with his life."

That combination of sensibility and urgency — the encyclopedic brain brimming with references to old movies and real-life experiences, waiting for just the right opportunity to download — is the dominant trait that distinguishes Scorsese from other filmmakers of his generation. In *Wiseguy,* the nonfiction bestseller by Nicholas Pileggi that *GoodFellas* was based upon, the wife of the main character, a Mafia soldier named Henry Hill, described how during their courtship he would escort her to the Copacabana nightclub: "On crowded nights, when people were lined up outside and couldn't get in, the doormen used to let Henry and our party in through the kitchen, which was filled with Chinese cooks, and we'd go upstairs and sit down immediately." Somehow, Scorsese translated those forty words into a seamless three-minute Steadicam shot, an exhilarating and revelatory blend of cinéma vérité and ballet — choreographed to the perfect music, "Then He Kissed Me," by the Crystals. When the camera at last delivers us to the big room at the Copa, Henry Hill (Ray Liotta), whom we've seen crossing palms with twenty-dollar bills, and his future wife (Lorraine Bracco) momentarily disappear, and a pair of briskly efficient waiters hoisting a linen-draped table enter the frame to give the couple the VIP treatment. Offscreen, some poor schmucks waiting to be seated whine futilely to the maitre d'.

How was it that Scorsese knew to build that scene that way? Or, rather, how was it that Pileggi's book found its way into the hands of the only film director alive who just happened to know by heart, along with a zillion other potentially but not necessarily useless facts, the protocols of the Copacabana in the fifties? "I'd been there a lot when I was fifteen or sixteen," Scorsese told me. "And I saw this go on all the time. I had to explain it all to the crew. 'Make sure we see the money. Money, money, money, money. Slipping money here and there, slipping money here and there, slipping money. Even if you don't see the cash, you see the hand movements.' Henry's greasing his way all the way in. This guy's like a king. This is his reward. The Copacabana was like, I don't know, like Buckingham Palace, especially if somebody like Sinatra was performing. It was as sanctified in my world, where I came from, before making movies, as you could get. Especially when you're younger, you get down there and you think you've got a great table and suddenly three more tables come flying into the room and these wiseguys, all these gangsters, come in and you can't say anything. You're finished."

"Marty never talks about his art," Pileggi has said. "All he ever wants to know from me is 'What really happened? What was he really talking about? How was he dressed? Where were they standing? What did his wife say?'"

Marty hates plots? It's a reductive, not-to-be-taken-too-literally way of saying that Scorsese is, among other things, a cultural anthropologist (with an unscientific devotion to the notion that character is destiny). Reviewing *Mean Streets,* Pauline Kael, in an unalloyed rave, described it as "a true original of our period, a triumph of personal filmmaking" and observed that "every character, every sound is rooted in those streets." In contexts as diverse as Las Vegas *(Casino),* Tibet *(Kundun),* Edith Wharton's New York *(The Age of Innocence),* and the Mob's outer boroughs *(GoodFellas),* Scorsese anatomizes the codes and rituals of whatever subculture he fixes his lens upon. He's an articulate, generous explainer, and his elucidations of what he was thinking when he first imagined that shot or made that cut reveal a rigorous self-awareness and a mind that's at once phenomenally cluttered and coherent. All that shelf space inside his cranium, it seems, is jammed with subtext — the footnotes, in effect, of his inspirations, footnotes that, as often as not, prove no less edifying or entertaining than the main text.

NO LONGER YOUNG, not yet old, Scorsese is, at fifty-seven, contentedly married (to his fifth wife) and the father of an infant daughter (as well as two grown daughters). According to Raffaele Donato, a film historian who has worked for Scorsese for fifteen years and along the way has become a close confidant, "Fellini used to tell Marty, 'As you get older, you're getting as handsome as De Sica.'" Well, not quite Vittorio De Sica, who had wavy silver hair and a dolce-vita radiance, but handsome, yes, in a worldly way: wide jaw, easy smile, bony nose, espresso eyes, and thick dark eyebrows hoisted like a furled awning, as if to say, "Behind these frontal lobes, everything is open for business." Each morning, he puts in a half hour on an exercise bicycle, a regimen that helps maintain his trim, bantam-rooster physique. But he has a history of shaky health, and he's heedful of the physical demands of filmmaking, the weeks in a row of twelve-hour shooting days followed by months of nocturnal postproduction marathons. He keeps a supply of inhalers handy for the asthma that has shadowed him since childhood, an affliction that, in retrospect, had a distinct upside; he couldn't run around with the other kids, but by studying street life from the living-room window he educated himself in the nuances of body language. Plus, his parents felt guilty that he was a shut-in, so they took him to see a *lot* of movies.

He now lives far from the Elizabeth Street tenement, on the East Side, in a brownstone he bought in 1987; he works there and in a suite of offices occupying half a floor in a midtown building. Door to door, it would be about a ten-minute walk, except that Scorsese's natural gregariousness makes it hard for him to tell intrusive strangers to back off, so he gets around town with a car and driver. He has no listed phone number, nor does his production company, Cappa Films. ("We find that people who really want to get in touch figure out a way.")

At this point in his life, Scorsese says, unless he's grappling with a movie budget he almost never thinks about money, as opposed to the eighties, "when I thought about it a lot, because I had none." A business manager advises as to what he can and can't afford. An avid book collector (recently, of first editions of novels that have been adapted as movies, as well as of Melville, Hawthorne, Joyce, Greene, and Huxley, among others), he began thirty years ago compiling an enormous collection of old movie posters, most of which are stored at the Museum of Modern Art. He doesn't have an agent, as such, but when situations arise that call for someone to represent his interests in a forceful manner — typically, dealing with certain people at certain movie studios — he often relies upon the Hollywood potentate and testicle squeezer Michael Ovitz. This arrangement dates to 1987, when Scorsese was despairing that he'd never be able to find a studio to back *The Last Temptation of Christ*, a story he believed he'd been put on earth to bring to the screen. Four years earlier, Paramount Pictures had pulled the plug just as production was about to get under way. A come-on Ovitz used in the wooing was "You know, Marty, you could get paid for being a film director." (Though not, as it turned out, for *Last Temptation* itself, which, financed by Universal, had a bare-bones budget of seven million dollars, a cast of splendid actors virtually all of whom worked for scale, and a director so fervid he agreed to work for nothing.)

Ovitz tapped into Scorsese's deepest dread: that a day will arrive when he'll no longer be able to make movies. He understands the marginal nature of his Hollywood citizenship — the category reserved for those whose work is revered but rarely does boffo box-office. (No doubt, it's harder for him to account for the bizarre fact that despite five Academy Award nominations, he has never won.)

In 1990, Scorsese showed Brian De Palma, an old friend, a rough cut of *GoodFellas,* and De Palma reacted with mock outrage: "You made the best movie of the eighties" — *Raging Bull*— "and, god-damn it, we're barely into the nineties and you've already made the best movie of this decade, too!" De Palma might have added that *Mean Streets* and *Taxi Driver* ranked among the best movies of the seventies, the decade when Hollywood reinvented itself. No wonder that in recent years Scorsese has received several awards of the lifetime-achievement variety, usually bestowed during black-tie ceremonies that test his ability not to squirm as moist-eyed colleagues deliver heartfelt testimonials. (Steven Spielberg: "Marty is the most honest filmmaker of our generation and in my opinion he is the best director in the world today," etc.) Guided by a blend of pragmatism and Sicilian fatalism, Scorsese regards such tributes warily, as if they were a warning that gray eminence lurks around the corner. He knows how abruptly even the most original talents can discover that their services are no longer in demand. Despite Scorsese's championing of his still-vibrant genius, Michael Powell couldn't really get work toward the end of his life. Fellini faced comparable circumstances, and Scorsese intervened on his behalf, as well. (Of Powell's *Peeping Tom* and Fellini's *8½*, Scorsese has declared that they "say everything that can be said about film-making, about the process of dealing with film, the objectivity and subjectivity of it, and the confusion between the two.")

Scorsese's worshipful respect for his forebears is, in a sense, indiscriminate, extending to the institution of cinema itself. In the early seventies, he attended a screening at the Los Angeles County Museum of Billy Wilder's 1955 comedy *The Seven Year Itch* and was appalled by the quality of the print, the color of which was so faded that everything looked pink. This wasn't an isolated case, he knew, and it led to a daunting, but ultimately successful, campaign to force Eastman Kodak, the leading manufacturer of color-film stock, to develop and bring to the market an affordable, durable product. Then, in 1990, Scorsese enlisted Woody Allen, Francis

Ford Coppola, Stanley Kubrick, George Lucas, Sydney Pollack, Robert Redford, and Steven Spielberg, and created the Film Foundation, the goal of which was to heighten awareness of motion-picture history and, specifically, to encourage the restoration and preservation of millions of feet of endangered films that mainly resided in the not very well protected archives of the studios. Scorsese had already helped pay for the restoration of certain favorite movies — André de Toth's *Ramrod*, Raoul Walsh's *Pursued*, Abraham Polonsky's *Force of Evil* — and he continues to do so. The Film Foundation shares office space with Cappa Films, and preservation advocacy and artists'-rights advocacy have evolved as a parallel enterprise to his work as a filmmaker.

What does it mean that Scorsese possesses this immense and astonishingly accessible knowledge of cinema? To the typical eight-dollar-ticket buyer on a Friday night, probably not much. And it makes understandable why one of his most interesting works — *A Personal Journey with Martin Scorsese Through American Movies*, a brilliantly condensed and ingeniously autobiographical film-history survey that he undertook, in 1994, at the request of the British Film Institute — didn't turn up in many neighborhood theaters. Film history vis-à-vis Scorsese began in 1946, when at age four he was taken by his mother to see *Duel in the Sun*, a King Vidor Western that starred Jennifer Jones and a villainous Gregory Peck. He was mesmerized: "The bright blasts of deliriously vibrant color, the gunshots, the savage intensity of the music, the burning sun, the overt sexuality . . . the hallucinatory quality of the imagery has never weakened for me over the years." Scorsese's pedagogy in *A Personal Journey*, propelled by enthusiasm rather than by dogmatism, pays homage to a handful of relatively obscure filmmakers — Samuel Fuller, Anthony Mann, Jacques Tourneur — and barely touches upon or omits many celebrated works by celebrated directors (Hitchcock, Huston, Wyler). Facing the camera, he makes plain his mission: "I've chosen to highlight some of the films that colored my dreams, that changed my perceptions, and in some cases even my life."

Typical is his discussion of Elia Kazan's *America America*, the story of Kazan's uncles' journey from Turkey to America, a classic immigrant experience: "I later saw myself making the same journey . . . from my own neighborhood in New York, which was in a sense a very foreign land. My journey took me from that land to moviemaking — which was something unimaginable! In fact, when I was a little younger, there was another journey I wanted to make: a religious one. I wanted to be a priest. However, I soon realized that my real vocation, my real calling, was the movies. I don't really see a conflict between the church and the movies, the sacred and the profane. . . . I believe there is a spirituality in films, even if it's not one which can supplant faith. I find that over the years many films address themselves to the spiritual side of man's nature, from Griffiths's *Intolerance* to John Ford's *The Grapes of Wrath* to Hitchcock's *Vertigo* to Kubrick's *2001* . . . and so many more. It's as if movies answer an ancient quest for the common unconscious. They fulfill a spiritual need that people have to share a common memory."

JUST IN TIME for the Venice Film Festival, late last summer, Scorsese assembled a rough-cut version of the first two hours of *Il Dolce Cinema*, a treatise on Italian film that will have grown to six hours by the time it's completed, later this year. Though *Il Dolce Cinema* seems a logical sequel to *A Personal Journey*, its conception actually predated the American documentary. For nearly a decade, *Il Dolce Cinema* percolated in conversations between Scorsese and Raffaele Donato, who in 1985 left the film department of the Museum of Modern Art to work as Scorsese's archivist. Donato has described it as "an even more personal journey than *A Personal Journey*" — an assessment Scorsese shares.

The genesis of *Il Dolce Cinema* can be traced to a brief trip to

Sicily that Scorsese made, somewhat reluctantly, in the late seventies, in the company of Isabella Rossellini, who would later become his third wife. They'd been vacationing in Rome when Rossellini proposed a two-day detour to Palermo and the exurban villages of Polizzi Generosa and Ciminna — respectively, Scorsese's father's and mother's ancestral hometowns. From Palermo, he phoned his mother, Catherine, in New York, and she gave him the name of a relative to look up. Arriving in Ciminna on a summer Sunday afternoon, Scorsese and Rossellini approached some men gathered in a small plaza, mentioned the person they were looking for, and were greeted with stony indifference. They continued strolling through town, Scorsese told me, asking the same question and making no progress. "Finally, a young man walked up to us and said, 'You want to meet this person, come with me.' He took us to a house where there was a woman with a child. She came out and said her husband was away on business. So I said we were cousins, I was a filmmaker, and I was interested in meeting him. The problem was my mother had given me the name of someone who was in hiding. I guess his wife thought I was the police or the member of a rival gang. Basically, we'd shown up, a couple of strangers, and dropped the worst possible name. That's why we were received that way, just like you see in the movies."

And, just like in the movies, clearing up the misunderstanding involved comic convolutions worthy of Pirandello. A brother of the fugitive cousin heard what had happened and ascertained that a famous American relation had been treated with great disrespect, which led to a falling-out between the brothers, which naturally became the talk of Ciminna. An elaborate letter of apology was written — the situation demanded nothing less — but . . . how was one to dispatch the letter? Years passed. Whenever American visitors came to Ciminna, they would be asked, "Where do you live?" If the answer was New York, they were then asked, "Manhattan?" If the answer was "Manhattan," the next question was "Uptown or downtown?" Did they know Elizabeth Street? Did they know

Charles and Catherine Scorsese, the parents of Martin? Finally, a woman materialized who indeed knew Elizabeth Street and Charles Scorsese, only he'd moved. But, she said, "I know where he goes to take a shave." Good. She was given the letter. Back in New York, she left a message at the barbershop and wound up hand-delivering the letter and reading it aloud in the Scorseses' kitchen.

By now, the letter was almost ten years old, but its invitation to come to Ciminna for a family reunion still stood. Which is how two years later, in 1990, Charles and Catherine went to Sicily — their first visit — where they were joined by their son the filmmaker. Donato also came along. (In the intervening years, Scorsese's marriage to Isabella Rossellini had come and gone, as had his fourth marriage, to Barbara De Fina, who began producing his movies when he was directing *The Color of Money* and, post-divorce, has continued to produce them.) In Sicily, Scorsese and Donato did what they always do — talked about movies, especially Italian movies, discussions that, according to Scorsese, "would go on for hours, about how certain films depicted the ways of life, the philosophy of the people." Scorsese's return to Ciminna, where, as it happens, Luchino Visconti shot *Il Gattopardo (The Leopard)* — based upon Giuseppe Tomasi di Lampedusa's exquisite tale of life among the Sicilian aristocracy during Garibaldi's campaign for Italian unification — had an especially stirring effect.

Scorsese: "I think one of the reasons I hadn't been eager to go when Isabella suggested it in 1978 was because I wasn't yet ready to accept that part of myself. The cultural connection between Sicily and where I grew up — whatever's been translated into Sicilian-American — has something very severe and strong about it, especially on my father's side. He wasn't a despot, but he had certain thoughts about what was right and wrong, a morality, based on that land. I knew that when I saw *The Leopard* in its first release, in 1963. These movies weren't just movies; they were all about the filmmakers and what they had to say, their art form, their version of cinema, their music. You know the funeral music in *Divorce*

Italian Style? We grew up hearing that in the street on the Lower East Side. That was so much a part of me, and one way it stayed with me was that for years my American side was fighting with my Sicilian side. I guess I didn't want to go to Sicily that first time because I felt if I stayed there too long I'd wind up in front of one of those cafés on Sundays drinking coffee, dressed in black, and I'd never make another film. The feeling that I belonged was so primal it was a little unsettling."

Donato: "Every movie that Marty's made, that he's talked about, that he loves, that's impressed in his mind, has some early family association for him. Movies for him aren't abstract, cold, critical, objective things. They're the air you breathe, what you eat. I like the metaphor from the Catholic Mass — Mary Pat Kelly also talks about this — the idea of transubstantiation, the wafer and the wine, body and blood. I think cinema for Marty is like that. When he discusses a film, it has a way of turning into flesh and blood."

With almost evangelical earnestness, Scorsese expresses his desire to introduce "classical Italian cinema" — De Sica, Roberto Rossellini, Pietro Germi, Francesco Rosi, Pier Paolo Pasolini, among others — to audiences unfamiliar with their work. His own familiarity with Italian cinema dates back half a century to weekend broadcasts by a New York television station of fare that wouldn't have had much of an audience in, say, Omaha — *Paisan, Open City, The Bicycle Thief, Shoeshine.* The impact of specific images was enhanced by the context in which Scorsese absorbed them — the Elizabeth Street living room, where he and his brother, Frank, their parents, maternal grandparents, and uncles communed with a sixteen-inch RCA Victor television. On the other side of the living-room wall was the 8-by-12 bedroom he shared with Frank, who was seven years older. When the plaster wall cracked next to where Marty slept, in the bottom half of a bunk bed, he covered it up by painting a face with penetrating eyes, then spooked his parents by explaining that the eyes watched him while he slept. "The eyes were sort of magical to me, what they saw," he told me. "The idea would be: viewing, always viewing, always see-ing, your eyes being on everything."

SCORSESE ARRIVED in Venice burdened by jet lag, fatigue, and general stress. He and Thelma Schoonmaker had endured a string of seven-day workweeks, alternating between the editing of *Il Dolce Cinema* and the postproduction polishing of *Bringing Out the Dead*. Simultaneously, he and his frequent writing partner, Jay Cocks, were working on what was supposed to be the final draft of the screenplay of his next feature, *Gangs of New York,* an adapta-tion of Herbert Asbury's history of an unheavenly nineteenth-cen-tury city plagued by corruption, poverty, crime, and savage tribal warfare. What else? Oh, yes, his wife, Helen Morris, was confined to bed all but one day a week — the safest place to be for a fifty-two-year-old woman with Parkinson's disease entering the last tri-mester of pregnancy. The first night in Venice, despite his comfort-able accommodations at the Hotel Cipriani, Scorsese dreamed he was being stretched in several directions. Earlier that week, in New York, he'd had a dream that plunged him back into final exams at the Catholic seminary he attended for a year during high school. ("Yes, we know you aren't going to become a priest, but you still have to take the tests.") The night after that, he'd found himself caught up in an epic battle between Gypsies and Sicilians, and the Sicilians were losing. Nightmare-wise, he was on a roll.

The Scorsese entourage included Donato; Schoonmaker; his producer and ex-wife, Barbara De Fina; his personal assistant, Gretchen Campbell; his media handler, Lois Smith; and some dev-ilish-looking professional muscle, a couple of nightclub bouncers from Rimini, who wore matching black pinstriped suits and Oak-ley shades and answered to the same name, Francesco. The screen-ing of *Il Dolce Cinema,* or at least the first two hours of it, would be the crowning event of the festival, following the awards ceremony and Scorsese's presentation to Jerry Lewis of a Golden Lion statu-ette for career achievement (an honor he'd received himself, in

1995). That evening, Scorsese wore a black suit, white shirt, gray striped necktie, and, on his left lapel, a tiny red bar that signified his elevation to the French Legion of Honor (something else he had in common with Jerry Lewis). During the ride from the Cipriani to the festival site, on the Lido, the mood aboard Scorsese's water taxi was subdued, inclining toward lugubrious. As we were about to dock, De Fina mused, "Well, is this the most cheerful group of people in Venice, or what?"

"It's always tense before you go over the top," Scorsese said, gritting his teeth and for all I knew quoting from *All Quiet on the Western Front* or *From Here to Eternity*.

"What could go wrong?" I asked.

"The kudos or the bomb," he said. "You never know. And you only learn that by thinking you know."

In this instance, it was definitely kudos. Scorsese sat in the balcony, flanked by Giorgio Armani, who was the film's executive producer (his reward for contributing two hundred thousand dollars of its initial financing), and by the screenwriter Suso Checchi D'Amico. From my vantage point a couple of rows away, I didn't see Scorsese budge during the screening, but he might well have been muttering. Nick Pileggi recalls sitting next to him during the premiere of *GoodFellas,* at the Ziegfeld Theater, in Manhattan: "As we're watching, I'm getting these elbows. He's saying, 'See? We let that shot run a little too long.' And 'Look at that, we should have taken that out.' I say, 'Marty, it's too late now. We're at the opening. You're wearing a tuxedo.'"

As the credits for *Il Dolce Cinema* rolled, the entire audience rose and faced the balcony, applauding warmly. This was followed by lots of kisses and hugs, including a full-body wrap from a tiny, wizened, gray-haired woman who was weeping and speaking in Italian, with Armani translating. Armani hosted a dinner that evening at a restaurant near St. Mark's Square, and on our way through the square I asked Donato who she was. Her name was Marcella De Marchis, and she was Roberto Rossellini's first wife —

actually, the only woman he ever married and therefore his widow (and, if you defined the term broadly, sort of one of Scorsese's former in-laws). What had she been saying?

"She described the emotions she was reliving as she watched the clips from *Paisan* and *Open City*," Donato said. "She'd never seen anything on Rossellini done in such a simple way, with such great taste, where you could explain what he was trying to do and capture what he was all about. And she was responding to the fact that this was, on Marty's part, obviously a labor of love."

I wondered if "labor of love" meant that Scorsese wasn't taking any compensation.

"As far as I know," Donato said, "it's a pure labor of love."

Had *A Personal Journey* also been pro bono?

"Well, that one was a little different. For that one, Marty didn't want any money, but as payment he asked the British Film Institute for a copy of *A Kid for Two Farthings*, a 1955 picture by Carol Reed, who also directed *The Third Man*. And they promised it to him, but there have been some problems with the restoration. They've never been able to pull all the elements together. So, now that I think of it, he's never actually collected."

A FEW DAYS after returning from Venice, Scorsese informed me, "What we're going to do is give ourselves a little film festival, which really gets the energy going." He still had to figure out the shape and content of the final four hours of *Il Dolce Cinema,* and the most expeditious approach was to watch a bunch of Italian movies that he'd seen many times but nevertheless felt he needed — and, remarkably, was able — to look at with a fresh eye. So, over the next few weeks, I spent several afternoons at the Cappa offices, inside a cozy, gold-carpeted screening room equipped with twelve cushiony green armchairs. Some of the films came from a collection Scorsese oversees — a few thousand sixteen-millimeter and thirty-five-millimeter prints, which he stores at the Museum of Modern Art and at Eastman House, in Rochester, New York. (These are separate from his video collection, which at last count included roughly 25,000 titles.) We saw Pietro Germi's *Divorce Italian Style,* Ermanno Olmi's *Il Posto* and *The Fiancés,* Luchino Visconti's *La Terra Trema,* Michelangelo Antonioni's *Blow-Up,* and Francesco Rosi's *Salvatore Giuliano.* Thelma Schoonmaker was always present, usually joined by Jay Cocks and his wife, the actress Verna Bloom, and occasionally by Raffaele Donato and Kent Jones, a programmer for the Film Society of Lincoln Center and a cowriter of *Il Dolce Cinema.* Afterward, Scorsese and Schoonmaker would consider which clips they might include in the documentary, and he and Cocks, who for nine years reviewed movies for *Time* and for almost thirty years has watched a movie or two a week with Scorsese, would exuberantly analyze the ingredients, as if deconstructing a savory meal.

It became clear to me that Italian cinema matters to Scorsese as something far more than intellectual fodder. He was explicit about which passages in which films corresponded to specific motifs in his own work — a sorting out, it seemed, or a way of illuminating his understanding of who he is. A shot of empty coat hangers in an empty room at the end of *Il Posto* inspired a shot of a forlornly dangling light bulb in the final scene of *Raging Bull:* "That just stuck in my mind as a symbol of loneliness. In *Raging Bull,* Jake La Motta is back, ready to go into the ring, only it's a stage. He's readjusted his life. He's made peace with himself and the people around him, but he's alone. And those images — when you're sitting alone in a room, you see those little details. If I'm alone here, my eye catches the wall socket under the wainscoting there. The inanimate object makes you aware of your own loneliness, of being by yourself."

Of the cinematography of *Salvatore Giuliano,* he said, "I think we translated that black-and-white intensity into the color of the neon in the streets of New York at night in *Taxi Driver.* It has a truth and honesty to it that's really devastating. It deals with humanity on a primal level. In *Taxi Driver,* the way Travis looked, the way he glanced up and down the street, comes from some of this. *Salvatore Giuliano* was an inspiration for that, and to a certain extent for *GoodFellas*. And certainly we looked at it again for *Raging Bull*, just for the black-and-white."

Scorsese invited me to at least one screening that I suppose he wished he hadn't. One afternoon less than a month before the premiere of *Bringing Out the Dead*, he and Schoonmaker settled into the back row of a multiplex theater in the Viacom Building, at Forty-fifth and Broadway, to inspect a print of the film that had just been put through a process called skip-bleaching, the purpose of which was to subtly heighten the contrast between light and dark tones. As the film played, Scorsese's own tone sounded anything but lighthearted. The basic flaw, he felt, was that now there was too much contrast. Throughout the screening, I could hear him moaning, "Oh, my God, Thelma. No good . . . There's like a haze over the picture. It's an overall problem . . . Oy. No good." He sounded like an alarmed mother — oddly, like a stereotypical Jewish mother — whose child had just wandered in after a nasty bicycle spill.

"I gotta tell you, the picture's subject matter is depressing. The areas we shot in the city are down," he told Schoonmaker afterward. "Each frame looks quite beautiful, but cumulatively, I think emotionally, we're cut off from the picture, and it's more depressing than it should be."

The problem could be fixed, but a cleaned-up print might not be ready in time for a preview two days later.

"Who's coming to that screening?" I asked.

"Oh, I don't know," he said. "Who knows? It's open to the world now. Everybody's there — families, ushers, we're dragging people off the streets, who cares at this point. Everybody's gonna see it now. That's the end. It's all over. It's gonna go out to theaters and get reviewed. I can't take it. Oh, God. Oy. That's it. It's going out into theaters. Some people may actually come to see it. Oh, God."

I was reminded of an anecdote about the editing of *Raging Bull* (for which Schoonmaker won an Oscar). As the film's opening date became imminent, the people around Scorsese recognized that he was having difficulty letting go. Finally, the producer, Irwin Winkler, invoked a deadline of midnight on a Sunday. If the lab didn't start printing the next day, the picture wouldn't be ready to open the following weekend. Midnight approached, and Scorsese was still fiddling with a scene in which a minor character orders a drink from a bar at the Copacabana. The problem was that Scorsese couldn't clearly hear the words "Cutty Sark."

Winkler said, no, that wasn't the real problem. "Marty, that's it," he decreed. "The picture is over. You have to give it up. If you can't hear 'Cutty Sark,' it's just too bad."

"I'm taking my name off the picture."

"People are going to look at this picture one hundred years from now and say that it's a great, great movie," Winkler said. "Because you can't hear 'Cutty Sark,' which, by the way, everybody else says they can hear, you're taking your name off?"

"Yes, I'm taking my name off the picture."

Fine, take your name off, Winkler told him, but it's going to the lab.

A well-traveled tale — recounted in more than one book about Scorsese — and, I think, easily misconstrued, seemingly a vignette about neurotic perfectionism but actually a wholly characteristic illustration of the multilayered subtext that underlies his finest work. *Raging Bull* is, in the Scorsese mythology, the pivotal event. In the late seventies, his personal life was a mess. He was living in Los Angeles, treating himself to a second adolescence following the collapse of his second marriage (to the writer Julia Cameron). After *Mean Streets, Alice Doesn't Live Here Anymore,* and *Taxi Driver,* which were in varying degrees critical successes, he made *New York, New York,* which was anything but. He agreed to direct Liza Minnelli in a Broadway musical, *The Act,* but, recognizing that he was out of his element, left the production two weeks before it opened (and quickly closed). He was more than mildly depressed.

Drug abuse, and abuse of his body in general, culminated in a ter-rifying episode of internal bleeding. Robert De Niro came to see him in the hospital and asked, in so many words, whether he wanted to live or die. If you want to live, De Niro proposed, let's make this picture — referring to *Raging Bull*, an as-told-to book by Jake La Motta, the former world middleweight boxing champion, that De Niro had given him to read years earlier. *Raging Bull* be-came, in Scorsese's adaptation, the story of a severely flawed hu-man being's quest for redemption. Which is to say that it was about his own quest for redemption. "I put everything I knew and felt into that film, and I thought it would be the end of my career," he said years later. "It was what I call a kamikaze way of making movies: pour everything in, then forget all about it and go find an-other way of life." He genuinely believed it would be his last Holly-wood studio project.

And the "Cutty Sark" line — what was that all about? Well, it was the whiskey of choice of Scorsese's father and his contemporaries, and the reference was a wink and a nod to them. The part of the bartender at the Copacabana, meanwhile, was played by Dominic Lofaro's father, who in real life was a bartender at the Copacabana. Dominic Lofaro? One of Scorsese's best friends from childhood (now dead), "a very interesting guy, as close as I could get to an intellectual in my neighborhood, he read books, he saw plays." Dominic was, along with one other pal, someone with whom the young Scorsese felt comfortable revealing his pencil-and-water-color storyboards, the frame-by-frame blueprints of movies he imagined one day making. He'd begun drawing them at around age ten and stopped at fourteen — actually, stopped only tempo-rarily, to resume when he arrived at film school at New York Uni-versity — having completed his pièce de résistance, "The Eternal City," a seventy-five-millimeter saga set in ancient Rome, broken down into close-ups, wide shots, medium shots, moving shots. As a full-grown professional, Scorsese laid out storyboards that were legendary for their specificity, their evidence of his matchless ability to visualize and map a movie in his head, along with sound-track music, before he shot a single frame. Was it a coincidence that the storyboards for *Raging Bull* were the most elaborate he ever did? The fight scenes were diagrammed punch by punch, angle by angle. The unforgettable footage of the masochistic La Motta / De Niro's face exploding in his climactic third fight against Sugar Ray Robinson was conceived and laid out shot by shot to mirror the shower scene in *Psycho.* . . . Cutty Sark? I would go on, except that with Scorsese you never really get to the bottom of this stuff.

THE LATE MOVIE CRITIC Gene Siskel once asked Scorsese what he regarded as the most emblematic image in his body of work. Scorsese's answer was the title sequence of *Raging Bull.* It's a slow-motion wide shot, its foreground a frame within the frame, delineated by the three ropes of a boxing ring. In the middle distance, the focal point, a robed, hooded figure inside the ring — La Motta, but we don't yet know that — shadowboxes. The background is bathed in fog. What I'd remembered about this tableau was its depiction of a lone warrior who must battle to survive, but when I looked at it again recently I decided I'd misremembered and misinterpreted it. I'd forgotten a handful of silhouetted background figures, barely discernible in the fog. And the fighter in the ring seemed no longer a ponderous metaphor but simply a man simultaneously at work and at play, moving air molecules with his arms and legs — something a newborn baby does just as instinctively and effectively. Was he a stand-in for Scorsese? Sure, to a degree. I also think Scorsese was one of the adumbrated shapes in the background — a camera flash goes off a couple of times — a witness, neither more nor less guilty than the dancing shadowboxer.

Two consecutive evenings a while back, Scorsese and I met at his home — in a warmly furnished parlor-floor living room, surrounded by neatly ordered bookshelves and framed posters of Jean Renoir's *Grand Illusion* (the only other significant wall hanging being a sixteenth-century crucifix) — where we covered, among other diverting topics, anger, guilt, pain, suffering, and violence. Our second conversation preceded dinner with Helen Morris, a fine-boned blond woman with finishing-school manners and Old New York bloodlines. She and Scorsese met in 1995, when she was an editor at Random House and was working on the second volume of Michael Powell's memoirs. Four years ago, they started living together, and last summer they married. Their infant daughter, Francesca, escorted by a nanny, made a couple of appearances while we talked, and Helen's deaf but excitable West Highland white terrier, Silas, also dropped by.

The joys of new fatherhood and domestic tranquillity notwithstanding, Scorsese had had, by his reckoning, "a rough fall." In late October, *Bringing Out the Dead* opened, accompanied by mixed but generally positive reviews. However, its grosses the first four weeks totaled only $16 million; by Thanksgiving it was fading fast; and by the time the Christmas-holiday movies turned up at the cineplexes it had all but disappeared. Like *Kundun,* his previous and more lavishly praised endeavor, it never really found an audience. Inevitably, this box-office disappointment did nothing to leaven the atmosphere during discussions with the studios that had provisionally agreed to finance his next film, *Gangs of New York.* The budget for *Gangs* — $83.5 million — would make it his most expensive picture. News items in the trade papers announced that Disney and Miramax would put up the money, Leonardo DiCaprio would star, and production would start in midwinter. During 1999, Scorsese and Jay Cocks wrote and revised nine drafts of the screenplay. Each time they were done, they assumed they'd solved whatever problems had nagged them. But as the New Year arrived nothing was firmly resolved, including the question of whether the movie would get made.

To bring *Gangs of New York* to the screen would fulfill a vision of the city Scorsese had ruminated upon since childhood. On Prince Street, between Mott and Mulberry, next to Old St. Patrick's Cathedral, the parish where he attended parochial school and served as an altar boy, stood a cemetery whose aged stones bore mainly Anglo, rather than familiar Italian, surnames. Who were these people? What had this corner of the world looked and sounded and smelled like when they were its inhabitants? Scorsese had absorbed fragments of century-and-a-half-old oral history — suggestive accounts of harrowing turf battles between mobs of nativist Protestants and recent-immigrant Irish Catholics — and in 1970 he happened upon the Herbert Asbury book, which gave a context to these inchoate emanations of the old neighborhood. He and Cocks wrote their first draft of *Gangs of New York* in 1976, and though the project lay dormant for more than two decades, it has withstood the vicissitudes of Scorsese's career and refused to die. What's in it, ultimately, for the auteur? Nothing more, really, than a chance to portray a city that millions of people think they know in a manner that no one has previously imagined imagining.

"If I get to make *Gangs of New York*," he said, "I will have gotten to make every picture that I really, really wanted to make. If I don't get to make it, I'll move on to something else."

But not so fast . . .

"Once I know that we're moving forward with *Gangs,* there are certain things I have to come to grips with in the script. The violence is the main thing. The violence is tricky, but that's the way those characters behaved. I have to figure out how to shoot it. At the end, when everyone's covered in dust and ashes, that's got to be very stylized."

Stylized violence. I thought, Well, Father Principe would be pleased. Father Principe was the priest from Old St. Pat's who, when asked what he thought of his former acolyte's interpretation of redemptive blood sacrifice — exemplified by the famous shootout at the end of *Taxi Driver* — said, "Too much Good Friday and not enough Easter Sunday."

When the words "Scorsese" and "violence" are linked in my mind, I advert to the scene in *Casino* where a psychopathic gangster named Nicky Santoro, played to the hilt by Joe Pesci, puts a guy's head in a vise after torturing him for two days because he refuses to give up some information. Before tightening the vise and slitting the victim's throat, he implores him, "Please don't make me do this!" By which we're led to understand that Nicky's just a working guy trying to keep his own head out of the vise. Earlier, we've seen Nicky the loving father cooking breakfast for his young son in his suburban kitchen. Later, we see him and his brother get beaten bloody with baseball bats and buried alive in the desert.

"I'm not interested in violence that way anymore," Scorsese said, convincingly. "A lot of these guys" — in *Gangs of New York* — "don't even have guns, they use bats. Well, I did that in *Casino.* I don't want to do violence like that again. I can't even watch that scene. It's upsetting, because I like those characters. And as far as the head in the vise is concerned — I should have played the whole thing on Joe's face and the other actors' faces but never shown the bulging eye in the vise. It has to do with the humanity of it. What it did to them mattered as much as what it did to the guy whose head was in the vise. If you can't show the humanity — let's say, the battle scene at the beginning of *Gangs of New York* — then you have to find a way to do the violence in a nongraphic way, so that it doesn't become literally just scene after scene of people smashing each other across the head. Because that's what they did. Fighting was a pastime. What you have to understand about these gangs is that they relate directly to Anglo-Saxon tribes and Irish Celtic tribes. The fact that one is Protestant and the other's Catholic, that's just a place you come from. You're not arguing over the tenets of religion. These were warriors, and their gods were war gods. I'm dealing with making a film about barbarians. If I were younger, there's no doubt that I'd be out there to shock. Here I don't necessarily want to portray violence anymore in such a way that you lose half your audience halfway into the picture. Why should I?"

Implicit in all this is the question that *Gangs of New York,* like every new venture, evokes for Scorsese: How do I muster whatever it takes to keep making these movies, telling these stories, when the process itself is steeped in pain and suffering?

"It comes out of a very Catholic point of view," he said. "I think it's very delicate. People say, 'What do you have to complain about? You make these movies, you do pretty much what you want.' And I think the problem is that talking about quote suffering unquote makes me sound like someone who takes himself way too seriously. But there's no other way I know to do the work. On a personal level, things are OK. But the work alone is extremely painful. On the set, I'll look like I'm having a great time, but in the trailer, in the preproduction phase, in the editing room, it's painful to pull it all together. Maybe 'suffering' is a bad word — but I don't really celebrate anything. I stopped, like, in the mid-seventies, celebrating. . . . *GoodFellas* felt good because a lot of people liked it, but just because a lot of people liked it doesn't mean it's really a good picture. And that's the other issue: How do I feel about myself and my own work ultimately? Something I'll probably never know is whether a picture's really good or not. I only know if it's right. In other words, I know that what I did was the way it should have been done."

"Why isn't 'right' synonymous with 'good'?"

"I'm not sure."

"Then what do you mean by 'good'?"

"I don't know." A three-beat pause.

"OK. Will it communicate to other people? Will it communicate to other people in the future, when the culture's changed? Will it speak to a different culture?"

So it wasn't very complicated. Scorsese merely desired what any artist desires: universal recognition and immortality.

On another occasion, Helen Morris said, "In the Catholic catechism there are all these absolute 'no's. Once you see how the world works, you get over these things. Marty never really has. You think of him as a child looking out the window and seeing people behaving badly. He could recognize it as a normal human instinct, but he understood that they have to get punished. He developed a sympathy for people doing bad things, studied the gangsters in the neighborhood, some of whom were good people. That dichotomy between Joe Pesci's character in *Casino* being very good to his children and being a horrible person otherwise — guilt and sin and what you can do and can't do — it always comes down to the fact that you're going to get punished."

ONE SNOWY DAY not long ago, I got a call from Scorsese's assistant Gretchen Campbell, telling me that she was faxing something he thought I should read. A few minutes later, it came chugging out of my machine, a fourteen-page introduction to the Loeb edition of Philostratus's *Life of Apollonius of Tyana.* I read the text, which said, among other things, that according to popular legend when Apollonius, a holy man and miracle worker of some sort who was born around the beginning of the Christian era, died he ascended bodily to Heaven. This was good to know, but why had Scorsese sent it?

"You and I had that conversation a while back about Simon the Magician and Apollonius of Tyana," he said the next time we spoke, by phone. "And I told you Simon the Magician was thought to have raised the dead twice, and that he disappeared in the presence of the emperor. Anyway, I recently saw a couple of television documentaries on the ancient world, and they sent me back to Philostratus. I first read Philostratus in 1983 or 1984, when I was looking at background material for *The Last Temptation of Christ,* because I was interested in anything that discussed the pagans' answer to Jesus. And when I picked it up again the other day I realized I'd given you some wrong information.

"Simon the Magician comes out of the New Testament. In the book of Acts, there's a confrontation between Simon and one of the Apostles; there were often these challenges between magicians and Apostles. Simon could have been a composite of different magicians of the period. Apollonius also could have been a composite figure. Apollonius appeared in front of one of the emperors, but he didn't disappear. And it wasn't Simon who disappeared either.

"I'm interested in the ancient world because of the nature of what they thought. It's a hundred and eighty degrees from the world I know, which is Christianity. It's the closest you can get to, I guess — this will sound funny — but it's the closest you can get to what we would think of as extraterrestrials. Pre-Christian. I guess *Alien* depicts that. Or, a better example, the closest we've come to the alien persona on film is Fellini's *Satyricon*, which depicts a sense of a world gone awry, crazy, a world in which you can be a victim any second, a dangerous place."

"Where are you now?" I asked. "At home or the office?"

"I'm at home. I'm sitting up here in the den on the fourth floor, with two stacks of books on the ancient world. There are the main texts, and then there are the companion explanatory texts. The thing I really want to do these days is read Gibbon. But I don't have enough time. I get to look at these Roman and Greek classics — I try to find the time at least once a week. What have I been reading lately? Well, Philostratus. I'm very excited by that stuff. That's why I sent it to you. I couldn't rest until I got the confusion cleared up."

— 2000